An Ordinary Englishman

The Autobiography of Reuben Brooks F.C.A.

An Ordinary Englishman

The Autobiography of
Reuben Brooks F.C.A.

Reuben Brooks

The Book Guild Ltd.
Sussex, England

The Book Guild Ltd.
25 High Street,
Lewes, Sussex.

First published 1992
© Reuben Brooks 1992
Set in Baskerville
Typesetting by Ashford Setting & Design,
Ashford, Middlesex.
Printed in Great Britain by
Antony Rowe Ltd.,
Chippenham, Wiltshire.

A catalogue record for this book is
available from the British Library

ISBN 0 86332 739 7

CONTENTS

LIST OF ILLUSTRATIONS

In memory of my Granddaughter, dear little 'Nonie', whose imaginative essays gave me the confidence to write this book. I hope she would think I 'passed the muster'.

1

AN ORDINARY ENGLISHMAN

In my early twenties I was drinking in the bar of the Kings Head at Rochester with a group of friends and we were discussing some aspect of government policy. During the general talk one of the group, a Scotsman in the party, dismissed my opinions and thought to close the discussion by saying to me 'You are only an ordinary Englishman'. When I thought about it later I realized he was quite right. I was an ordinary Englishman along with millions of my fellow countrymen.

2

FAMILY AND VILLAGE LIFE

1990 was my golden wedding year when I was eighty years old. Golden weddings are always an occasion for old memories to be brought out so I decided that I would put mine down in writing.

My father was born in 1877 and my mother in 1882, both from farming families. Father was the youngest of a family of six. The eldest was a sister called Charlotte and then there were four elder brothers, Charles, Reginald, Philip and George. The family was descended from an ancient Kent family of yeoman farmers who could trace their ancestry back to 1577 from the parish registers in which Elizabeth I ordered all births, deaths and marriages to be recorded. My mother had four sisters, and six brothers. Her father was champion ploughman of Kent.

The families lived next door to each other in a place called Sparrows Castle in the hundred of Hoo between the estuaries of the Thames and Medway.

Father left school at the age of twelve after he had learnt the three Rs. The children all left school as soon as possible as it cost 4d. per week to attend school and with the large families which were usual in those days it was a relief when they were able to leave school. Owing to the depression in farming my father's eldest brother, Charles, emigrated to Canada, whilst Philip and George went to sea and became captains of coasting sailing barges. Philip had the *Venta* and later the *Velosia* and George had the *Glenmore*. Father started work on a neighbouring farm and one of his first jobs was scaring birds in the cherry orchard with another boy of the same age. They were given a shotgun with live cartridges to do this work and, as might have

Author's mother

Author's father

been expected, the boys started to lark about and the other boy was wounded. The police conducted an investigation and they confirmed that it was an accident. Father lost his job and his elder brother, Captain George Brooks, took him on as cook/third hand on the sailing barge *Glenmore*. His duties in that capacity were to do the cooking, clean out the cabins and forecastle and help on deck when needed.

Father was last in the family and was much younger than his sister, who was the eldest, and his brothers. His father was fifty years old when he was born and his sister's eldest children were older than he was. His sister had seven children. The eldest daughter, named Bella, became matron of the first Borstal institution, which was established near Rochester. She often spoke with affection of 'her boys', who kept in touch with her when she retired. Of her brothers, two emigrated to California but came back to England in 1914 to enlist in the British army; two other brothers were captain and mate of the barge *Glenavon* who were drowned on the Goodwin Sands. They were last seen clinging to the rigging as the barge sank. The youngest brother served as mate on my father's barge. Captain Philip Brooks' son became an accountant with Nobels, the explosives company which later became part of Imperial Chemical Industries, and Captain George Brooks' son went as mate on his father's barge.

Father was married at twenty-five to my mother, Ethel Ann Squires. She left the village school at twelve after learning her three Rs. It was the custom then for country girls to be recruited into domestic service because they were used to hard work and had to leave home to make room for the other children. She went to work as a kitchenmaid in a city merchant's house in the London suburb of Forest Hill.

* * *

Father was kind, generous, helpful and considerate to others and a loving family man. I have been out walking with him when a tramp crossed the road to ask him for a copper to get a cup of tea. He always gave tramps money and I said to him that they probably spent it on beer, but he said that if only one was genuine it was worthwhile. He had a fine tenor voice and was in great demand at village concerts when he was home.

He had a large repertoire of songs which were popular at that time, in addition to the traditional country songs. All his family had fair hair and grey eyes, typical of the Jutes who conquered Kent under Hengist and Horsa. They were called 'the men with the big noses' in France.

My mother's family, in contrast, all had black hair and brown eyes. They must have been descended from the original inhabitants of Kent who were conquered by the Jutes. She was loyal, hard working and efficient, with a temper, when aroused, like her father's and with a possessive love of her children which made it difficult for her to give them up when they left home or got married. She rose to be housekeeper in charge of six servants by the time she left to get married at twenty-one. Her sisters all married. One brother took over a farm in Norfolk. One served in the Royal Navy. One was a sailmaker, and the rest went to sea. One of them was lost at sea from my father's barge. Mother was the second eldest in the family and was the one who held the family together. She settled their arguments, looked after them when they were ill and entertained them at Christmas and during holidays. If anybody wanted help they sent for her.

I did not know my father's parents, as they died before I was born, but my mother's parents lived in an old farmhouse in the village of Wainscott which they turned into the village shop, run by my grandmother. My grandfather, when I knew him, made a living in various ways. He had stables and kept horses for cartage work, carrying goods to the nearest railway station at Strood, and had a waggonette for taking people on outings, and he also attended the local markets, buying and selling cattle. He had a big black beard and dark eyes and a temper easily aroused, which made him a fearsome person to us as small children. He had a large walnut tree in his garden and in the autumn he would climb up into the tree and thrash it with a long stick to dislodge the walnuts. He seemed to enjoy this and it was our job to gather the nuts up as they fell to the ground.

Wainscott was a village of straggling terrace cottages at each end and older cottages and farmhouses in the middle with the village school and public house, which was kept by my father's nephew. The houses were all on one side of the road with orchards and the village green on the other side and fields at the back running down to the River Medway at Upnor. It was situated in a valley between two hills, Spakes Hill which went up to Frindsbury, leading to Strood and Rochester, and Lodge Hill at the other end, going to Chattenden and out to Hoo and the Isle of Grain on the Thames marshes. A small river called the Wain ran through the valley at the bottom of the village in the water meadows and eventually reached the Medway at Whitewall Creek, opposite Chatham Dockyard.

After they were married my parents moved to Wainscott and rented a farm worker's cottage called Ivy Cottage, next to an old farmhouse occupied by the village carpenter and his family. The cottage had three bedrooms upstairs, a parlour, kitchen and scullery downstairs and an outside lavatory with mains water. As children we loved to visit the carpenter's workshop next door to smell the wood shavings which littered the floor and watch him making doors or window frames or coffins. They had an earth closet at the bottom of the garden with two seats side by side, one for grown-ups and a small one for children, which we liked to use sometimes when mother was not watching. The carpenter got drunk frequently and staggered home after the pub shut, bumping from side to side, first into his house and then into ours. His wife was a motherly woman who always gave us hot cakes to eat when we called in to see her.

Our home was simply furnished but it did have an upright piano. Lighting was by oil lamps and heating by coal fires, although the fires in the bedrooms were only lit in the case of illness and in the parlour for special occasions. There was a copper in the scullery to boil the water for washing the clothes, which were stirred by a wooden copper stick and lifted out to be scrubbed on a metal washboard with an outsize bar of Sunlight soap. After that the clothes were wrung out by hand, then put through the mangle and hung up to dry. In the summer they dried on the clothes line in the garden but when the weather was bad they were dried indoors, filling the room with condensation. When they were dry enough the clothes were ironed with a flat iron heated on the kitchen range. Cooking was done by a coal-fired kitchener and as we had no bathroom kettles of water had to be heated up on it to fill a bath tub for washing and bathing.

The villagers were poor but not poverty-stricken. When the women greeted each other they did not ask after their health, they always said 'Has your husband got plenty of work?' The men were employed as farm labourers, general labourers, road menders or lengthsmen, keeping the verges clear. Some went to sea or into the forces. There was also casual work to be had on the farms in the spring and at harvest time and fruit picking. It was usual to keep rabbits and chickens and grow vegetables in the garden and some families also had smallholdings.

At harvest time, when the corn was cut, the women went gleaning to gather up the loose corn to feed their chickens. The corn was cut by a machine attached to a steel cable which was drawn to and fro across the field between two traction engines, one at each end. There was great excitement among the children when the traction engines arrived, pulling their cabins behind them. When the corn was cut the sheaves were stood on end in groups of six or eight, called stookes, which were ideal for playing hide and seek. When the sheaves had dried out they were taken to the barn or made into large corn ricks with thatched roofs decorated with corn dollies to await the arrival of the threshing machine. The day the threshing started the boys and men gathered round the rick with sticks to kill the rats as they bolted out. The men always tied up their trousers below the knee with twine for fear that a rat might run up their leg.

After the corn harvest there was hop picking. Each family had a bin and when the vines had been cut down from the hop poles the hops were picked off into the bins. The foreman was told when the bin was full and he came round and threw out the leaves which had also collected in the bin, and pressed the hops down until he was satisfied the bin was really full of hops, and then he issued a ticket to enable the workers to collect their pay. The children were supposed to help with the picking but they soon got bored and went off to play and only appeared again in time for the picnic. Fruit picking provided another opportunity for casual work for the grown-ups and plenty of fruit to satisfy the children.

Earlier in the year, about June, depending on the weather, the hay was cut by a horse-drawn mower and carted into the farmyard to be pitchforked up to the workmen building the hay stacks. This also needed some casual labour and playing in the hay attracted the young ones who were supposed to be helping.

There was no public transport in the village. The only way to get into town was by walking the one and a half miles to the top of Frindsbury Hill and catching a tram which ran through the Medway Towns out to another terminus at the village of Rainham, or by getting a lift with a carter or someone with a pony and trap. One of the favourite pastimes of the boys was to jump up behind a cart for a ride and those who could not get on, usually the smaller ones, would shout out 'Whip whip behind the cart, mister' and the driver would then lash out with his whip and force the boys to jump off. Apart from the excitement of getting on, riding on the back of the cart was not much fun because the roads were not tarmacked and it set up a cloud of white dust which smothered the riders.

Our home was always clean and tidy because Mother kept up the standards she had been used to in service. As Father was always away at sea she ran the house, brought up the children and managed the finances. We were well clothed and ate well, although as a boy I always seemed to be hungry. Visitors were always welcomed with refreshments. Mother organized her days. Saturday was baking day when she made cakes, pies and puddings for the following week. On Sunday a joint was cooked or steak and kidney pudding. Monday was washing day with cold meat and Tuesday was drying day with the rest of the cold meat. Wednesday and Thursday were turning out and cleaning days and Friday was shopping day when the greengrocer, butcher, fishmonger, grocer and baker called with their vans. Friday night was bath night and clean clothes and a dose of syrup of figs. We had fruit or Kentish fruit pies in season for afters and high tea every evening, with a special meal on Saturday evenings after the baking was done.

Mother always went to church on Sundays, up the hill to Frindsbury, and we went to Sunday school. The parson told his congregation not to have anything to do with the Mormons. The Mormons were very active in the village at that time, trying to get people to join them and emigrate to America, so I suppose the parson was afraid of losing his congregation. Mother also belonged to the Mothers Union, which was run by the church.

We said our prayers every night with a special prayer for those in peril on the sea. My bedroom was above the kitchen and I could hear my mother reading from her prayer book before she went to bed. Father was not a religious man but like a lot of seafarers he read the Bible and could quote passages from it. He always attended the Missions to Seamen services when he was away. I think he enjoyed singing the hymns as well. Mother was a very good manager and any money left over after paying all the bills she put into the Post Office Savings Bank. Father had no holidays but could sometimes get home for two or three days when his ship was loading or discharging cargo and then, of course, it was like a holiday for the children, but as Mother remarked 'It's all right for their father, he doesn't have to be with them all day and every day'.

Sundays were very tedious. We were not allowed to play games but when Father was at home and Mother went to church all restrictions were relaxed and we had a fine old time. During the weekdays we went to the orchard to pick baskets of cherries and had a competition to see who could pick the most doubles and hang them on our ears like earrings. We went down to the river at Upnor to picnic and paddle. Motor boats used to run trips from Strood Pier to the beach at Upnor for the day. We also had outings in Grandfather's waggonette. On one occasion the shaft broke and the horses ran away. My father was nursing me on his knee at the front next to my grandfather who was driving, and he jumped clear with me in his arms when the horses bolted. The waggonette ended up in the ditch.

I suppose because there were so many in the family the sons had descriptions attached to their names to distinguish them. I do not recall this being done with the girls' names. One of my mother's brothers was called Mad Jack because of his terrible temper, a second was called Uncle Dido, which was the name of his ship when he was in the Royal Navy, and the third was called Jimmy Squarefoot, I do not know why. Mother continued this practice with her sons-in-law. One was called Postie because he worked in the Post Office, another one who managed a branch of Burtols the Cleaners was Burtol Bill, and there was Motty whose real surname was Mottram. Joe Burgess, who was my sister Lydia's dancing partner, was Joey the Jazzer.

The Christmas parties were big affairs in our house. All the relations came. There was lots of food with beer for the men and wine for the women and lemonade for the children in bottles with marbles at the top, held there by the gas to stop them leaking, and fruit and nuts and cakes and jellies. There were games and singing to the piano. Aunt Emma always sang *Jerusalem*. This is not to be confused with Blake's poem of the same name which was set to music and adopted by the Women's Institute. Aunt Emma's *Jerusalem* ran something like this:

17

'Jerusalem, Jerusalem, Hark how the Angels sing Hosanna to God in the highest, Hosanna to the King'.

This was sung in a very high key but Aunt Emma had a very strong soprano voice and she could reach the top notes with great effect. It was listened to in silence, which was only broken by Grandmother whispering to the children 'Stop wriggling and keep still and take your feet off the staves of those chairs'.

When Father was home he always had to sing, mostly his country songs. One I remember had a chorus which sounded like 'Rye Toodle, Rye Toodle, Rye Toodle, Rye Ay'. This was a great favourite and everybody joined in. Until we were old enough to join in we watched in amazement at the grown-ups playing games, such as Spinning the Plate, where a plate was spun and the spinner called out a number and if it was your number you had to get to the plate and keep it spinning. If it stopped spinning before you got to it you had to pay a forfeit. There was always Musical Chairs and a version of Blind Man's Buff where each player was named after a railway station and had to change stations when they were called with another. The caller was always Uncle Bert who lived in London and was a guard on the South Eastern and Chatham Railway. He was Aunt Emma's husband. In another game a ring, usually a wedding ring, was threaded onto string and everybody sat round in a circle and passed the ring round under the cover of their hands so that the person standing in the middle could not find it. The game was played whilst everybody sang a song starting with 'There was a jolly miller who lived by himself. As the mill went round he made his wealth, one hand in the Hopper and the other in the bag. As the mill went round he made his grab'. There was always singing at these parties with everyone joining in, as there were no gramophones or radio. When the parties were held in Grandmother's house she was always afraid the floor would collapse into the cellar. Other family meetings were not so happy. During the 1914-18 war there were gatherings to say goodbye to the young men when they were being called up or rejoining their regiments in France. The war was never mentioned. The talk was of the family and mutual friends and looking at photographs over a quiet drink. Nobody cried whilst the young men were there. Later their parents could not bring themselves to open the door when the telegraph boy walked up the garden path.

When the people in the village became too old to support themselves they had to go and live in the workhouse, which was situated in Gun Lane, Strood. The villagers called it the 'Spike'. Mother visited the workhouse once a week, usually on Wednesday afternoons, and took in books and magazines and tobacco, sweets and cakes for Christmas for the old people living there. They used to wait at the gates looking for her. Included in the magazines my mother gave them were early issues of Charles Dickens' stories my father had inherited from his mother, which was rather a loss. Father was a great reader. He supported the Liberal party and read the *Daily News* or the *Daily Chronicle*, which were later amalgamated and became the *News Chronicle*. Mother was always too busy to find time to sit down and read.

When Grandmother died her youngest daughter, Grace, who had stayed at home to look after the shop, married a former sergeant in the Royal Horse Artillery who had been badly wounded at the battle of Mons and had been billeted on them during the war. They emigrated to Canada and took up a grant of land in one of the prairie provinces. The fare for the steamship crossing was £10. My grandfather was too independent to go into the workhouse. He made his sons contribute 5s. a week each for his support and as he had six sons and some savings he lived comfortably and still attended the weekly cattle market and no doubt did a bit of dealing. Mother was good at patching and darning but she never had time to learn dressmaking. Consequently an aunt made flannel vests for me to wear and pinafores for the girls, which they all wore at the village school. Clothes were handed down in the family but as I was the only boy I did not get any hand-me-downs. My usual clothes were a jersey, corduroy trousers, stockings and boots, until I went to school in the town when I had to wear school uniform and a cap.

One day a bullock escaped from the cattle market at Rochester. It was chased all the way through the town by a crowd waving their sticks and shouting 'Look out! Mad Bull! Mad Bull!' The poor beast was frightened and kept on running. Eventually it reached Wainscott and somebody opened the gate of Grandfather's stable yard and when the animal ran inside the gate was shut and it was cornered. A man went up the village to fetch Grandfather and he came down in a very bad temper.

The crowd sat on the stable yard walls and waited to see what would happen. I don't suppose any of them had been to Spain and seen the running of the bulls through the streets of Pamplona but they all seemed to expect to see a bull fight when Grandfather entered the stable yard. But Grandfather never did fear man or beast. The animal was exhausted and confused. He went up to it, spoke quietly to it, and calmed it down. He gave it some feed and water and tied it up to wait for the owner to come and collect it. Then he went over to the people who were watching and told them to clear off and not to act like a pack of bloody fools in future. The family ties were very strong whilst the grandparents were alive and this provided a certain stability and a standard of behaviour which had to be maintained in their presence.

Two brothers of Grandmother who had emigrated to New Zealand and established themselves as sheep farmers always sent over two lamb carcasses for Christmas.

Father bought the grandparents' house when it was put up for sale and they were likely to be evicted. After the 1914-18 war when Grandmother died and Grandfather moved out he sold it to the son of our next door neighbours who wanted to turn the village store into a butcher's shop. Although the property had increased in value since he bought it my father sold it for the price he gave for it because the young man had served in the war and wanted to establish himself in business. Actually this man sold the premises to the Co-op at a good profit a few months after my father had sold it to him.

I went away with my father every summer practically as soon as I could walk and some memories of these trips have stayed with me all my life. I remember warm summer nights; stars were out and the moon was shining. There was hardly any wind and the only sound in the stillness of the night was the quiet lapping of the water against the side of the barge as we drifted along. My father softly sang negro spirituals and songs of the American South by Stephen Foster, whilst I listened with the crew, seated on the hatches. Even now, thinking of these occasions and remembering the haunting tunes makes me feel sad. Some other times still upset me. When Father was bound for the Thames or Medway he would send a telegram to let us know the day he expected to be home. But this was subject to the vagaries of the wind and sometimes he could not make it.

I knew when he was expected home and I walked all the way to the top of the hill at Frindsbury where the trams stopped to meet him there. I would keep watch all day, hoping to see him coming with his free and easy walk, and kit bag over his shoulder. When it turned dark and he did not come I walked back home, tired and hungry, to be met at the door by my mother, who guessed where I had been but still demanded to know what I had been doing. All I could repeat between sobs was 'He didn't come, he didn't come'. As I grew older other times were more exciting. If we ran short of coal for the galley fires we tied up when it was dark alongside a coal lighter and the crew filled a few buckets with coal whilst I kept watch for the river police. When we made a trip to France the crew bought as much perfume and brandy as they could afford and sent me up on deck with the excess over their allowance whilst the customs officers were on board.

My father's elder brother, Captain George Brooks, was a tall strong man and owing to his size and strength he was called 'Navvy'. He was a hard man to his crew and to his own family and in his dealings with others. When my father joined Uncle George's ship he was treated with the same hard discipline as the rest of the crew. Father said it was like serving under Captain Bligh of the *Bounty* must have been. The mate said they were treated like trained dogs. None of the crew had a day off. When they were in port they had to paint the captain's house or dig his garden. On his first voyage with Uncle George the weather was very rough and father was battened down in the galley and owing to the movement of the barge and the heat in the confined space, for the only time he felt sick and hammered on the hatch to be let out. The only reply he got was to stay where he was and get on with his work. Uncle George was a fine sailor and navigator and a good judge of weather.

Weather lore was taught and remembered by rhymes or catch phrases such as 'Red sky at night shepherd's delight, red sky in the morning sailor's warning,' 'Evening grey and morning red makes a wise sailor shake his head,' 'When the sun goes down as clear as a bell it's an easterly wind as sure as hell, but when the sun goes down behind a bank its a westerly wind and the Lord we thank.'

This last saying was particularly used in the old sailing ships when they were homeward bound across the Atlantic. Clouds also foretold the weather. If they were shaped like mares' tails they meant wind and if they built up like castles in the sky they meant rain. Navigation at night was helped, when another ship was sighted, by remembering 'Green to green, red to red all clear go ahead.' I found these very useful when racing offshore in my yacht or making a passage.

The third hand or cook slept in the fo'c'sle on a canvas cot and did the cooking there and carried it along the deck in all weathers to the saloon. There were no life lines on deck and when the barge was beating to windward in a strong wind and loaded, the leeward deck would be constantly under water, so the cook had to take his chance to get aft on the windward side. If he was caught by a wave he dropped the food and hung on to the shrouds or anything else he could get hold of to save himself from being swept overboard. The lavatory consisted of a wooden bucket kept in the fo'c'sle which was filled with sea water and a wooden plank placed on it for a seat. The result was then thrown overboard and the bucket cleaned by dowsing it in sea water. The accommodation aft consisted of a saloon with small cabins for the master and mate, one each side. There was a coal stove for heat and a hanging oil lamp for light under the skylight. Furniture consisted of a table, two chairs, a settee, lockers and cupboards for food and utensils. The main meal of the day was dinner at midday. When the barge was in port there was fresh meat and vegetables, but when these ran out at sea a piece of salt beef was soaked in a bucket of fresh water to get out the salt and make the maggots float to the top, looking like little Michelin men in the tyre advertisements. This was boiled with carrots and potatoes and for afters it was usually plum duff followed by cups of tea. No alcohol was kept on board. When bread ran out we ate ship's biscuits which were so hard they had to be soaked in water or tea before we could eat them.

Sailing a barge was hard labour for the captain and crew. All the work had to be done manually. There was no machinery and in small ports the crew had to do the discharging and help with loading and stowing the cargo. The wheel house on a coasting barge was open at the front, and the helmsman was exposed to the elements. This helped the captain see everything that was going on and lend a hand when necessary. When the wind and/or tide were favourable a sailing barge got under way whether it was day or night. The captain did not turn in, he laid down on the settee fully clothed. If both the wind and tide were against the direction the vessel had to sail it was a case of down anchor and wait for a change in wind or tide. That was the difference between a sailing ship and a steamship. A barge worked with Nature but a steamship forced a passage whatever the weather, if it could.

The navigation aids on a barge were a compass, a log which was streamed aft to register the distance travelled through the water, a lead to measure the depth of water, Admiralty charts and tide tables and a flag to show the direction of the wind relative to the point of sailing. Father's master's ticket covered the area from the Baltic in the north to the Mediterranean in the south and all round the British Isles, including Ireland and the Channel Islands. The training and discipline instilled in my father by his brother, Captain 'Navvy' Brooks, stood him in good stead. He became a fine seaman and could navigate all the coastal waters and short sea routes from his own knowledge and experience and soon acquired the ability to forecast the weather, which was essential for a sailing barge captain. Father was fair and considerate but firm with the crew. He used to inspect their living quarters regularly to see that they maintained the standards of cleanliness he insisted on and that everything was shipshape. On one inspection I heard him say to the men 'This place looks like a whore's garret. Get it cleaned up right away'. It was some years later that I found out what a whore's garret was.

The difference between my father and his brother, Captain 'Navvy' Brooks, is illustrated by an incident which happened before the 1914-18 war. The dockers were on strike and called for support from the watermen, lightermen and bargemen. My father supported the dockers and tied up his barge but Uncle George stayed at sea and creamed off the freights, earning sufficient to build a fine house for himself at Hoo.

Father was a moderate drinker and smoker. I never saw him lose his temper and the only time I heard him swear was when a steamship nearly ran us down when we were sailing up the Thames. In theory steamships are supposed to give way to sailing ships but my experience is, if you are in a sailing vessel you either get out of the way or you run the risk of being hit. On this occasion it was only my father's quick action in going about between a string of lighters tied up to a buoy and the steamship, and then immediately coming about again before hitting the lighters which avoided a collision. We were left rolling in the steamship's wake with the sails flapping, the sprit banging to and fro and the mast vibrating dangerously as though it would jump out of its casing.

He always acted quickly in an emergency and knew exactly what to do. When his barge sprang a leak and the pumps could not keep pace with the water flooding in, he ran the vessel up on the sands near Littlehampton and saved her. On another occasion in Belgium the barge was being towed down the canal to Zeebrugge. There were six barges on the tow and they were made fast fore and aft in pairs side by side. Father's barge was in the second pair with another pair being towed behind. The bow rope broke and as the stern was still held fast this allowed the bows to swing outwards towards the canal bank. Father immediately shouted to the tug to slow down, threw another bow rope to the other barge alongside and ordered the stern rope to be slackened off. The new bow rope was made fast and hauled in to bring the barge against the other barge, the stern rope was refastened and we were on our way again. He always took great care of the vessels he commanded. When the barges had to go through Rochester Bridge to get up the Medway he always employed a man called a huffler to help lower the mast and raise it again after clearing the bridge, but some captains tried to manage on their own and the mast often came down to the cracking and breaking of the rigging.

Father's first command was a barge called *Glencoe* owned by Mr Little, who had a fleet of barges which he managed. On occasions when his barge was discharging in the Thames the owner would tell him to meet him at Cannon Street station where he would pay my father and the other captains the money due to them. Mr Little invariably left it late to catch the five o'clock train and there followed the spectacle of three or four captains running after him and being doled out a sovereign each before the train left. Father was glad to leave his employ and became master of a large coasting sailing barge called *Glenway* when it was bought by Mr Wilks, who lived on the coast at Deal in sight of the sea and could watch his barges sailing up or down the Channel. Mr Wilks left full control of the vessels to the masters. My father engaged the crew, negotiated the freights, collected the payment and maintained and repaired the barge. Father had no bank account so he collected the freight money in cash, which was paid in gold before the 1914-18 war. When he came home after collecting freight money he emptied a bag of gold on the kitchen table and divided it into three, one heap for the owner, one for the maintenance and repairs of the vessel and one for the wages and keep of the captain and crew. He made up his accounts which he sent to the owner with his share, retained one share for the ship's expenses, and out of the third share he kept sufficient for the crew's wages and his own expenses and handed the rest to my mother. When the war broke out gold was replaced by Treasury notes which came to be known as Bradburys after the name of the man who signed them. We saw no more glistening heaps of gold on the kitchen table, but I still have a gold half sovereign which my mother gave me as a souvenir.

Father was a modest man. He was awarded the usual Merchant Navy medals for service during the war. The authorities sent him the ribbons and he was asked to attend to receive the medals but he did not bother to do so and never wore the ribbons. He always joked and said he would collect the medals if there was a pension attached to them. When the life of the sailing vessels came to an end in the mid 1920s, he was approached by Mr Metcalf, the owner of a firm who were building up a new fleet of motor ships, to go over to Bremen in Germany to take command of the ship they were having built there. Mr Metcalf knew my father well because my father had often carried freights for him in his sailing barge, sometimes quicker than his own motorized barges could do. Father accepted command of the ship, which ended his career in sailing barges after forty years. He did not wear his captain's uniform but he did compromise by wearing a cap with the owner's badge on it to show that he was master of the vessel.

3

CHILDHOOD

I was born on the 31 October 1910. I was a sensitive child and wanted affection but I did not get it after I ceased being a baby, except from my father when he came home and would take me on his knee. I still sat on his knee when I was ten years' old, despite the taunts I received from boys of my own age. Mother loved us dearly but she had all the responsibility of bringing up the family and making all the decisions on her own. She would do anything for us but she had to maintain a strict discipline to keep six children in order and she could not unbend. The only times she gave me a kiss on the cheek was when I left to go away with my father. The other thing which prevented her from showing affection towards me was the way I behaved. I was independent and determined to get my own way from an early age. I had an enquiring mind and I wanted to explore new places and try out new things. I could not understand why people tried to stop me, so I was always in trouble. When my sister Ethel was five she went to the village school. I was two and a half yeas old and she was my playmate so I went after her and kicked on the schoolroom door to be let in. Ethel had to take me back home but as soon as she had gone I went back and started to try and kick the door down again. This went on for a week or more before the teacher finally gave in and allowed me to join the class.

So I started school at two and a half and all during my school career, including the school I went to after leaving the village school, I was two years younger than the average age in my form. My mother actually fostered my independent spirit as I grew up by always advising me to 'Be your own Master.' She was born under the sign of Scorpio and so was I and I must have inherited a lot of my characteristics from her. I understand that a boy takes two thirds of his genes from his mother. This explains why the Spaniards always killed the bull at a bull fight. The bulls inherit their fighting instincts from their mothers, not from their fathers. I was not aggressive but I always reacted strongly against aggression. My wife says my temper is on a short fuse.

I was creative rather than ambitious. I liked to initiate enterprises and plan their future progress and see them through to completion. I was always impatient to get things done. One of my favourite sayings was 'It's only a ten minute job.' My interest was in whatever I was doing and so long as I could provide a good life for my wife and family I was happy.

The village school was an old Victorian building surrounded by a concrete playground. There was no central heating and the lavatories were right at the bottom of the playground as far away as possible from the classrooms. In winter there was a fire one end of each room, surrounded by a large fireguard. When it rained heavily the boys coming in from the outlying cottages and farms were soaked to the skin. They were allowed to stand six at a time in front of the fire to dry out and the steam used to rise in clouds from their clothes. They never missed school because of the weather. I think the parents were afraid of the school attendance officer.

If a child attended school for a year without being absent once the boy or girl received a medal and was awarded a bar to the medal for full attendance in each following year. My eldest sister, Minnie, held the school record for a medal with six bars until she left to go to the grammar school. We received a sound grounding in reading, writing and arithmetic and religion. A lot of the basic training was done by repetition which helped the backward children, but those who were capable of going further were given every encouragement. My sister Ethel set another school record. She was the only pupil ever to gain a scholarship to the grammar school and we were all given a half-day's holiday to celebrate her achievement.

The other occasion when we were given a half-day's holiday was on the annual Empire Day. We paraded around the flagpole, the Union Jack was raised, we all saluted the flag and sang a song, ending in 'We salute thee and we pray God to bless our land this day.'

Ethel was rather unlucky at school. She had a front tooth knocked out by a boy with a catapult whilst she was playing in the school playground. At other times she was accident prone. When I was coming down the road with her she fell into the road, which had recently been tarred. Her arms and legs were covered in tar, which had to be cleaned off by a liberal application of butter. One evening she went to visit the next door neighbours and fell into the cesspool. Fortunately it was practically dry. Workmen had been pumping it out and had left the cover off.

I was happy at the village school except for one thing which upset me. On Monday mornings the headmaster would come in and call out four boys from the front row to stand before the class. We sat in alphabetical order and, as my surname began with a 'B' I was always one of the four. He took a large white handkerchief from his breast pocket and instructed each of us to hold one corner. He then said 'When I say, Hold it, Drop it, and when I say Drop it, Hold it'. He proceeded to say 'Hold it, Drop it, Drop it, Hold it' in quick succession. This caused absolute confusion in our minds and we just dropped the handkerchief on the floor. The headmaster then produced his cane and whacked us about the legs to drive us back to our seats, saying 'That will teach you to wake up in the mornings.' I thought it was very unfair, as I was the brightest boy in the class and I was always invited to his daughter's birthday party.

At Christmas time we were given a bun and orange. Once we had an outing to visit the London Zoo. We marched down to Strood railway station, a distance of about two and a half miles, carrying our sandwiches and caught a train to Charing Cross, where we changed to the Underground for Regents Park. I felt sick in the enclosed space but soon recovered when we got out into the fresh air and thoroughly enjoyed seeing all the animals.

Games were played at different times during the year. In the summer the boys played Five Stones or Castles. Five Stones consisted of four pebbles placed in a square with another stone in the middle against a wall. A tennis ball was thrown to knock a pebble out and bounce back from the wall to be caught by the thrower. If no pebble was hit or the thrower could not catch the ball on the rebound the other boy took his turn with the ball. The winner was the one who knocked most pebbles out. Castles was played with cigarette cards. One or more cards were placed on end against a wall and each boy tried in turn to flick a card at the ones against the wall to knock them over. The winner gathered up all the cards which were left lying on the ground after he had knocked the castles over. A boy who won at this game could gradually build up his sets of cigarette cards of footballers or cricketers or motor cars. Bowling of hoops was very popular with both boys and girls. The girls had wooden hoops and the boys had iron ones made by the village blacksmith.

When the pond was frozen over in winter we made slides on it, although going on the ice was forbidden in case of accidents. There was no skating because nobody had any skates. At Halloween we hollowed out the insides of turnips, carved a horrible looking face on the outside and put a lighted candle inside. When it was dark we knocked on the windows of a house and when the curtains were drawn back we pressed the lighted turnip against the glass to scare the people inside. A man usually came to the door but we ran away before he could catch us. We did not adopt the American custom of 'Trick or Treat.'

Whip tops was a game played to spin the tops. One type of top was called a 'Flying Dutchman'. It flew through the air if it was whipped hard enough. I gave my Flying Dutchman a hard whack and it flew through the shop window of the village grocer. He rushed out of his shop and I ran away but he had recognized me and shouted 'I'll have the police on you'. I knew the village policeman would go to my mother and ask 'Will you deal with him or shall I, Mrs Brooks?' and my mother would reply 'I'll deal with him.' From past experience I knew that meant a good hiding so I always stayed out as late as I could, sometimes after midnight if it was not too cold. However, the result was always the same; my mother was waiting for me and started to deal with me by saying 'Get your clothes off and let me know when you are ready for bed.' I called out when I was undressed and she came up to the bedroom. I was laid face down on the bed and given a good hiding with the back of a hairbrush on my bare bottom. I always shouted as loud as I could, hoping the next door neighbour, the carpenter's wife, would hear. If she did hear and thought the beating had gone on long enough she would come in and ask 'Don't you think you have punished him enough, Mrs Brooks?' My mother always stopped then and

29

I was put to bed, but I suffered terrible nightmares. They were always the same. I dreamt I was falling into a black bottomless pit, but before I reached the bottom I woke up screaming and crying. My sister Lydia, who was the second eldest, used to come into my room to comfort me and get me to sleep again.

She was the one in our family most like our father, very fond of children. She did not go to grammar school but remained at home to help my mother look after the house and do the cooking. She became a better cook then my mother. In the summer she went fruit picking to earn some pocket money and as she started work at six o'clock in the morning, my sister Ethel and I took her breakfast to her in the orchards at eight o'clock before we went to school.

I belonged to a group of village boys under the leadership of the son of the carpenter. I was only five years old and the other boys were about ten but I was allowed to join because my friend next door decided who could be admitted. We did not call ourselves a gang as this had the meaning, to our minds, of a lot of ruffians, whereas we were just high spirited, although we were often in trouble. We looked for birds' nests and collected eggs but we took only one from each nest and left at least two. The boy who discovered the nest or who reached it after a difficult climb was the one who had the egg. We did not walk through growing crops but we did take fruit, chestnuts, blackberries, mushrooms and woodnuts, in season, to eat when we were hungry. When we were camping we also dug up potatoes to roast with pigeons, which we knocked off with our catapults, and sometimes we found a rabbit caught in a trap to add to our meal. I imagine that these traps were set by poachers, as the gamekeeper had no need to trap rabbits, which he could always shoot.

The gamekeepers who looked after the woods at Cobham Hall for Lord Darnley were rather difficult. We always went into Cobham Woods to get chestnuts and if we were caught the gamekeeper confiscated all we had collected. There was no point in trying to run away. He had a gun and although I don't suppose he would have fired at us we were frightened and gave up our chestnuts without arguing. The village constable toured all the lanes on his bicycle. When he saw us in the orchards or trespassing he did not bother to chase us because he knew us all by sight. He reported us to our parents who said they would deal with us and I knew I had another late night and a good hiding to come.

I had an egg collection which my mother gave away to the Girl Guides whilst I was in hospital.

When the school doctor visited the village I was examined and I was sent home with a note to say I only had one lung, but no action was recommended. Presumably if you only had one lung nothing could be done to give you another one. My parents were very upset but they had to accept the situation. There were no X-rays and the doctor had reached his decision by tapping my chest and listening to my breathing through his stethoscope. Actually he had discovered something wrong with my chest, as was proved fifty years later, but he had arrived at the wrong conclusion. In any case it did not affect me at that time.

We had a lot of fun catching sticklebacks and collecting frog spawn from the river. The sticklebacks did not develop but the frog spawn turned into tadpoles and then to frogs which we put back into the river. I tried freshwater fishing from the streams on the marshes but found it rather dull sitting waiting for a bite, so I usually went off to find ducks' nests and collect a few eggs. The river Wain was too small for swimming except when it was in flood and we went down to Whitewall creek where it joined the river Medway. Rafts of logs were kept in the water there and we used them as diving platforms. The water was deep and I soon learned to swim by breaststroke and backstroke. We were not supposed to be there and were always chased away if we were seen.

We did not smoke. We tried a Woodbine cigarette to find out what it was like but we did not continue with it. We found we did not like smoking and we did not carry on with it long enough to develop a liking for it. But more importantly we were told 'Smoking spoils your wind' and we were afraid that we would not be able to keep up our running and playing games like football.

We were too young to drink alcohol. My father's nephew and his wife kept the village pub called The White Hart. They had a son of my age and my mother forbade me to go and play with him because of the horrible language I might hear. Nevertheless, I did go to play with him in the afternoons when the pub was shut and as they had an early tea before it re-opened I stayed to tea and then went home in good time to have my supper.

There was one bad accident arising from our game of climbing onto the back of carts for a ride. A cart was coming down Spakes Hill from Frindsbury and, following the usual custom, the driver had put a skid pan under one of the rear wheels to lock it and so help to hold the cart back. One boy could not get on the back of the cart and he stood on the spokes of the wheel which was prevented from turning by the skid pan. Unfortunately, the iron chain which held the skid pan in position broke, releasing the wheel to turn round, and the boy was thrown under the wheel and killed.

When I was born my mother told my father she wanted to call me James after my paternal grandfather, but my father said I must be christened Reuben. She said 'In that case you must have him christened yourself.' I was not christened until a year later when Father came home. Actually the choice of Reuben was the right one because it means 'Behold a Son' and as I had five sisters and no brother it was very appropriate. My friends all call me Brooky, my business associates addressed me as Reuben and my junior clerks referred to me as 'Der Führer' when they were talking amongst themselves. The daughter of my father's brother, Captain Philip Brooks, was not so fortunate with her name. Her father wanted Helen, her mother insisted on Ellen, a compromise was arrived at and she was christened Helen Ellen. She trained as a secretary and went to America, where she took a job with General Motors and married her boss, who was one of the directors of the company.

The outbreak of war in August 1914 widened our horizons considerably. We had two sergeants billeted on us until the army camp at Lodge Hill was large enough to take all the men. They were regulars, aged about forty, and both had large moustaches. We had only three bedrooms and they slept in the outhouse. We did not have to feed them because they had all their meals at the camp, but except for that we treated them as part of the family and did their washing and mending, and saw to it that they were properly turned out. The children cleaned and polished their buttons and badges. We wanted them to be the smartest soldiers in the village. When the camp was large enough they were accommodated there and we did not see them after that until the day we heard the regimental band strike up as it neared the village, escorting the soldiers marching away to the front. As they came through the village we recognized our two sergeants and we ran up to them and kissed them goodbye and cried. The other women in the village greeted the men who had been billeted with them and gave them gifts of cigarettes and chocolate and scarves and gloves. The boys followed on behind them, trying to keep up, but eventually we fell out at the top of Frindsbury Hill, whilst the troops went down the hill to catch the train at Strood Junction on their way to Dover or Folkestone. We never saw them again. The camp at Lodge Hill was expanded to take in extra troops and we did not have any more soldiers billeted in the village. Although when they marched away we always followed the band.

One day an aeroplane landed in a meadow near the village and it seemed that everybody ran down to see it. It was a biplane with an open cockpit and lots of wire and struts to strengthen the wings. It appeared that the pilot had engine trouble and after working on it for about two hours he decided to take off again. The plane was dragged to the other end of the meadow and turned round so that he could take off into the wind. He ran the engine up, waved goodbye, and had no difficulty in getting into the air.

There was an airship base on the Isle of Sheppey at the mouth of the river Medway. Airships were a frequent sight but one day, when I had gone down to Strood pier to meet my father, an airship came over with an aeroplane fastened beneath it. Apparently the idea was to launch the aeroplane from the airship. Whilst we were watching the front of the aeroplane detached, but it was still made fast at the tailend and hung suspended by its tail. We saw two bodies fall out of the aeroplane. One fell into the water off Strood pier and the other into Strood dock. The men were both dead when they were taken out of the water.

The soldiers practised digging trenches and dugouts and when they had gone back to camp we explored what they had done. Some of the dugouts were very deep and water had filled the bottom, making them dangerous to go down. Side rooms were built in them and sometimes interconnecting tunnels, which were very exciting to boys with a vivid imagination. Grandfather, my mother's father — I did not know my father's parents who both died before I was born — could always see an opportunity for making an honest penny. He still ran the village shop so he loaded his cart with confectionery, fruit, lemonade, cakes and buns and drove out to the places where the soldiers were working. He invited me and my cousin Roly, the son of my mother's eldest brother, to go with him and lend him a hand. We first visited the site where the soldiers were digging the trenches. The officers gave the men a break when we appeared and they crowded round the cart to buy what they wanted to eat and drink. When the officers called them back to work we moved on to Blacklands Farm which had a large pond where the engineers were practising building pontoon bridges. They took a break and bought what they wanted. Then we packed up and drove back home. As a reward for our help Grandfather gave both of us what he called a speckled orange. This was in fact an orange which had started to go mouldy and which he could not sell. We pointed this out to Grandfather and he said we could cut the mouldy bits out and eat the rest. When we got back he asked us to be at the shop by eight o'clock the next morning to help him load up. We followed the same routine as the day before and were again given a speckled orange each. We discussed what we should do the next day. I told Roly that when I helped a smallholder to feed his pigs on a Saturday morning I was always given 2d. Roly was a year or two older than I was, so we were both only little boys, but we did help to load the cart, serve the soldiers while Grandfather collected the money, pack the cart up and clear up the rubbish. We knew Grandfather would not pay us any money, but we did think we were entitled to more than a mouldy orange. Whilst Grandfather was at the front of the cart we each took a penny bar of toffee from the back which we had decided was a fair reward for our work. We also accepted the speckled orange we were given, in case Grandfather became suspicious if we refused, and threw it away when we got home.

We knew all the wartime songs, of course, but we sang a parody of our own at the time of the Dardenelles campaign when Charlie Chaplin was becoming known, which ran 'Oh! The moon shines bright on Charlie Chaplin, his boots are cracking for want of blacking. Oh! The moon shines bright on Charlie Chaplin, they ought to send him to the Dardenelles.'

There was an ammunition depot near the army camp, where shells were filled for the Royal Navy and then carried by a light railway to the Gun Wharf at Upnor to be put aboard the battleships anchored in the Medway or fitting out in Chatham

Dockyard. Shortly after leaving the depot the line crossed a bridge over the main road and the train had to slow down to take a sharp right hand bend before picking up speed for the run down to the Gun Wharf. The father of one of the boys in our group was the engine driver, so our friend was able to keep us informed when a shipment was to take place. The shells were loaded on flat-bottomed wagons and where the train slowed down we hid in the woods and then rushed out and jumped up onto the last wagon for a ride on top of the big fifteen inch shells. The train slowed down again when it reached the gates at the entrance to the Gun Wharf and we jumped off and ran away before the policeman guarding the gates could catch us. One of the battleships, *HMS Bulwark*, blew up and sank in the lower reaches of the Medway when taking on ammunition and most of her crew of 700 or 800 men were killed.

In 1917 I was involved in an event which put me out of action for a while. When we were exploring the trenches we were always looking for souvenirs to take home and one day we found a hand grenade or Mills bomb, as it was sometimes called. We took it to an old stableyard on the outskirts of the village, which the council used for dumping road-making material, to examine it. The pin holding the lever in place had been pulled out and the lever was missing. It could have been a dummy for practice throwing or a dud which had failed to explode. The boy who had picked it up said 'There is one way to tell. Let's light a fire and throw it in.' This seemed a dangerous thing to do, even for us, so we had to find a way to avoid being hurt. The stable yard was enclosed by a low wall with a five barred gate opening onto the road. It was decided to throw the hand grenade into the fire and hide behind the wall in case it went off. We lit the fire and threw the grenade in. The wall was about twenty yards away and we ran as fast as we could to get over it. I was the youngest so I was a few yards behind the others and as I scrambled over the wall I heard the bang of the grenade exploding. I pulled myself up on the other side and when I did so I felt something warm running down my left leg. I was wearing shorts and I put my hand inside to find out what it was. As I did a lump of flesh fell onto the ground. I thought at first I might pick it up but then I decided the best thing to do was to get home as quickly as possible. Our house was about fifty yards away in the centre of the village, and when I got there

I just sat on the kitchen floor and could not get up. The immediate reaction of my mother when she was told I was in trouble, was always to cry 'I'll kill him! I'll kill him' to relieve her feelings. But this time it was really serious because I was losing a lot of blood and getting weaker every minute. Fortunately, one of the girls next door was courting a sergeant in the Royal Army Medical Corps and he happened to be there. he came in and stopped the bleeding and bandaged me up; then we had to think about getting to the doctor's. There was no doctor in the village, the nearest one being at Frindsbury. I was put in the baby's pushchair and my sister Lydia pushed me all the way there. I was taken into the surgery and the doctor told me not to look while he put eight stitches in. I did look, of course, and saw that he used a kind of thin gold wire which was tied into a knot and then clipped off. He gave us a supply of dressings with instructions to change them every day and we set off home. It was all down hill on the way back. The difficulty was to stop the pushchair from running away but Lydia managed it and put me to bed when we got there. About a fortnight later we went back to the surgery to have the stitches taken out. This was more painful than having them put in. Unfortunately, when the grenade went off some workmen were coming down the road after their shift finished at the munitions depot. They complained to the police, which meant another visit by the village policeman to my mother, who said she would deal with me as usual, but the policeman said the last escapade was more serious and if I had been older he would have had to handle it himself. When my father came home I heard my mother say to him 'I can't deal with him this time, you will have to take him with you.' He pointed out that he was loading a cargo for France and it might be dangerous. Her reply was to the effect that our village was only across the river from Chatham Dockyard and a stray bomb could come our way. When the Germans were trying to hit the dockyard they had on one occasion damaged the Naval Hospital at Gillingham whilst Uncle Dido was a patient there, recovering from being torpedoed.

The next morning Mother said 'You're going with your father this trip.' I was overjoyed because I had not been allowed to go since the beginning of the war. She packed a kit bag made out of an old pillow case with a change of clothing and my toilet things, kissed me on the cheek and off I went with my father.

My wound had healed well and although it left me with a hole in my left thigh it did not cause me any trouble. We went aboard the *Glenway* and as it was not allowed to carry passengers I signed on as a cabin boy at a wage of 1s. a week and my keep. We had a fair wind down the river, out to the Nore, along the north Kent coast, round the North Foreland and dropped anchor in the Downs to wait for the rest of the convoy. Some vessels were already there and more arrived during the day. The convoy got under way the next day, shepherded by three or four navy destroyers. There must have been forty or fifty ships, ranging from quite large steamers down to the sailing barges. The steamers went ahead and the sailing barges tagged on behind, with the result that it was a very ragged convoy and the destroyers had a difficult task trying to keep in touch with everybody. They dashed about at high speed and hailed us. 'Can you make more speed, Captain?' Father shouted back, 'Yes, if you can give us more wind.' We had a man on watch, keeping a look out for submarines, and Father was given a Very pistol and a supply of flares to signal if anything was sighted. Nothing was seen and we arrived in Calais and docked ready for unloading, which meant a delay of four or five days because of the congestion in the docks, and we were one of the last in the queue. It was the first time I had been abroad and I made the most of the opportunity to explore the town when I went shopping with my father for provisions, and he bought some perfume for me to take home to Mother and the girls. The odd aeroplane came over during the day to drop a bomb, if possible, on the docks and there was some shelling from long range guns. Night time was busiest for air raids. It was considered too risky to stay on board the wooden vessels to sleep so my father and the other captains spent the night aboard an iron dredger. I soon went to sleep on my father's lap, whilst all the men passed the time smoking and yarning. They smoked clay pipes, which could be bought for a halfpenny each, and their yarns were always of what had happened to other captains, their ships, the voyages they made, the weather they encountered, the accidents which occurred, and the freights they carried. They never spoke of leisure activities such as football, the reason being they were never at home, but always at work either at sea or, if they were in port, loading or discharging cargo.

When they were ashore I noticed that all the captains used

one pub or café and the crews went elsewhere for their entertainment. There was no rule about it but it seemed to be the accepted practice. I sailed with my father all the summer and went back to school in the autumn. Sometimes the voyages were at night time and then nobody turned in below. I slept on deck in the wheel house instead of on the bunk in my father's cabin. The watch during the night was very tense. If the wind broke the surface of a wave the lookout thought he could see the periscope of an enemy submarine, but they were all false alarms. The ship's boat was kept slung out, hanging from the davits in case we had to get away quickly. We never had to sail in convoy on the way back to England, probably because we were carrying no cargo. I became quite a mascot with the other captains, who gave me money, and after each trip I went home feeling quite rich and put the money in the Post Office Savings Bank.

I could not get into much trouble during the winter and in 1918 I again spent the summer with my father. 1919 was the same, but as the war had ended I did not have to sign on, as passengers were permitted. The end of the war meant that my father could go further afield for his freights. The countries of Europe were getting back to work and rebuilding their damaged towns and villages, so there were a lot of cargoes about. Father secured a contract for return freights to and from Belgium. We sailed over to Zeebrugge where I saw the damage to the mole made by the English raid during the war and the three ships which were sunk to block the harbour and which had been towed to one side to clear the fairway. We sailed up the canal to the town of Nieuport, where we tied up alongside the quay. Several other barges were trading there, including the *Leonard Piper*, whose captain was Frank Day, my father's cousin. He had his two sons aboard, one of whom was my age and the other a year younger. We got on well together, exploring the remains of the trenches and going out in the ship's boat belonging to the *Glenway*, which my father had taught me to handle. He gave me plenty of pocket money to share with my cousins and as the sailing barges were windbound for two or three weeks we had a marvellous holiday before the wind changed and they could get down the canal and put to sea again.

The captains used to meet in one particular café to talk, have a drink and smoke. They all knew each other and had heard my father sing. Every evening when the talking flagged someone would say 'Give us a song, Dave.' Music was not allowed in the cafés at that time because everybody was supposed to be hard at work rebuilding the town. I have noticed that anyone who can sing well is always willing to entertain others. My father stood up and sang a selection of songs in English which everybody enjoyed, including the Belgians. Each evening the café was full as people came to hear the English captain sing. We were invited to stay for supper by the proprietor and his wife after the café shut and I remember a dish I particularly enjoyed, baked hare stuffed with prunes. When my cousins and I were out in the ship's boat we rowed up the canal to a place which had been a yacht haven and there were still some yachts looking as though they had been left since before the war and were in a bad shape.

I was a great reader and one of the books I enjoyed most was called *Deeds that Won the British Empire* I do not remember who wrote it but it described one of the tactics the Royal Navy used in the old days, called 'cutting out'. This was in the time of Admiral Hood and Nelson, when we were fighting the French and Spaniards. The enemy ships stayed in port, guarded by the guns of the forts ashore, and would not come out to fight the English fleet, which was waiting outside. The Royal Navy therefore manned their ship's boats and rowed with muffled oars into the enemy port under cover of darkness. Some of the men scrambled up the sides of the enemy ships and overpowered the guards, another group cut the anchors and the foretopmen went aloft to shake out the sails. The sailors who had remained in the boats started towing the ship out to sea and when the wind caught the sails the ship got under way before the forts could get their guns to fire.

I planned a similar expedition to cut out some of the yachts from their moorings and tow them away. We could not do this at night. It had to be done during the day, so I decided to carry it out at midday when most people would be at lunch. With my crew of two we rowed into the yacht haven and put a tow aboard four of the yachts nearest the entrance. We rowed as hard as we could and once we had got them going it was easy to keep them moving. Off we went down the canal past the wharf where the barges were tied up. I did not have a clear idea how far we were going to take them but this was solved for me when there was a shout from the bank and I saw a policeman riding a bicycle on the tow path and shouting at us. We continued on for another ten minutes and then cast the yachts adrift and rowed as hard as we could back to the barges, while the policeman decided what to do about the drifting yachts. We got back on board, ate our lunch and said nothing about what we had been doing and strangely enough nobody else said anything about it either.

The crews of the barges usually spent their evenings on shore together but one lad fancied a waitress in the café they frequented and visited her on his own. He came out of the café and was set upon by her boyfriend, aided by his friends, and was beaten up. The following morning the dockers came along the quay to go to work and the lad from the barge recognized the man who had attacked him amongst the group. He immediately leapt up the ladder and got hold of his attacker, but the other dockers interfered. The crews on the barges saw what was happening and ran up onto the quay, including my father, and they formed a ring round the two who were struggling to let them fight it out. It was a good hard fight until the Belgian called it a day and gave up.

Two days later the wind changed and a tug was ordered to tow the barges down the canal to Zeebrugge so that they could get to sea again. The trip across was uneventful and I was greeted by my mother with the news that she had entered me for the preparatory school of the Sir Joseph Williamson Mathematical School at Rochester and I was to take the entrance examination next week. Some of the boys failed but, thanks to the teaching I had received at the village school and my love of reading, I passed the examination easily and joined my new school in the autumn term.

4

GROWING UP

Rochester lies in the Valley of the River Medway, surrounded
by hills. It was a natural crossing place even before the Romans
came and established one of their fortified camps there. Main
roads from four directions meet to cross over the iron bridge
which has replaced the old bridge built in the Middle Ages by
Sir Robert de Knollys and Sir John de Cobham. Coming from
Wainscott by the route I had to take to get to the Mathematical
School, I walked up the hill to Frindsbury on the main road
which led out to the Thames Estuary. Frindsbury was formerly
a village on its own, but had become a suburb of Strood. The
road ran down Frindsbury Hill to Strood High Street, where
the London Road from Strood Hill joined it from the right at
the Angel, named after the pub of that name on the corner.

At Strood Junction two railway lines met, the London
Chatham and Dover and the South Eastern and Chatham.
Strood dock by the river was the Medway end of the Thames
and Medway Canal, which was cut under Frindsbury Hill to
emerge from the tunnel at Higham and continue across the
marshes to Gravesend where it joined the Thames. The South
Eastern and Chatham railway bought out the canal company,
drained the water out of the tunnel and put their trains through
it. The line then ran alongside the canal to Gravesend and on
to London by way of Dartford and Greenwich. This destroyed
a link by which barges could avoid sailing all the way down the
Thames round the Hoo peninsular and up the Medway to
Strood.

The High Street had some good working class shops and along
the river on one side was a timber wharf, the pier, and the oil

41

and cake mills. By the river on the other side were the large engineering works of Aveling and Porter whose main product was the steam roller. These steam rollers, with their famous emblem of the White Horse of Kent on the front, were to be found working on the roads all over the British Empire. A friend who was posted out to India in the Second World War said he saw one still working on the North West frontier.

The railway bridge to Rochester ran alongside the road bridge to the other bank of the Medway, where they parted company. A medieval building stood at the end of the bridge by the entrance to the castle grounds. Known as the Bridge Chamber, it was the place where travellers had to report before being allowed into the city. Inside the grounds enclosed by the castle walls was the Norman keep, one of the best preserved in England, although unfortunately the internal floors had been allowed to collapse.

On the opposite side of what was formerly the moat was the cathedral, also built by the Normans, and a row of houses for the canons called Canon Row but known locally as Hell Fire Corner. The grounds there were the Vines, named after the Monks' Vineyard, and included the Kings School, which claimed to be founded by the monks and to be the oldest school in England. The clergy were, of course, prominent in the social life of the city and the dean of the cathedral was a governor of the Mathematical School and a frequent visitor to the classrooms. The High Street was a mixture of old and new buildings, with some high class shops, notably Dales, the grocers, Cobbs, the men's outfitters, Leonard's ladies shop and Ogden's, men's hairdressers. The buildings associated with Dickens' stories are well known, in particular the Bull Hotel where Mr Pickwick's party stayed on their outing to Maidstone, and the Seven Poor Travellers Almshouse where seven men are given a bath, dinner, bed and breakfast and a shilling in the morning to help them on their way.

Not so well known, but worth a visit are the Guildhall opposite the Bull Hotel, the old Corn Exchange underneath the 'moon faced clock', the house where James II sheltered for the night on his way to Sheerness to escape to France, and the museum, housed in what was a Tudor merchant's home near the former art school. The other schools in the town in addition to the Mathematical School were the Boys Technical School and the

Girls Grammar School.

Corporation Street ran round the back of the High Street and the weekly cattle market was held there. It joined the High Street at the bottom of Star Hill where the main road to Maidstone came into Rochester. The town had a large modern cinema and small repertory theatre where several actors and actresses appeared who later became well known. The High Street continued past the station into Chatham High Street.

Apart from the river, which was always busy, the only industry was Short Bros aeroplane works. They became famous with their production of flying boats, which opened up the air route from Cairo to the Cape for Imperial Airways. During the 1939-45 war they built the Sunderland Flying Boats, which were the backbone of the RAF Coastal Command, capable of keeping watch far out in the Atlantic and hunting down the German submarines.

Rochester had a hospital, St Bartholomews, and also an aerodrome which was used by light aeroplanes, except for a period during the war when Short Bros assembled the Sterling bombers there.

Chatham was essentially a navy town. It had the royal dockyard where Nelson's flagship, the *Victory*, was built, and barracks for the seamen and marines. The shops and public houses catered for the navy. Certain pubs were used exclusively by sailors, notably the Long Bar, and any soldier who poked his nose in got short shrift. There were three theatres, the Theatre Royal which put on plays ranging from Sir Frank Benson's Shakespeare productions to the musical, *Rose Marie*; the Empire was a vaudeville theatre and Barnards was a music hall which still had a chairman to introduce the acts and where there were bars at the back of the stalls and circle. Mother took us to the Christmas pantomimes and the musical plays at the Theatre Royal but as young men we always frequented Barnards or the Empire. After passing the dockyard the road went up the hill to Gillingham and on to Canterbury and Dover.

Gillingham was a military town with a few shops and a cinema. The Royal Engineers were established there in Kitchener Barracks, Lord Kitchener having been a Royal Engineer, surrounded by playing fields overlooking the river, with two or three small forts built in the last century to protect the dockyard at Chatham. The open country on top of the hill

43

was called the Lines, where the troops used to hold their reviews.

The Medway Towns had two breweries to supply the thirsty sailors and soldiers and the civilians. Style & Winch were in Rochester and Budden & Biggs in Strood. They were both family firms. Budden & Biggs had a large sign outside in bold letters advertising Budden & Biggs Body Building Beverages. We used to ride on their carts to get to school in Rochester, when the river flooded. When I bought our first house at Gads Hill near Dickens' old home, Colonel Winch, the chairman of Style & Winch, lived in a large house on the opposite side of the road. He arranged for a small group of us from the badminton club to have fencing lessons in the warehouse at the brewery by the foreman who had been one of his sergeants, or corporal, which I believe was the correct term in the cavalry. He taught us the use of the epée and the sabre, a heavy sword for cavalry charges, and after the lessons we had a pint or two of beer from one of the barrels. I had several illustrations of the comradeship which grew up between the officers and men in the 1914/18 war.

A friend who went up in the train to London with me had been a sergeant in the army under an officer who established a company making Marmite when the war was over. He invited the sergeant to become his works manager. The basic ingredient of Marmite was the mash left over after beer had been brewed and as the breweries did not know what to do with it, the new company offered to collect it free of charge. This arrangement continued until Lord Davidson, King George V's physician, wrote an article pointing out the benefit to health of Vitamin B which was contained in brewery mash and used to manufacture Marmite. The result was a rush of other manufacturers to get in on the act and instead of getting the mash for nothing the price rocketed, although Marmite is still in business. Another man I knew in the city was an NCO in the Northumberland Fusiliers and his officer took him into his shipping business after the war and he became the managing director.

Colonel Winch's family were well known in Kent. They were land agents and auctioneers and one branch established themselves as stockbrokers in the city under the name of Arthur B. Winch & Co. Peter Winch was the senior partner and I was a half commission man with his firm. In actual fact the commission paid was only one fifth, but apart from this I

44

collaborated with him on several deals. He was a member of the Council of the Stock Exchange and I invited him to the box owned by my clients at a Royal Ascot meeting to discuss a public quotation we had in mind. Unfortunately Peter was killed when his car skidded off the road and hit a tree as he was driving to collect his children from boarding school for their half term holiday, and his firm was amalgamated with another.

The Mathematical School was established by Sir Joseph Williamson, who succeeded Samuel Pepys as Secretary of the Navy. It was a free school for the sons of freemen of the city to provide officers for the navy. David Garrick, the famous actor/manager, was a pupil there, as was Admiral Sir Cloudesley Shovell, but he could not have been paying attention in class because he navigated his fleet onto the rocks off the Scilly Isles when returning from the West Indies. The ships were wrecked and he was drowned with most of his men. The school buildings were Victorian; situated in the High Street opposite Leonards, the ladies shop, the sixth form boys were able to signal from the school library to the girls in the shop to arrange meetings.

One side of the school was built up against the old Roman wall which enclosed the upper yard and if we wanted to play a trick on a new master, we prised up the floor boards of the form room adjoining the wall and crawled underneath into the dungeon. When he came into the room to take the class there was nobody there.

The preparatory school consisted of three forms. I started in the first form, where Miss Christine Lee was the form mistress. She was young and pretty and very kind to the new boys so I was very happy after the rough and tumble of the village school. She was the Cub mistress and took us camping during the Easter holiday on a farm. We slept in a barn with straw palliasses; I was very comfortable after being used to camping with the village boys. Some of the boys who were away from home for the first time were upset and one cried so much he had to be sent home the next day, despite Miss Lee's efforts to comfort him. I enjoyed the games and the tracking in the woods and I won the archery competition. Our lunches usually consisted of cold meat, but when it was my turn to prepare the food I made a hot stew of corned beef with potatoes, onions, carrots and cabbage, all in together, which was voted a great success.

After the holiday we went back for the summer term. The

first week I was leaning one day against the wall outside the room where tuck was being sold during mid-morning break, waiting for a friend, when a boy jerked my feet away from under me and I fell down. I got up and hit him. A master who was on duty in the corridor took us both down to the gym and asked the gym master to arrange for us to settle our differences with the gloves on. We went to the gym when afternoon lessons finished and had a set to. I managed to make the other boy's nose bleed and the gym master, Mr Bailey, said that was enough and called a halt. After we got dressed he asked if I would like to join his boxing class. I thought it was a good idea to defend myself, so I joined and took part in exhibition bouts at the gym displays, where I was billed as the Strood Hill Slosher or the Frindsbury Frightener. I had an advantage because although I was normal height for my age I had very small bones and was very light. I never exceeded eight stone all the time I was at school, and since being grown up my weight has been between nine and nine and a half stone.

I continued to see the village boys and join in with their games and expeditions at weekends. I was climbing a high tree when a bough broke and I fell to the ground, fracturing my left thigh. The problem then was how to get me to hospital, because there was no ambulance service. Since the war, motor cars had been appearing on the roads and the village greengrocer had bought a small van. My mother took the mattress off my bed and put it in the van; I was placed on top, the doors were fastened with string, as the mattress was longer than the inside of the van, and we set off for St Bartholomews Hospital in Rochester. I had a bed in the men's surgical ward. Men were still visiting the hospital to be treated for wounds received during the war. The next day I was taken down to the operating theatre, a wad of cotton wool was placed over my face, chloroform was sprinkled on it until I was unconscious and the broken bones were set. I was terribly sick when I came to. The bed was very hard as though there was a board underneath the mattress, and my leg was in traction, consisting of a cord fastened to my foot which went over a pulley at the end of the bed with weights at the bottom of it. The leg was not in splints but it had what I can only describe as thin sandbags fastened to each side. If I moved, even slightly, the cord came off the pulley and as every nurse who came by my bed looked to see if the weights were in place,

I was continually being told 'You naughty boy, you've moved again. You must keep still.'

How can a boy of nine be expected to keep still, lying on a hard bed for weeks? I was very unhappy. The year 1920 had a fine summer and I was in hospital the whole of the summer term. I hated the food, which was on a par with the meals cooked for us by the midwife who attended my mother when the babies were born, and we refused to eat. On Wednesdays and Sundays Mother brought me in hot meals of meat pies or steak and kidney puddings, with Kentish fruit pies and cream or custard. There was a locker beside my bed where we kept our own tea, sugar, eggs, butter, biscuits and fruit. The night nurses used to come and borrow tea and sugar to make a cup of tea when they were on duty. Miss Lee, my form mistress, came to see me every week and brought me in letters describing what had been going on at school, written by the boys as part of their work in the English lessons. One night the man in the next bed caught it alight when he smoked his pipe under the bedclothes. It was quickly put out but Matron was very annoyed and told him what she thought of his behaviour in putting the whole hospital in danger.

When the broken bones had healed both my legs had stiffened up and every morning a nurse massaged them and gradually bent them at the knees to free them, which was very painful. I was allowed an invalid chair to propel myself about and one day when I raced up the ward in it, I turned it over and it fell on top of me. The doctor thought I might have broken my leg again, but it was all right, although I was refused the use of the invalid chair again. I was in hospital for about ten weeks, and when I came out I was given a pair of broomsticks without the brushes on the end to use as crutches. Although I had missed out on my schooling for the summer term I was put up to the second form for the start of the new school year.

I was only in that form for a term when I was transferred to the third form and from there into the big school, so I had passed through the preparatory school in a year. By this time I had become like all the other boys. I had lost my country accent. I said 'garage' instead of 'garrige' and 'waistcoat' instead of 'westkitt' and I was ready to cope with life in the big school. But I missed my friends from the preparatory school. I still saw Miss Lee, because I continued in the Cubs and, of course, the gym master was in charge of his class throughout the school. I was particularly sorry to leave Form Three because the form master, Bob Morris, was in charge of cricket and as my cousin had been a member of the first eleven when he was at school and still played for the old Williamsonians I received special attention. The master had served in the Royal Horse Artillery during the war and entered teaching immediately afterwards, without going to university, but he was one of the best teachers, despite the fact that he had no degree.

As I still belonged to the Cubs I kept in touch with my friend Robert Passmore, who was the pack leader. I first met him when we both took the entrance examination; although we lost touch when we left the Cubs, we renewed our friendship when we left school and have remained friends ever since.

The fees for the preparatory school were four guineas a term and five guineas for the big school. The scholarship boys entered the school at the age of twelve in the upper third forms but despite the fact that I was two years younger, I could still get into one of the top places and win a form prize.

There were three grades of punishment. The lowest was called PD, which stood for Punishment Drill in the old days. Boys were kept in after school in the evenings and drilled for an hour in the lower yard by the gym master. This was abolished after the war and the drill was exchanged for extra lessons. The next punishment was detention, when the culprits had to come back to school on Wednesday afternoons and miss games. The third was a caning by the headmaster. Waiting outside his study to be called in was the worst part of it. The caning was actually carried out by the porter in the presence of the headmaster. The final punishment was expulsion, which was really final so far as the pupil was concerned. I only witnessed one expulsion. Some boys used to come to school by train, which crossed the main road by a low bridge before entering Rochester station. One boy who must have been seeing too many cowboy pictures, had made a loop on the end of a rope and as the train passed over the road he leaned out of the window and lassoed a passer-by below. The poor man was dragged along by the neck before the boy released his hold on the rope. The man was taken to hospital suffering from shock and bruises but with no broken bones. The police came to the school and the boy was caned and expelled. I do not know what action the police took.

There was unofficial physical punishment handed out by the masters but the boys accepted that as part of school life. The geography master hit his pupils with the map pole and the mathematics master used the biggest book he could find. Other teachers threw chalk at anybody they could not reach, but it was always possible to dodge that. I got on well with all the masters. If you did your best and tried hard they were very helpful and would respond to your efforts so that it was possible to have a happy relationship with them.

Although I say I got on well with all the masters, there was one I could not stand. He took the Latin class when I got to the middle school. If you misbehaved he called you out to the front of the class and asked 'Will you have a PD or a clout?' If you said 'I'll have a clout' he got hold of your face and took some time tilting it to one side until he got it at the right angle and then he gave you a tremendous blow across the cheek. I had seen this happen to other boys and when I was called out, I said I would have PD. He replied 'You will have both and that will teach you not to be a coward'. I protested he was being unfair but to no avail and I got both, but I was not going to put up with that sort of thing so I applied to drop Latin and take extra French in its place. My application was granted and I enjoyed my extra French lessons with Mr Tregenza, a Cornishman, who lent me books from his own library to read and took a great interest in my progress. This extra work paid off because when I matriculated I obtained a special distinction in oral French. The Latin master was also the Scout master and when boys left the Cubs they usually joined the Scouts, but I joined the Cadets instead to get away from him. This is why I lost contact with my friend Rob Passmore, as he was not in my form.

His family originally came from the West Country and his father was a Methodist lay preacher. He lived in Rochester and I went to many parties at his house. His mother owned the best café-restaurant in the town, called Tea Tables, with tennis courts in the garden, and it was great fun to have a game of tennis and then cool off with an ice cream soda. We had many outings together with Miss Lee, looking for fossils in the chalk on the downs and visiting pre-historic sites such as Kits Coty House, a cave dwelling formerly inhabited by the ancient Britons.

It took me some time to get used to the organization of the

big school, which had between 400 and 500 boys. I could not sort out who the captain of school was. Eventually I identified him as the big young man who had a moustache, wore a bowler hat, and used the masters' entrance and common room. I thought he was a master at first. The school was divided into four houses — Bridge, for boys from across the river, which included me, Castle, for those living in Rochester, Pitt for pupils in Chatham, named after William Pitt, Earl of Chatham, and Tower for those who lived in Gillingham, named after the tower intended to reach Heaven which had been built by the Jezreelites but never finished. Prefects were appointed to keep order in the houses but they were not very popular with the boys. They had their own common room and on one occasion a home-made stink bomb was thrown into their room and the door locked from the outside so that they could not get out. They hammered on the door and shouted until the porter appeared to let them out. Nobody owned up so the whole house was put in detention and lost its half day holiday.

I was made captain of the junior cricket and soccer teams and whilst still a junior I sometimes played for the senior side. I was very agile and could avoid a lot of the heavy tackles by the big fellows but I did get knocked about. In the final match for the senior house football championship we met a team composed of nearly all the school first eleven and after a hard game we were beaten 3-1. I was sitting on a bench in the changing room, counting my bruises before getting dressed, when the captain of the opposing side, who was also captain of football for the school, came over to me, slapped me on the shoulder, and said 'Well played, young-un'. I had read Sir Henry Newbolt's poem but I never thought I would play a part in it and all I could say was 'Thank you'.

After I had been in the school for about three years our headmaster had a breakdown and resigned to take up an appointment later at Oxford University. He was a brilliant mathematician but we did not get to know him personally because he was always engaged in administration and did not have time to take a class. He used a simple way of measuring the height of buildings by taking the angle at the base from a measured distance and calculating the result by a geometrical formula and illustrate how mathematics could be put to practical use. The new headmaster was a rugby supporter and he changed the school games from soccer to rugby. A new games master was appointed to train the new teams but I refused to join. I had a well-developed sense of self-preservation and I was not going to get involved in brawls with fellows weighing ten or eleven stone and risk getting my neck broken when I only weighed eight stone, so I joined the hockey club. This was more my line and complemented my cricket, where I continued to captain the team.

Cricket under the guidance of Bob Morris was very strong. There were six school teams and net practice every evening during the summer at the cricket field beside the river. In the corner of the field were the open air swimming baths. They were filled by water from the river which was absolutely clear, with no pollution, and full of fish. At the start of the summer term Mr Bailey, who was also the swimming instructor, chose a band of boys, of whom I was one, to clean out the baths ready for the new season. The baths were left full of water during the winter. We had to put on our bathing costumes and then, using brushes and brooms, we cleaned the baths as the water was gradually let out. At the end we had collected several buckets of fish which we took home, after having a shower to get the mud off, and the baths were refilled from the river. Each form had one period a week for swimming lessons. We hurried as fast as we could — we were not allowed to run through the High Street — to get as much time as possible in the baths. We arrived hot and sweating and if we hesitated on the side before getting in the water, the gym master shouted 'Get in while the sweat is on you'. I could already swim so I got my life saving badge without any trouble. The most difficult part was swimming underwater to retrieve an object from the bottom. I swam for the relay team at the sports but I was not really fast because I never learnt the crawl, which was just being introduced. However, I did dive from the top springboard through a paper hoop to earn a few points for the house.

I still did well at my lessons, particularly on the academic side, English language and literature, history, geography, French and also, of course, mathematics. I was not very keen on physics, chemistry, geometrical and mechanical drawing, painting or woodwork. Mr Rigg, the English master, encouraged me in my reading and as I now had access to the school library I progressed from G.H. Henty, Edgar Rice Burroughs and R.M. Ballantyne to Robert Louis Stevenson, Sir Walter Scott, Charles Dickens, John Buchan and so on, in addition to the set books at school, including the works of Shakespeare and the poems in the *Oxford Book of Verse*. Several people have put forward theories arguing that Shakespeare's plays were not actually written by him but by various other people, such as Sir Francis Bacon. Ronnie Rigg had his own ideas about it. He produced a paper to prove that the plays were written by Henry Wriothesley, the Earl of Southampton, who was Shakespeare's patron, and had the plays published in Shakespeare's name.

Invicta Cinema where Uncle George Rase was manager

On my way to school I had to walk to Frindsbury and I was given 1d. a day to ride on the tram to Rochester, which cost a ½ d. there and a ½ d. back. If it was fine I walked all the way there and back and saved the money. I either bought tuck with it in the morning break or kept it until the end of the week. On Saturdays I went with my sister Ethel into Strood to go to the pictures. Uncle George Rase, who was my mother's youngest sister's husband, was the manager of the new cinema called

Strood Invicta, built there just after the war. He was the engineer at the Kent Electric Power Company Works but he became manager of the cinema because the owners wanted somebody who knew all about electricity to install and run the machines. His eldest daughter, Nin, played the piano for the silent films, the second daughter Betty was in the box office and his son Arthur ran the projectors, while a third daughter showed the patrons to their seats and sold ice cream. Uncle George stood out front in his evening dress and as he was big and stout he cut a fine figure of a man. Ethel and I hung about outside the cinema until the first house finished and then if there were two spare seats, Uncle George let us in for nothing. We always had to occupy the front seats, which meant that we had to look straight up at the screen and all the pictures appeared in an oblong shape. When Uncle George booked the big pictures he also had to take what was known as a 'B' picture, as they were rented out in one package, so there were two films and the newsreel at each performance. We saw the stars in the evenings — Lillian Gish, Charlie Chaplin, Rudolph Valentino and others — but if we went in the afternoon we saw the special children's programme with William S. Hart, a cowboy who fought the Red Indians, and Pearl White tied to the railway lines by the villains but always rescued in the nick of time. These were serials and it was absolute bedlam when they came on with the shouting and screaming of the children. After the evening shows, as we had not spent our money, we bought a hot potato from a barrow and ate it as we walked home.

I did not always go to the cinema on Saturday afternoons; sometimes I attended dancing lessons at the Co-op Hall. The boys had to wear suits with white gloves and dancing pumps instead of shoes, whilst the girls showed off their best dresses. The dancing master wore full evening dress, his wife played the piano and his daughter danced with those boys who had not got partners. She was our age and very pretty so there was great competition to get her as a partner. We enjoyed the lancers and the quadrilles and the other set dances most. When I see 'Mr Pastry', Richard Hearne, portraying the lancers on the television it brings it all back to me — the way we whirled the girls round off their feet very often and how the dancing master threatened to stop us coming again to restrain us, when the proceedings looked like getting out of hand.

My mother made me take piano lessons under a Professor Sellen. I like music but I did not like practising and sometimes I could not even remember what piece I was supposed to have learnt when the professor came. He eventually gave me up as a bad job.

We repaid Uncle George for letting us go into the cinema without paying by distributing leaflets to the houses in the village, advertising coming attractions. When Charlie Chaplin's film, *The Kid*, was going to be shown we dressed up Peter — Uncle George's youngest son who was the same age as Jackie Coogan — as The Kid and took him round with us. We called at a large country house on the outskirts of the village. It was a warm sunny afternoon and as we walked up the drive we saw three maids on the lawn making a show of beating carpets hung on a line between two trees. They were girls of about sixteen or seventeen and seemed to be enjoying themselves, laughing and giggling. When they saw us they came over to say hello and find out what we wanted. We showed them the leaflets and they made a great fuss of Peter. After a while one of them said 'Poor little fellow, he looks tired out, would you all like some tea?' Naturally we jumped at the chance, the girls stopped their work and we all went into the house. They sat us down in the kitchen and we had a lovely tea of toast, jam and cakes, which put more life into Peter. We left without seeing a sign of the master or mistress of the house; presumably they must have been away for the day.

The end of the war brought great changes to the village. The one which most affected it was the building of a large council house estate in the orchards on the opposite side of the road from the village houses, destroying all the trees.

The other event was the coming of a bus service from Rochester out to Hoo. The first buses were single deck petrol electric vehicles made by Tilling-Stevens at Maidstone. If we went to Hoo we had to get out of the bus at the bottom of Lodge Hill, walk to the top of the hill and then get into the bus again to continue our journey. When double decker buses were put on the route the top deck was open to the weather. Mackintosh sheets were attached to the wooden seats to cover the passengers up if it rained, but several of them were always missing.

Frindsbury suffered a similar fate when a council house estate was built on land bordering a long avenue of trees leading to the ancient church, which involved destruction of the trees.

I still saw my village friends at weekends and during the Easter holidays, which coincided with bird nesting time and camping at Allhallos beach if it was fine enough. A farmer who grazed his cattle on the marshes tried to stop us camping at Allhallows by saying we were not allowed on the beach but I pointed out that the land between high and low water was the property of the Crown and if he thought we were trespassing, he should bring the local policeman down. We did not hear any more from him.

Wednesday afternoons were usually taken up with sport, but if I had nothing on I would explore the countryside on my own. One Wednesday afternoon I had been sentenced to detention. I decided to chance it and not go back after lunch. I was not down to play in any of the teams because I was supposed to be in detention, so I had the afternoon free. I went to an old disused chalk quarry and climbed up to have a look at a jackdaw's nest. It was always easier to climb up than to get down and after inspecting the nest I continued to climb to the top. When I reached it a hand was extended to me and helped me up. The hand belonged to one of my schoolmasters who was out for a country walk with his wife. He looked at me and said 'I thought it was you Brooks, aren't you supposed to be in detention?' I had to agree I was, and he instructed me to 'Come and see me in the morning if you don't break your neck beforehand'.

There was plenty of work for everybody in the first two or three years after the war and Father shared in the upsurge in trade by securing some very good freights. Mother was used to managing on very little money but she always bought the best she could afford. In 1921 we went for a month's summer holiday to Margate and stayed at a private hotel. At that time all the guests still dressed for dinner, but the children had high tea and went to bed early. We spent our days on the beach, paddling, swimming, making sand castles and playing cricket. Mother had fruit for us to eat during the morning and we could always get ice creams and drinks at the Normandy Cafe. There was a Punch and Judy show on the beach and donkey rides. Sometimes we walked over the cliffs to the 'Captain Digby' public house and in the evenings went to see the concert party. My youngest sister, Barbara, who was only three, fell off a groyne into deep water and was saved by a young man who jumped in to save her. I made friends with a boy my own age who had to spend the whole summer at the seaside on his own because he had a weak chest. He showed me where the best rock pools were when the tide went out and always won the competition on the promenade to hook tin fish in a drum, which the owner vibrated to disturb the water and make it more difficult to hook the fish. The prize was a bar of chocolate, which we shared. There were also the swings and roundabouts on the sands or a trip in one of the motor boats from the harbour.

The following year we spent a month in the summer on holiday at Ramsgate. The sands were not so extensive as Margate's but the harbour was more interesting, many more boats including large ships entering and leaving after discharging their cargo. We enjoyed ourselves just as much. The third year we went to Sheerness on the Isle of Sheppey. This was not developed in the same way as Margate or Ramsgate, because it did not have the sand. The beaches were mainly shingle and rocks where we searched for cockles and winkles.

We travelled everywhere by train second class because in those days there were three classes, first, second and third, with plenty of porters to carry your cases.

In 1922 the farmer who owned the cottage where we lived wanted it for one of his farm workers so we had to get out. My parents took the opportunity to move nearer the town, which was more convenient for shopping and the schools we attended. They bought a small Victorian house in a row called Jersey Road. It was not much different from the cottage at Wainscott, the only advantages were a dining room as well as a parlour and gas lighting and fires. The lavatory was still outside, the cooking had to be done on a coal fired kitchener, the washing with a copper in the scullery and there was no bathroom. The difficulty regarding a bathroom was got over by installing a bath in the back bedroom with a gas geyser. The only drawback was that I occupied the back bedroom so all baths had to be taken early before I went to bed.

Jersey Road was at the top of Strood Hill, the London Road, and Uncle George Rase and his family lived in a modern house at the other end so I saw a lot more of Cousin Arthur, who also went to the Mathematical School. Nin, his eldest sister who played the piano at the cinema, was a pupil at the Girls

Grammar School. She went on to Goldsmiths College to get her teacher's degree and became head of a large comprehensive school at Snodland, a village just outside the Medway Towns. Betty, who looked after the pay box at the cinema, took a secretarial course and became a secretary at the War Office, being posted to the headquarters of the army in Palestine and later to Malaya before returning to the War Office in London. All my sisters still lived at home except the eldest, Minnie, who left at eighteen to train as a nurse. She was most efficient dealing with all the infectious cases from the East End of London, spending six months at a time in the isolation hospitals which handled the smallpox and diphtheria patients, and if they unfortunately died she laid them out in the mortuary for the funerals. My second sister, Lydia, started training as a nurse but she caught double pneumonia. Minnie obtained leave from her hospital to nurse Lydia at home. The bedroom was fitted up just like one of her own wards, with cylinders of oxygen and all the necessary medical equipment. Nobody else was allowed in the bedroom. She nursed Lydia night and day through the crisis until she recovered. Lydia owed her life to her. Later Minnie left the nursing service to become assistant to the manager of the Post Office Regional Office and married a postman but did not have any children.

Lydia, who had previously stayed at home to help Mother look after the children, obtained a post for which she was ideally suited. She ran one of the homes established by the London County Council for the care of orphaned children between the ages of three and ten, with a small staff to help her. They were one big happy family in a comfortable house with a large garden and all the children called her Mother. An added advantage was Lydia's good cooking and the parties she could arrange for them. She left to get married to Norman Chittenden, who was a motor engineer, having trained for seven years before the 1914-18 war as an apprentice at Robins & Day in Rochester. This firm had the agency for practically all the makes of car which were made, ranging from Rolls Royce and Lanchesters down to Jowetts, Beans and Fords. Their stores, holding spares, occupied a tremendous space because they were laid out on the floor for each make of car. When Ford said that they wanted sole agency Robins & Day told them to take their agency away because they could see no future in Ford cars. The firm was the first acquisition made by Rootes Brothers when they started expanding from their base at Maidstone.

They lived at Bromley, where Norman was manager of a garage until 1939, when he became an engineer with the RAF at Cardington and they lived at Gerards Cross. In 1946 they moved to Strood and bought a house in Brompton Farm Road. Lydia did not have any children, which was sad for her after the happiness she had taking care of the children at the LCC home.

Ethel continued her studies at the Girls Grammar School, where she had won the scholarship and passed the matriculation examination for London University with distinction in German. It was intended that she should enter Goldsmiths College to get her teacher's degree but Mrs Shepherd, the vicar of Frindsbury's wife, persuaded Ethel to become governess to her two young daughters. Ethel was Brown Owl in charge of the Brownies and was greatly influenced at that time by Mrs Shepherd, the Girl Guides captain. She invited her friends to send their children to be taught by Ethel, who did not receive any extra payment for teaching them. Father was very annoyed when he came home from sea but he had to accept the situation. When the children were old enough to go to school Ethel became governess to Lord Jowett's family. She kept in touch with Mrs Shepherd's elder child after the girl grew up and they spent several holidays together. When Ethel left Lord Jowett she taught in the village school at Fordcombe near Tunbridge Wells and married the village baker. She had one child, Barbara, who married and has two sons. Ethel was separated from her husband, who later died, and as she likes travelling she has spent many holidays abroad after retiring, sometimes with her grandsons or Mrs Shepherd's daughter, visiting Russia and the Mediterranean countries.

Gladys, who came after me, attended Gordon Road School and finished her schooling by staying on as a pupil teacher until she was sixteen, when she made a start at a private nursing home in Blackheath before leaving at eighteen to train as a student nurse at Hither Green Hospital. She qualified at twenty-one and remained there until 1939 when she became an ARP nurse for the duration of the war. When the war ended she took charge of the first aid clinic at Wingets, a big engineering company in Strood, where she met and married Norman Taylor. They had one little girl who married and who now has two girls herself.

Barbara was my youngest sister, born just after the 1914-18 war ended. After leaving the Girls Grammar School she was apprenticed for five years to a ladies hairdresser. When the 1939-45 war broke out she enlisted in the WAAF and was stationed at the headquarters of Fighter Command for the duration of the war. After the war she met and married Bob Harvey, who had been a pilot during the war, but they did not have any children.

Because I lived in Strood, within walking distance of the school, I lost my allowance of one penny a day to ride on the trams. Except for the fact that I could not save up to go to the pictures it did not worry me much because, having the run of the school library, I took out so many books that I used to walk home along the street reading them and sometimes bumping into people on the way. The family called me a bookworm and my mother thought that as I read so many books and won the Graham Bequest for Religious Knowledge at school each year, I should become a parson.

Reading books as I walked along nearly got me into trouble. When I reached the road next to the one where we lived I bumped into three boys a few years older than I was, who refused to let me pass. They were obviously out to provoke a row but I recognized the biggest, who worked for Mr Davis, the local grocer where we shopped. I went up to him and said 'I know you. You work for Mr Davis and if you don't stop annoying me I'll tell him what you are up to. If he knows you are upsetting one of his best customers he won't like it.' I had no more difficulty from those lads and after that the oldest one always said hello when he saw me.

During the school year we had the house concerts at Christmas. They were all enjoyable and some of them were very good. The best show was put on by Tower House. The assistant headmaster, Mr Pattenden, was in charge of Tower House and as he had a good voice and was a first rate actor he was always the star turn. I acted in the sketches for Bridge House but my voice was not good enough for the singing parts. The concerts always ended with the school song where my voice was lost amongst the 400 odd others as we sang: 'All hail to the colours of dark and light blue which float in the flag of the school where we one and all have a life's work to do beneath its beneficent rule. Long long may it flourish and always appear the cradle of honour and truth so we through our life will always revere the shrine of our studies in youth.'

The song was written and composed by the music master, Percy Fearnley, with a good rousing tune.

It was a tradition to stage one of the Gilbert and Sullivan operas each year in the school hall. The woodwork class built an extension to the stage for the large number of performers, the art class made the scenery but the costumes were hired. Mr Pattenden was stage manager and director, taking one of the leading roles as well, while Percy Fearnley trained the chorus and orchestra. I tried to get in the chorus without success so I had to be content with helping in the office. The opera was put on every evening for a week and was very successful. The mayor, with other prominent citizens, attended in full evening dress. It was one of the social highlights of the year in Rochester.

The Cadets had an annual camp run by the army near Herne Bay. Several other Cadet Corps attended in addition to our own. It was so soon after the war that the organization was based on the routine of that period. Everything was done by bugle calls. In order to remember them we sang words to the music, including 'Get out of bed, get out of bed you lazy buggers,' 'Come to the cookhouse door boys, come to the cookhouse door,' 'Fall in A, fall in B, fall in every company.' Mornings were taken up by drill, the afternoons were free for swimming or football matches unless we had a field day. On Sundays we had church parade.

Since I lived in Strood I had to find new friends outside school, so I joined St Mary's Church Boys Club. The vicar of St Mary's was the Rev. Hubert H. Treacher. He was an apprentice at Chatham Dockyard until the war when he joined the army and was commissioned on active service. After he left the army he was ordained and later became head of the Church Army. He was supported at St Mary's by a young curate who ran the boys club to keep them interested and active in the church. He was keen on amateur dramatics, which had a religious theme, bringing home the teachings of Christ to the boys. He suggested performing the 'Little Plays of St Francis' and I joined the members of the cast. I was Brother Bernard, one of St Francis' followers; the curate played the part of St Francis. We met at his lodgings for afternoon tea and rehearsals, until we were good enough to appear at the church hall. The play was set in a prison cell. St Francis was the patron saint of birds and we gazed out of the cell window, trying to attract the birds outside, longing to be with them but prepared to be locked up inside rather than renounce our faith in God. The curate also organized outdoor activities to maintain the boys' interest. He took a party of us to camp on the Isle of Grain where we slept in the church hall and were fed by the ladies of the parish. He was very interested in cricket and organized a cricket contest. We had enough members to make up three teams, each of which was named after a county side. I was captain of one team called Nottinghamshire because one of the boys wanted to be Larwood; I had to be A.W. Carr. Everybody enjoyed it so much that the camp was repeated the following year.

In 1924 the Empire Exhibition was held at Wembley. The school laid on a coach to take each form to see it. Unfortunately, two days before my form was to go I was thrown down during a wrestling match and fell heavily on my shoulder. It hurt so much that I called into the doctor's surgery on my way home and he said I had dislocated it. He put it back in, strapped it up, made me a sling and I went home. I did not want to miss the opportunity of going to Wembley so I joined the coach two days later. I was in agony on the coach and as I walked round the Exhibition. I tried to avoid anybody bumping into me but if I had to stop suddenly to avoid them the jarring sent excruciating pains shooting through my shoulder. The Exhibition was exciting, I saw as much as I could but I did not enjoy the day.

It is possible to shrug off injuries when one is young but in old age they seem to come back. My shoulder creaks and groans now when I use it and I suffer from a permanent backache because the leg I broke is slightly shorter than the other one, which throws my spine out and puts pressure on one side.

The General Strike in 1926 was called to support the miners' strike. The older boys were allowed off to help the authorities where they could and I worked in the office producing the Gazette, giving the official news bulletins. It only lasted a week but some of the boys had exciting jobs. One of my friends at St Mary's Boys Club was an apprentice on the railway and he became a fireman on a train, realizing every boy's ambition to help drive one.

As I was now sixteen my sister Lydia suggested I should go on holiday with her. I still had the cash I was given on my trips to France in the Post Office. Lydia wrote to a boarding house in Folkestone, advertised in the local paper. This seemed very nice and we booked a fortnight's holiday, paying a week in advance. We arrived at the boarding house and were shown our rooms but when we went to bed we discovered that the landlady had removed the electric light bulbs from the bedrooms and left a candle with one match instead. When we spoke to her she said she had to economize. She also economized on the food, serving margarine instead of butter and most unappetizing meals. We were used to good food at home and this was the last straw. We had paid for a week and so we had to stay but at the end of the week we arranged for Lydia's boyfriend to send her a telegram saying we must return home at once. We told the landlady, she asked to be paid for the second week, we refused and she turned nasty and threatened 'I will sue you if I find you still in the town.'

However, we found another boarding house to stay in and spent a very pleasant second week. We saw all the shows — I particularly liked the *Maid of the Mountains* — walked on the leas, listened to the band, played tennis and thoroughly enjoyed ourselves.

I passed the matriculation examination for London University with honours and special distinction in oral French, thanks to my friend Mr Tregenza, the French master. I then had to make a decision on whether to go to university or take a job. I decided on a job and remained in the sixth form until I found one. I was offered two. The local paper, the *Rochester Chatham and Gillingham News*, needed a junior reporter at £1 per week and when they approached the school the English master, Mr Rigg, recommended me for the vacancy. At the same time a London firm of accountants wanted an articled clerk and I was offered this position. I could never see myself owning a newspaper but if I qualified as an accountant there was always the prospect of owning my own business. Although it meant a great sacrifice for my parents to keep me during the five years I would have to be articled they agreed if that was what I wanted they would support me. I therefore left the Mathematical School at the end of the autumn term in 1927 and commenced my articles on 1 January 1928 at the princely sum of 5s. per week.

Captain Brooks (Author's father) first motor ship after decline
of sailing vessels

The year 1928 was a bad time for my parents to take on the
additional financial burden of supporting me during the five
year term of my articles. The life of the sailing vessels had come
to an end. My father spent more time tied up in port and going
the rounds of shipbrokers to find freights than he did at sea.
Eventually, in 1929, he took command of Mr Metcalf's new
motorship and brought it over from Bremen to England.

The year 1929 saw the start of the Great Depression which
affected trade all over the world, and shipping was one of the
first to suffer. It was said that there were so many ship's captains
out of work in Gravesend that you could crew your ship with
them because they were desperate to get to sea again. Where
I had seen the great J class yachts, including the King's yacht
Britannia, racing off Southend with their tremendous press of
sail and the numerous crew handling the sheets, there was now
a line of merchant vessels anchored with only a watchman on
board and the rust slowly eating away at their hulls. Father's

salary was £4 a week, out of which he had to pay pilot's fees, but as he never took a pilot this did not worry him. Father engaged a Captain Smith as mate, who had been master of a deep sea cargo vessel. As I only had two weeks' holiday a year from my work and had to fit in other arrangements I joined my father on short trips to south west ports, including Fowey for china clay and Par for stone, but I found them rather boring after being used to sailing vessels.

Having command of a motorship was a great change for my father. Whereas everything had to be done manually before now, machinery was used to heave up the anchor, work the winches, haul in the mooring lines, take the strain on the steering wheel, uncover and replace the hatches and there were no sails to hoist. The bridge was enclosed and fitted out with all the navigational instruments. The accommodation was sumptuous compared with what my father had previously been used to. The crew consisted of a mate, chief engineer, second engineer, cook/steward, and three seamen. They were all accommodated aft with the officers having separate cabins, my father's being large and particularly comfortable. There was also a spare cabin for use as a sick bay or to accommodate passengers, which I used. There was a large well furnished saloon, a fully fitted kitchen, central heating, electric light and constant hot water for showers. Captain Smith found it strange being a mate on a smaller vessel but he developed a great respect for my father. On one trip they loaded coal in Blyth, Northumberland, for the gas works at Salcombe in Devon, and cleared the harbour in thick fog. The fog continued all the way round the coast. Captain Smith was nervous because he was used to checking the position on his previous ship by taking sights of the sun, but my father continued to navigate the ship and alter course when necessary until he ordered the crew to drop anchor and stop engines.

When Captain Smith asked, 'Where are we?' My father replied, 'We're there, of course, outside Salcombe. When the tide changes the fog will lift, and we can cross the bar into the harbour.'

Captain Smith said, 'How do you know?'

Father just laughed and said, 'I can tell by the colour of the water.'

In the evening the fog lifted, they went in on the tide and made fast at the coal wharf where the gasworks manager greeted them with great relief, explaining that he had not had a delivery of coal for two weeks because of the thick fog and he was down to his last hundredweight.

As soon as the ship had been moored up ready for unloading in the morning, there was a clatter of boots on the dockside receding in the distance, followed by silence. Captain Smith looked around and wondered what had happened to the crew. Father told him, 'They've gone up to the pub. If you want a drink you'd better hurry.'

On another occasion, when the ship was on a return trip down the west coast to round Lands End back to London, the winter gales reached hurricane force and Father ran for shelter under the lee of Lundy island. They sheltered there for four days, during which time the crew were sick and anxious for their safety, but Father remained calm, checking that the anchors were holding, making sure everything was battened down, surveying the weather and keeping the engines running at slow speed to take the strain off the anchors. As soon as the wind dropped they were able to get under way again to everybody's relief. When I was on board while the ship loaded cargo in London, the second engineer suggested we should have an evening in town. I was only too pleased to agree. We went to the Prince of Wales Theatre to see a revue. We had seats in the front stalls and in the first act the girls came down off the stage to give us a glass of wine. We had supper afterwards in the Trocadero before we went back to the ship. Captain Smith later became marine superintendent of the company.

In 1929 I volunteered for the RNVR as a sub-lieutenant in the London Division on *HMS President*, but in 1931 the country's economy collapsed and the Government made very severe cuts in their expenditure. The wages of the men in the armed services were reduced, as a result of which the navy mutinied at Invergordon. This was settled by arresting the leaders, court marshalling them and at the same time meeting some of the men's grievances. The navy list was cut, including the RNVR officers, and I had a nice letter from the Admiral Commanding Reserves thanking me for my services, regretting the necessity for dispensing with them owing to the economies brought in by the Government.

I renewed my friendship with Robert Passmore. He had been working at Short Bros as a draughtsman on the design of the wings of the flying boats. He left Short Bros and with finance from his father he started a business manufacturing wooden portable buildings in the railway arches at the Strood end of Rochester Bridge. It was an uphill struggle but he gradually succeeded and although he could not draw much money out he had the use of a motor car, a model called the Segrave Coupé named after the famous racing driver. This enabled us to get about and we would drive out to the country, have lunch at a village pub and go for a walk in the Surrey beech woods.

The firm of accountants I was articled to was small, with only one principal and three clerks. The offices were in Chancery Lane, opposite the main entrance to Lincolns Inn. I lived at home and in addition to my train fares my parents had to pay the cost of a correspondence course with the Metropolitan College and the examination fees. I had the 5s. a week I was paid for my spending money. I usually took sandwiches for lunch, which I ate in Lincolns Inn Gardens, watching the tennis or the girls' netball matches. Sometimes for a change I would go into a Lyons or ABC teashop with one of the other clerks and have a brown roll, a portion of butter, a slice of cheese and a tomato, which came to 4½ d, so I was able to give the waitress a ½ d. tip. If we had time to spare I ordered for 1d. a cup of coffee which I drank whilst we had a game of dominoes. I had a school friend, Ken Sawyer, who was a student at the London School of Economics on the other side of Lincolns Inn Fields. I used to meet him to have a cheap lunch with the students and occasionally attended lectures by Professor Laski on economics, which was on the syllabus for my accountancy examinations. Nobody seemed to pay any particular attention to my presence at the lectures. Professor Laski was very left wing; his talks were always slanted towards government control and socialism, whereas I was studying the basics of economics by Adam Smith. The students mostly talked of working for a government department when they left university, instead of going into industry or commerce, and my friend Sawyer became a schoolmaster. He rowed in the London School of Economics eight and I joined him at the Boat Club. They rowed in the Head of the River Competition after the Oxford and Cambridge Boat race but in the opposite direction. When it was over we visited the other clubs' boat houses along the river to celebrate and then as many as possible got into an old Lagonda open tourer owned by the Boat Club to get back to London West End and continue the party.

My office hours were from nine to five on weekdays and half day Saturday. I walked down to Strood Station at seven o'clock to catch the seven thirty train to Charing Cross. The train arrived in London at eight thirty, giving me half an hour to walk from Charing Cross to the office in Chancery Lane. I travelled up with three friends from my schooldays; one worked in a bank, another for the London County Council and the third for an investment trust. We usually played bridge on the way but not for money, as we had none to spare. I did not see them in the evenings because my time of returning was very uncertain if I was working outside London and had to complete what I was doing before leaving.

I checked the accounts of a building company in Slough, a small country town in those days and nothing like the sprawling place it is today. I waited on the platform for a train to Paddington, which stopped at nearly every station on the way, while the non-stop West Country expresses pulled by the great Castle class engines roared through at about eighty or ninety miles an hour to the cries of the porters shouting 'Stand away everybody', because the vacuum caused by the trains as they rushed past could have pulled passengers waiting on the platforms onto the line. Every month I wrote up the books of an engineering firm in Southend and to save time I caught the ferry from Gravesend to Tilbury, where I changed to a train for Southend. This service was worse than the Paddington one and to add to my misery in winter a thick fog on the river frequently stopped the ferry running. The way to get across was in a launch run by a boatman, who took so many on board there was only standing room. We could see nothing in the fog as he inched his way across but he always arrived at Gravesend pier. He charged 1s. each for the trip. I dread to think what might have happened if we had been run down by a ship. Fortunately, when the fog was so thick there was nothing else moving on the river.

I did have a narrow escape when a thick yellow fog typical of London cut visibility to a few yards. I had been working outside the town and arrived very late at Charing Cross station to find that the train I wanted to catch had gone. I was glad I was not on it. It crashed into the rear of a stationary train at St Johns station and the collision damaged a bridge carrying another line across the main line, which caused a train crossing the bridge to fall on the other two trains below. The casualties were increased to such an extent that dozens were killed and many more injured. It was one of the worst railway accidents for years.

Working late on many occasions, instead of reaching home by seven o'clock it was ten or eleven by the time I had my supper, leaving me two hours for studying before I got to bed at midnight or one o'clock. When I first started I had to make the tea, answer the telephone, post the letters, and collect parcels of books, able to make my way across the city through office buildings under cover, out of the rain. Our firm were receivers and managers of a pottery company with a warehouse in South East London. We ran the company of behalf of the debenture holders to safeguard their security whilst we tried to sell it.

In the course of our investigations we were unable to reconcile the reduction in stock with the sales figures and I was sent to keep a watch on the warehouse to see if goods were being removed illegally. I spent a miserable day hanging about in the rain, trying to avoid attention and act like a detective, but I discovered nothing wrong. We also managed a company selling brushes, not the household type, but very expensive toilet articles such as ebony backed men's hairbrushes and ladies' silver ones. The travellers came in once a week to collect their commission, which I worked out and paid them. They earned quite substantial amounts and when we had a free day before going on to another audit I suggested to the principal that I should go out with one of the other clerks and try to sell some brushes on commission. We packed a bag with samples and caught a bus to the West End to call on the big department stores in Oxford Street, who were the company's customers. We had a frustrating day persuading the buyers at the stores to place an order; either they were stocktaking or it was not their usual day in the month for ordering or we were not the regular travellers they were used to dealing with. We returned to the office tired out, carrying the heavy case of samples, and after paying for our bus fares we ended up with less than £1 commission between us. If I had any spare time after that I spent it in the office catching up with my studies.

We also managed three investment trusts and when we had

the shareholders' meetings I had to book a room at the First Avenue Hotel in Holborn, prepare the information the chairman required, make notes of any questions the shareholders might ask and be prepared to prime the chairman with the answers. When we had cases in which clients were involved at the Law Courts we put them up in Anderton's Hotel in Fleet Street. I worked on the books of the Musicians Union and Club which had offices and rehearsal rooms in Archer Street, off Shaftesbury Avenue. The musicians would meet up in Archer Street and if there was the prospect of an engagement a group would get together, book one of the rehearsal rooms and form a band. Ishbel Macdonald, the daughter of the prime minister, Ramsey Macdonald, was a trustee of the Union funds and I took a share transfer form for her to sign to County Hall where she was an LCC member. She was speaking in the council chamber so I listened to her whilst I waited until she was free. She was a good speaker, lucid in her arguments and with a clear distinct voice. When I met her afterwards to sign the share transfer she was very pleasant and thanked me for coming over to see her.

I tried to keep my weekends free for sport or swimming and outings in the country. I joined the Frindsbury Cricket Club, Tennis Club, Hockey Club, and Badminton Club. The cricket club had been formed by choirboys from Frindsbury Church about 1880 and the grounds which were owned by the church were at the back of the vicarage. The club ran two teams with a Colts team at weekends and a team on Wednesdays. I played for one of the two teams at weekends as I could not get time off to play on Wednesdays unless I was on holiday. The secretary of the club was Arthur Ring, who devoted all his spare time to running the club. He had been a good player when he was younger and still took a turn at the nets, coaching the batsmen, besides organizing bowling and catching practice. He arranged the fixtures, acted as umpire, stood in when we were a man short and travelled with the Colts team to their away matches. He saw that the club's pitches were in top class condition, often going over them with a small bag of weedkiller, dropping a pinch on any little weed which remained after the groundsman had finished his work. We played on all the best grounds, including those used by the county, at Mote Park, Maidstone, the Bat and Ball at Gravesend and the Royal Engineers ground at Gillingham. Some of the best playing fields were owned by companies, such as Sittingbourne Paper Mills, and Bowaters and Belmont; Lord Harris's ground was very pleasant.

Arthur Ring liked me and lent me his season ticket to go and see the county matches. This was at a time when the game included great personalities such as Frank Woolley, Tich Freeman and Leslie Ames for Kent, Jack Hobbs for Surrey and Patsey Hendren for Middlesex. We expected to see 400 runs on the board by tea on the first day and still leave time to have a go at the opposition. Some of the best matches took place during the school holidays when Kent would field seven or eight amateurs in the side from public schoolmasters, including John Knott, a batsman always looking for runs, and C.S. Marriott, a slow bowler, both of whom taught at Tonbridge School. I always bought my bats from Jack Hobbs sports shop in Fleet Street, signed by Jack Hobbs, costing a guinea. One Saturday I was captain of the side playing at Frindsbury; my father happened to be home and came to watch the match. I always opened the batting and on this occasion the wicket was easy and I enjoyed myself scoring freely all round the wicket. Our score board showed the total of runs and the number of men out but not the individual scores. I could see we would be able to declare at tea to leave us enough time to get our opponents out. My partner and I tried for a quick run but we misjudged it and I was run out. When I got back to the Pavilion I found that I had scored forty-nine runs. If I had known I would have waited to score the odd run to make it fifty while Father was watching.

I got on well with the principal to whom I was articled. He had the ability to check columns of figures whilst at the same time conducting an intricate conversation with a client, but after I had been at the office for a year he died. The firm was taken over by a former articled clerk who had established his own practice on the outskirts of London and my articles were transferred to him. The London business was run by the senior clerk and myself with juniors to help us. This meant longer hours for me and more late night studying, but I did not mind it. I welcomed the new responsibility and experience, sometimes going down to the other office to help them out. It all helped me to pass my intermediate examination after two years, which was the earliest date I was allowed to take it.

In 1929 Rochester staged a pageant to publicize the city and attract industry to the area. A pageant master was appointed and stands erected in the castle grounds with the castle forming the backdrop to the arena. Episodes in the history of the town were performed by various organizations. The Masons took the part of Roman soldiers establishing the city, the Royal Engineers were Normans invading the country and building the castle, the Co-op staged scenes from Dickens, and the army bands supplied the music. I had my fortnight's holiday and became a Roman soldier for two weeks. One week was spent on rehearsals, followed by the second week when we performed in the afternoons for the schoolchildren from all over the county and in the evenings for the main audiences. Trades shows by local industries had exhibitions to demonstrate their work and as we had to appear in the town in our costumes the city was full of colour and crowds of people who had come to see us. The floodlights were switched on for the evening shows and when all the performers were massed together for the grand finale, the costumes under the lights made the scene appear to be one vast flower garden. It was a fitting end to a marvellous fortnight.

I still received only the 5s. a week stipulated in my articles but I was able to do some work at home for local tradesmen in my spare time and earn extra money. I could pay for my own season ticket and share the car expenses when I went out with Rob Passmore. During our holidays we drove to London, and had supper at one of the restaurants before driving through the night to North Wales. We were able to remove the seats from the car, putting them outside under cover of a ground sheet, which gave us room to bed down at full length in the car. We toured North Wales, then down the beautiful Wye Valley to Ross-on-Wye, where we stayed at a Trust House Hotel for 7s.6d. a night bed and breakfast. It became a standing joke between us that as soon as we arrived at a hotel Rob wanted a drink and I had a wash. We drove back to London by way of Gloucester, the Cotswolds and Oxford to stop at the Grosvenor House Hotel for a large tea, costing 1s.6d. before continuing home. Another trip we made was to Scotland, leaving London after midnight, covering about 200 miles, because the road was clear at that time until we camped down about four o'clock in the morning. We were woken up by the noise of dogs barking and whimpering round us. When we looked out we found a pack of foxhounds all over the car until they were called off by the hunt servants. When we arrived in Scotland we camped outside

Glasgow and had a night out at the Empire Theatre. There was a lot of trouble at that time from the Glasgow gangs but we did not see any sign of them.

We crossed the border on the way back to Carlisle, toured the Lake District and stopped at Blackpool, hoping to spend a few days there. Unfortunately, we had run out of money. I had an account at the Westminster Bank at Gravesend so I went into one of their branches and asked the cashier to advance me £10 out of my account. They did not seem to take my suggestion seriously and when I persisted the cashier said they had no procedure to allow them to do this. I asked to see the manager to whom I repeated my request. He was very unhelpful until I gave him the number of my Gravesend account, the name of the manager there, including personal details he could verify if he telephoned him. The Blackpool manager telephoned Gravesend, spoke to the manager, confirmed my account was in credit and gave me £10 less 3s.6d. for the cost of the telephone call.

It was Wakes Week in some towns in Lancashire; all the bars and amusement centres in Blackpool were crowded with people spending their holiday money so we spent an interesting two days before leaving for home.

I continued my work and studies until I passed my final examination in 1932 and when my articles came to an end I was elected an associate of the Society of Incorporated Accountants and Auditors on 1 January 1933. The Society of Incorporated Accountants and Auditors had broken away from the Institute of Chartered Accountants in 1885 over some disagreement between the members but they came together again in 1959 when the society was integrated with the institute and I became a fellow of the Institute of Chartered Accountants. The senior clerk and I took our finals at the same time. Due to the work and stress involved in running the practice I had caught him up. Now, in 1933, I had to face up to my biggest job of all, finding employment in the middle of a world-wide trade depression when unemployment in the UK had reached an all-time high.

I arranged to continue working for the firm to which I had been articled, for no salary, provided they paid my expenses to come to London and allowed me to have the use of the office facilities and time off to attend interviews. This was convenient

Author aged 22

for me in my search for a job and I also kept up to date with accountancy practice. Having secured a base I planned my campaign. First I enrolled with Laurie & Co., the accountancy employment agency, then I approached all the tradesmen with whom my family dealt, drafting letters for them to sign addressed to the chairmen of the companies who supplied them with goods, such as Lyons, Unilever, Bovril, Glaxo, Huntley and Palmer, setting out my qualifications and experience and asking them if they could offer me a position as accountant in their company. They all replied that they had no immediate vacancy but would bear me in mind if one occurred and some invited me to meet them, although they regretted that they could not help me at the moment. I also arranged to have the names and addresses sent to me of all the new companies registered at Somerset House so that I could apply to them enquiring if they needed an accountant. I answered all the appropriate advertisements which appeared in *The Times*, *Daily Telegraph*, and financial journals. I volunteered for a commission as accountant officer in the RAF and applied for a vacancy in the Colonial Office advertising a posting to the South Sea Islands, but without success.

After nearly twelve months of searching Laurie & Co. arranged an interview for me with a firm of accountants in Gravesend. I saw the senior partner and was offered the appointment at a salary of £4 a week plus a small commission on the fees, which I accepted, starting work on the 1 January 1934. After all my efforts I had a job practically on my own doorstep. Perhaps that was the reason I got it; no doubt the firm preferred somebody who lived locally. They were very prominent in the town, with interests in several business activities. The firm was divided into three departments, estate agents, valuers and auctioneers with responsibility for the local building society and land company, a second department of property managers, insurance agents and rent collectors, and lastly the department which included the accountancy practice, stocktakers and brewery agents managing the transfer of licensed premises and hotels on behalf of the various brewery companies.

There were three partners, one from each department, who were also prominent in town affairs, either as mayor or members of the council and as Justices of the Peace. The firm had been collectors of taxes before this service was taken over by the Inland Revenue, and the accountancy practice had been built up by people coming in to pay their income tax complaining about the amount they had to pay and asking the firm if it would see whether the tax could be reduced. None of the partners were accountants, so they engaged Mr Turner, with several years' experience in the offices of a chartered accountant, but who had not taken his examinations. He ran the practice with the help of one assistant but the work built up to such an extent that further staff was needed and it was decided to employ a qualified accountant, who was me.

I had an office to myself and the partner advised me not to have anything to do with Mr Turner and his staff because they never did today what they could put off until tomorrow. This got me off on the wrong foot and relations were rather strained at first. I took over company and partnership accounts from Mr Turner because my knowledge of the law was still fresh but I realized that he was behind in his work because the number of cases he had to handle overwhelmed him. We therefore established a more friendly basis, he called me Brooky and I called him T, and I was able to learn a great deal from him about the organization of running a practice, particularly in the handling of income tax cases, which was to stand me in good stead when I had my own practice. My secretary was Miss Betty Ethel Glyn Jones, who occupied an office on the ground floor of the building with two other girls, Miss Cooper and Miss Kath Jones, whilst we were on the floor above. I was twenty-two and Betty was seventeen. She had just left training college so we were both starting out together. The first time she came in to take some letters for me I think we were both rather nervous. She knew that I had been asked not to have too much to do with the rest of the staff and I did not know how she would react towards me. She was pretty and I felt attracted towards her but for the time being I could not get to know her better.

I worked hard and was well liked by my clients, who often gave me something over the fees I charged them. When they did so I told them 'This won't reduce the fee I am going to charge you', but they still insisted on giving it to me as a token of their appreciation for the way I had done their work. I was able to earn commission on the fees I brought in and this helped me to contribute towards the cost of my living at home. I could also afford to expand my social life. T had been an amateur boxer as a young man and he was still interested in the sport. I went with him to see professional fights at the Albert Hall and to watch football matches between the big London clubs. I bought a secondhand Wolseley Hornet sports car to drive to work and call on clients.

The man from whom I purchased it took me for a drive to a public house a mile away, got out and said 'Drive it up the road while I have a drink and call for me on the way back.' I had never actually driven a car before but I had been hundreds of miles with Rob Passmore so I transferred to the driver's seat and set off. I soon got the hang of the controls and after three or four miles I stopped, but I had some difficulty in backing and turning round before I got back to the pub where the other man was waiting. He said 'What do you think of it?' and I replied 'It seems all right' so I paid over the money and took the car. The following day was a bank holiday, I telephoned two old school friends, told them I had a car and suggested a trip to Margate. The run down was uneventful but on the way back there was a long line of traffic returning from the coast. On the way out from Canterbury there is a steep hill at Boughton, the traffic stopped when we were halfway up and I came to a standstill. I had not practised an uphill start; consequently when I let the handbrake off the car ran backwards, the rear bumper coming down over the front bumper of the car behind. We were jammed together with dozens of cars behind us and all the drivers sounding their horns, as if that made any difference. I went down the line behind us and said to the drivers, 'I want four strong men to lift my car clear.' I soon had some volunteers and with my friends helping they lifted and freed my car, then held it until I got going.

Betty had a boyfriend called Eric Jones, who was no relation, but as I saw her every day and had a car to take her out I had the advantage over him, which proved decisive in the end.

I bought a tent for camping at weekends in a meadow at the back of the Allhallows on Sea Village pub, with a group of men and girls, including Ken Sawyer, who had graduated from the London School of Economics and was teaching locally. The railway recognized the possibilities of Allhallows as a seaside resort and ran excursions there at weekends, which turned a lonely out of the way spot, as I knew, into a popular place for a day's outing.

We also had parties which the landlord of the King's Head

in Rochester organized for us. He had three very pretty barmaids and when each of them had a birthday he applied to the local justices for an extension of license. We had the parties in a private room upstairs dancing to the piano, and we enjoyed ourselves whilst the landlord increased his takings. On Saturdays, after I played hockey or cricket for Frindsbury in the afternoon, we usually met for supper in the Sun hotel at Chatham and then went along to the casino in Rochester for a drink and dancing. Some of the top dance bands performed there and it was very popular with the girls in the towns. Ken Sawyer had a way with the girls and the night usually ended up with driving them home in my car, sometimes after a midnight swim in the nude at a roadhouse on the way.

We preferred Barnards Music Hall to the other two theatres in Chatham. It was the last surviving music hall in England to have a chairman on the stage to introduce the acts and keep the audience in order. Attendants brought round drinks; if you were in a box you had to be careful not to spill them on the people below. They also threw out anybody creating a disturbance, but if an act did not go down well the audience shouted its disapproval and the chairman took it off. This did not apply to the orchestra because if they were sent packing the show would have to close. One evening we occupied a stage box close to the musicians, who were really bad. We demonstrated what we thought of them in various ways during the show and at the end of the performance we showered them with torn up programmes. They insisted on calling the police who listened to their complaints, decided it was something to be expected at the music hall and went away.

The Wolseley Hornet car had narrow tyres, and driving home one night during the winter, when it was raining very hard, the front wheels caught in the tramlines and when I pulled them out the car skidded across the road and hit the kerb. This turned it over and the car finally came to rest with the chassis wrapped round a tree. I switched off the engine and climbed out through the window. Apart from bruises I was unhurt but the car was a write off. I bought a new car to replace it, called a Hillman Minx, a new model which Rootes Brothers had just produced.

I began to think seriously about my future and I decided to meet my acquaintances in the accounting profession again. I went on a course run by the society, at Cambridge University, attending lectures in the morning, punting on the river in the afternoon, having tea at Grantchester or visiting the golf course and ending up each day with discussion groups after dinner. I had previously purchased a dinner jacket suit for five guineas and a full evening dress suit for ten guineas from McCombie Brothers in Holborn. I took Rob Passmore as my guest to the Lord Mayor's banquet at the Guildhall, London to celebrate the fiftieth anniversary of the founding of the Society and talking with the people I knew at the dinner strengthened my resolve to get back to London.

Although Betty was still going with her boyfriend I was seeing her frequently out of the office as well as at work. I knew she was the girl I wanted and I decided to bring the matter to a head at the first opportunity. Her family always went away on holiday to the seaside in the summer and in 1936 they went to Great Yarmouth. I discovered that the eldest daughter's boyfriend, Fra Taylor, was going to join them so I offered to drive him up there. Everybody was surprised when I turned up, except Betty. I booked a room at the Two Bears Hotel and spent my fortnight's holiday with them. This was one of the most enjoyable holidays I have had. I joined in all the fun with the family, although I spent as much time as possible alone with Betty and by the end of the holiday we knew we were in love. When she returned to Gravesend Betty broke off her association with her boyfriend. We spent all our spare time together at the seaside, particularly Hastings where a new marina had been built, and there were many small restaurants to choose from for a meal. We also liked Greatstone, with its wide beaches backed by sand dunes leading to Dungeness, and its lighthouse. We visited London for dinner and theatre shows, sometimes inviting Betty's mother to go with us. This may seem strange to some people but I enjoyed her company and she liked coming with us. One evening in particular I remember when we had dinner together at the Cumberland Hotel and afterwards saw Emlyn Williams' new play *Night Must Fall*.

Betty's parents had seven children, four daughters and three sons of whom Betty was next to eldest with one sister a year older. Their mother was a fine looking woman and all the girls inherited her good looks. Betty and her sister were in great demand to sell roses on Queen Alexandra Rose Day because they attracted all the men and collected most money. Mr Jones

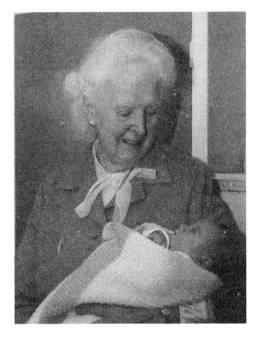

Betty's mother

Betty's father

had gone to sea as a boy apprentice on four masted sailing ships, learning the hard way, voyaging all around the world. He passed his examinations for master and also had what was known as an Extra Master's Ticket for those who had been trained in sail. He joined the Trinity House pilotage service on the Gravesend station as one of the youngest pilots and ultimately became the senior pilot. His family had a tradition of service with Trinity House; his father and brothers were pilots.

Mr Jones was a quiet man but he surprised the girls when he shouted orders to the men on the ship he was piloting and they were aboard for the trip up river. He was artistic, good at handicrafts and painting, a gift which the girls inherited. He made himself a one string fiddle to play and sang the solo verses when the pilots made a recording of the old sea shanties at the BBC. He had a serious stomach operation brought on by the bad food he had to eat on the sailing ships, and although he was a keen gardener he could not undertake the heavy work of digging, which had to be done by his sons when he rented an allotment during the war.

Mrs Jones ran the family with love and affection and the children returned her love throughout her life until she died at the age of ninety-two. She had to keep control of the four girls but they respected her for it. The three eldest girls and two of the boys married, the youngest son and daughter remaining at home to look after their parents. The family were well off compared with mine. They had a maid who lived in, also a daily woman, and all the children went to good schools with holidays each year at the seaside. Mrs Jones had an unhappy childhood. Her mother died when she was very young and she was in the care of a housekeeper. This influenced her in the way she brought up her own children. She was determined they should have a better childhood than she had.

I took Betty up to Donnington with my sister Lydia and her husband, the engineer, to see a motor racing meeting. The course was in a park where deer still grazed, making a further hazard for the drivers. The Bugattis and Alfa Romeos dominated the races. We were watching at the bottom of a hill where the road took a sharp right hand bend, when a wheel came off one of the cars, which ran out of control, crashing into the barrier of straw bales in front of us. Betty had her camera ready but we all scattered and she could not get the photograph she wanted.

Robert Passmore took up golf and he asked me to join him. I went into the railway lost property office near Charing Cross Station and bought a set of golf clubs, unused in their original packing, which had been sent down from Scotland and lost in transit. We went out to Bearsted Golf Club near Maidstone one morning, paid the green fees, bought some repainted balls from the professional and started playing. I was used to playing ball games so I was quite good at it. The last hole was in front of the club house where the caddies were waiting for the club members to appear after lunch. It was necessary to hit the ball to carry over a wide ditch on to the green. I was lucky and made one of my best shots from the tee, which landed on the green a few feet from the hole. When I put the ball down with one putt there was a buzz of talk amongst the caddies asking who I was, wondering whether I was a new member.

Bearsted was a nine hole course which was later extended to eighteen, set in beautiful countryside which I appreciated, but I found golf boring because I liked my sport to be exciting, with a spice of danger, and although I played the occasional game of golf with my clients later, I did not persevere with it. I preferred hockey and cricket, offshore yacht racing and flying, where I came into physical contact with my opponents or the elements. I cannot understand why business men take up golf for relaxation when all it does is to build up stress and frustration, trying to get a small ball into a hole. They would do better to leave their golf clubs behind and take a country walk.

A prominent Methodist business man wrote a play called *Tell England* which he financed himself and staged at a small theatre in Holborn. The hero was a Scout master and the heroine a Guide captain who triumphed over evil and came together at the end. It was so naive and the critics gave it such a bad write up it should not have lasted a day, let alone a week, but the backer kept it on to press his message home and it was taken up by young people who came in to see it several times and made a romp of it. The audience knew all the words before the actors spoke them and everybody joined in the play. I took Rob Passmore to see it and it lasted for a year instead of folding up.

I was always very keen to get back on the water and Betty wanted to start sailing so I looked around for a small boat. I saw a dinghy advertised in a yachting magazine lying at Wandsworth, which we went to see. It was high water and I stepped aboard from the bank to inspect it. The boat was a Sharpie which had a drop keel to give it stability. The owner also got on the boat, but he had forgotten to lower the keel and as he stood on one side the boat heeled over and sank. He slipped into the water up to his chin; my instinct for self-preservation prevailed and I stepped on his shoulders and then onto the bank, hardly getting my shoes wet. When he pulled himself up the bank I said to him, 'It's not the sort of boat I want. It's too unstable.' An old woman who was selling flowers nearby sympathized with him, saying 'You always were unlucky dear,' and even Betty did not like what I had done, although I pointed out that I could have been soaked to the skin with no dry clothes to change into. I bought a fourteen foot dinghy called *Marietta* instead, from a yachtsman in Leigh-on-Sea, and sailed it up to Gravesend. It was ideal for sailing in the estuary and with practice Betty became used to handling the boat when we went down the river on our trips. I cannot say the same when I tried to teach her to drive my new car. She had driven before but not the same model as mine, where the controls were different from those she was familiar with. I was impatient and finally she got out of the car and walked away, leaving me to drive slowly along beside her, asking her to get back in, which she finally consented to do. She later took lessons from a qualified instructor, becoming a very good driver, and I often wondered whether she might have jumped overboard and swum ashore if I had been as impatient whilst teaching her to handle the dinghy.

My mother never liked living in a terrace house with a small garden after being in the country with plenty of room to keep chickens and rabbits, although for a time she did have a goose at Jersey Road. This came about when my father picked up an exhausted goose at sea, lying on top of the water in the middle of winter. He had it taken aboard, thawed it out in front of the galley fire, and when it could eat fed it on porridge oats until it recovered. At the end of the voyage he brought it home in his kitbag, and it lived in the garden, and like all geese defended its territory against all comers. It was so aggressive that nobody would come to the house through the back garden. When my father came home he opened the garden gate and, not recognizing him, the goose flew at him, pecking him viciously on the leg through his trousers, leaving a painful bruise. That was the end of Billy the goose's life with us. We could not bear to kill it so we gave it to my mother's sister, Beatrice, who had a paddock where she kept chickens and ducks.

I decided that the best way to repay my mother and father for the sacrifices they had to make when sending me to a private school and during the five years of my articles, was to get them a modern house in the country with a large garden. I therefore bought a quarter of an acre of land in a cherry orchard owned by a local farmer near the village of Higham, a short distance out of the town, situated in Dillywood Lane. A friend drew up the plans for a three bedroomed house with a large living room, bathroom, electric heating and garage. He wrote out the specification, which Betty typed, and I sent to three local builders for quotations. I selected the one most suitable and as my parents had not sufficient savings to pay for the house I arranged a mortgage at four per cent through a solicitor I knew, making myself responsible for paying the interest. The builders made good progress but half way through the work they were made bankrupt, which was not unusual in those days, during the depression. However, I retained all the materials on site and arranged with the foreman to complete the work with the assistance of another workman. After the house was finished Mother moved in and I laid out the front garden with the help of my brother-in-law, Norman Chittenden. I engaged a part time gardener to make a vegetable garden in the top half of the large garden at the back of the house and to maintain it. A man in Bromley advertised his flock of White Leghorn chickens for sale, together with a chicken house. I arranged for one of the lorries which delivered farm produce to Covent Garden in the morning to stop off at Bromley on the way back and collect the chickens together with the chicken house. When he arrived I found that the chickens were in an open lorry covered by a tarpaulin. As we cautiously lifted the cover to get them out one by one, they made a bid for freedom and escaped all over the lane. It took us two or three hours chasing these birds before we collected them and penned them in. Norman erected the chicken house and my mother settled in to her new house among familiar surroundings. However, all was not well between Mother and me. As I have explained, she had a possessive love for her children and as I was her only son it was focussed on me. She knew that I was going with Betty and she hated the idea of it. I thought that if she met Betty she would change her mind, but I was greatly mistaken. When I took Betty home to meet my mother she accused Betty of robbing her of her only son and insulted her. However, I was as strong willed as my mother and rather than put up with the anger and abuse to which I was subjected I left home to live with my sister Lydia at Bromley.

Since my holiday in Great Yarmouth I had been thinking seriously about my future, in which Betty would now be involved. Everything was too comfortable and easy where I was employed and I realized that unless I soon made a move I would be there for life.

I was liked by all the staff and when they were shorthanded I volunteered to help them. I offered to collect the rents from weekly tenants, which involved calling on the small houses in the back streets of the town. As I had not done this before and I did not know my way about the district I was late getting round, and the housewives were standing at their doors with the rent money in their hands, looking for me. They had some jokes at my expense but they were also very helpful. They knew who were the bad payers and if I knocked at a house without getting a reply they advised me 'Don't waste your time there. She's in but she won't answer. You won't get her money.'

I also attended the change-over of the tenancy at public houses and hotels when the firm acted on behalf of the brewers and worked out the amount to be paid by the incoming tenant for the inventory. I went to a hotel at Allhallows-on-sea called The Pilot, which was being taken over by a man who had been marine superintendent for the P & O company in Hong Kong. He invited me to stay to lunch because he was preparing a special curry, but I was rather dubious about staying; my experience of curry had consisted of soggy rice and sauces too hot to eat. However, he said he had personally prepared the curry and I would change my mind when I tried it. A waiter brought the food in with a dish piled high with rice, and as the swing doors from the kitchen closed behind him they created a small draught which literally blew the top off the heap of rice, it was so light. That was one of the most enjoyable meals I have eaten and I have never had a curry to match up to it since.

I had gained experience in running an accountancy practice from Mr Turner and I was now ready to make a move. I contacted an agency handling the sale and purchase of accountancy practices, as I did not have enough private work to start entirely on my own. After investigating several propositions I was offered the opportunity of purchasing the share of a partner retiring from a small London two partner firm. I did not have sufficient capital to pay for it so I approached the bank for a loan but they would only advance sufficient funds to buy a one fifth share. I explained the position to the remaining partner, who agreed that I could take the one fifth share with the option of buying a further fifth when I had enough money. I gave notice to my employers in accordance with my agreement and commenced practice with my partner in 1937 from an office in Bloomsbury Square near the British Museum. Six months later Betty obtained new employment as secretary to the manager of APCM Bevan's Works at Northfleet.

In the summer we went on holiday to the Scilly Isles, driving down to Penzance, then taking the ferry *Scillonian* across to St Mary's Island. We took a leisurely drive, stopping on the way to see anything which we thought would be interesting. We visited General Wolfe's home at Quebec House in Westerham and lunch at Abinger Hammer where two small figures emerged with their hammers to ring the chimes of a clock which projects out over the narrow main street. We stopped to walk round Stonehenge and take photographs — Betty is a keen photographer — before continuing on to Honiton where we hoped to stay the night at a hotel, but unfortunately all the rooms were taken except for one double room. We looked at each other; Betty was really startled, and it flashed through my mind that she might be thinking I had arranged to reserve a double room. After a moment I turned to the manager, explaining that we needed two single rooms. He said he had an arrangement with people in the town to accommodate visitors and we could have two single rooms there, taking our meals in the hotel. I accepted his offer; we had comfortable rooms for the night and the meals in the hotel were very good. We stopped the next morning at Exeter to see the cathedral, Archbishop's Palace and Guildhall and have a meal before continuing on to Penzance by the evening, where I garaged the car. We had no difficulty in getting two single rooms for the night, which was rather a relief. We boarded the *Scillonian* in the morning.

* * *

The Scilly Isles lie twenty-eight miles south west of Penzance but the sea was calm and we had a pleasant voyage. We tied up at the quay on St Mary's and I went to find Thomas Hicks, who was to take us over in his boat to St Agnes, where we were to stay in his house. Eventually, when I found him, I discovered he was known as Tommy Cook because all the families on St Agnes were named Hicks except one named Smith, who came from the mainland, so they were known by their middle names and as Mr Hicks' full name was Thomas Cook Hicks he was always referred to as Tommy Cook.

St Agnes is the most westerly of the islands; the run across the Atlantic by the big liners was timed from the Ambrose light off New York to the Bishops Rock off St Agnes. We had comfortable rooms with cold water basins in them, there was no hot water, no central heating, and the lavatory was an earth closet at the bottom of the garden, but we were made most welcome and the home cooked food with fresh vegetables from the garden, milk, cream, eggs, chicken, fish and lobsters was delicious. The cost was £2.10s. per week each for full board and lodgings. The house was called Rose Cottage. There were no roads or hotels on the island. We had the use of a boat and spent our time fishing, sunbathing, swimming, exploring the rock pools and playing tennis. The only excitement occurred when the bucket came off the windlass of the main well on the island and all the sixty villagers gathered round to watch it being recovered.

Sometimes we went out with Tommy Cook's son to retrieve his lobster pots and collect the lobsters to await the arrival of the French fishermen, who came over in their boats to buy them. Whilst Betty and I were out fishing one day I caught something very large. We never saw what it was because it started towing the boat backwards whilst I hung on to the line and Betty rowed as hard as she could until eventually the line parted.

There were only two other visitors staying on the island, an elderly man with a young woman. He was keen on fishing but she preferred sunbathing in a smart bathing costume with her hair set in the latest style and her coloured nails carefully manicured. We did not see much of them but one day they were on the beach and the man was preparing his fishing tackle, but he had some difficulty in getting the lugworms which he had brought for bait out of a tin. He turned to the girl and asked her to get them out for him and when she enquired, 'What shall I get them out with?' he replied angrily, 'Dig them out with your nails'. She left the beach in a hurry and we did not see them again.

A smaller island called Gugh was joined to St Agnes by a bar which we could cross when the tide was out. It was a bird sanctuary with no people living there but hundreds of seabirds. We also visited the other islands, including Tresco, with its semi-tropical flowers and trees which flourished there in the warm climate due to its sheltered position. The islands organized a regatta once a year when races were rowed in eight oared longboats, which have been preserved on each island from the time they were used to row out to the old sailing ships, hoping to be the first to offer their services as pilots. When we left at the end of our holiday the sea was very rough. The small launch taking us back to St Mary's to join the *Scillonian* plunged into the waves and threw up clouds of spray, deluging us with sheets of water. But we had prepared against the weather, having been lent oilskins which covered us; otherwise we would have arrived in St Mary's looking like drowned rats.

The sea continued to be very rough on the crossing to Penzance and as the *Scillonian* was a small vessel it was thrown down into the trough, then climbed up to the crest of each wave. Many of the passengers were seasick and it is not very easy to stop feeling queasy when people are being sick all round you; but we managed to last out, although we were glad when we arrived in the harbour at Penzance. We stayed the night in the same hotel as before and I collected my car in the morning to drive home by a different route from the one we used when we came down. We stopped to see St Michael's Mount, visit Rostormel Castle and admire the views on the river Fal in Cornwall.

In Dorset we visited the Tolpuddle martyrs' memorial, then drove on into Hampshire to see the Rufus Stone in the New Forest and explore Winchester, with its statue of King Alfred and King Arthur's Round Table in the castle, finally reaching home through Sussex to Kent.

My father died in February 1938 from a heart attack at the age of sixty-one. I attended the funeral and returned home to support my mother. Relations between us continued to be strained but I ignored her outbursts of anger against my

87

association with Betty and in the summer we spent our holiday touring Scotland. My brother-in-law, Lydia's husband, made a towing bar for my car and I hired a caravan from a firm in Hither Green. It was well fitted out, one of the latest models with a sliding partition which divided the sleeping accommodation into two compartments to the satisfaction of Betty's mother. I had earned her respect and trust after the incident at the hotel in Honiton on our holiday last year. My plan was to drive up the east coast and return by the west after crossing Scotland. Our first stop was Cambridge University, where we explored the Backs, and I showed Betty round Gonville and Cais College where I had lodged during my accountancy course. We spent some time watching the end of the term play at Trinity College before leaving for York. We walked on the top of the city wall and were given a conducted tour of the Minster. We camped at a very pretty farm near Northallerton and crossed the river Tees in Durham to reach Alnwick, Northumberland, and explore the castle. At North Berwick we ran into a typical Scotch mist, the first bad weather since leaving home, but it was fine again by the time we reached Edinburgh.

At the castle I pointed out to Betty the name of the Scots clan from which she claimed her grandmother was descended, in the list of the clans who had surrendered to the English after the battle of Culloden. The small dark room in Holyrood Palace where Darnley, the Queen of Scots' husband, had her Italian courtier killed, seemed to symbolize the unhappiness she suffered at the hands of her Scottish lords and the Kirk of Scotland.

We camped at Perth and continued on to Arbroath, then along the coast of Banffshire to reach Inverness. We explored the castle and the site of the battle of Culloden and followed the line of the Caledonian Canal across Scotland. We saw an object out in the middle of Loch Ness which looked at first glance like the monster but on closer inspection proved to be the trunk of a tree with its branches sticking up in the air. We saw Ben Nevis in the distance and continued by the bonnie banks of Loch Lomond, eventually reaching Garloch and the outskirts of Glasgow. We camped for two nights at a farm near Glasgow to visit the 1938 Empire Exhibition. The farmer showed us round the site and the toilet block, explaining that there was mains water, pulling the chain of the cistern to demonstrate that it flushed and pointing out that there was plenty of toilet paper, but when we came to use the lavatory we found that he had substituted torn up newspaper in place of the toilet paper, so I deducted 1s. when I paid him the camping fee.

Although the exhibition was not as large as the Wembley exhibition we spent two interesting days visiting the many pavilions from all parts of the Empire.

On the way out from Glasgow we passed John Brown's yard where the *Queen Elizabeth* looked very forlorn, half built and waiting for the decision on whether to complete the ship. We called in the blacksmith's shop at Gretna Green but resisted the temptation to get married and drove on through the Lake District to stop at Grasmere and visit Wordsworth's cottage there. After the many nights camping we could not resist the lure of Blackpool, so we stayed there and went out on the town, taking a trip up the tower and dancing in the Tower Ballroom, after listening to Reginald Dixon at the organ. We crossed under the Mersey through the tunnel to Warwick to see the castle and on to Stratford-on-Avon for Shakespeare's birthplace and his tomb in the parish church. We took the quieter road through Banbury and Aylesbury back to London.

I had driven 3,000 miles without any trouble when I swept through the gates of the yard to return the caravan, but I was overconfident and the caravan caught one of the gateposts, ripping off the side, which was only made of plywood. The proprietor heard the crash and came running out of his office to see what had happened. I felt a fool as I apologized for my carelessness, but he was quite philosophical about it, saying that similar accidents had occurred before and that he must widen the entrance. I had paid for insurance in the hiring charge so there was nothing extra to pay and the owner explained that a new panel could be fitted to the caravan quite quickly.

Betty was able to learn a lot about cooking and housekeeping on the trip. When we were in Scotland she went into a butcher's shop and enquired, 'Is the beef English?' to which the butcher replied, 'No madam, all our meat is Scottish.' On another occasion she bought a lot of dried apricots which swelled up so much when they were cooked that they lasted all the holiday.

Besides being a good tennis player Betty enjoyed horse riding. One of her favourite rides was to a public house in the country called the Stone Horse, where the horse had a pint of beer whilst she went inside for a drink. She was riding with a friend when the other rider's horse was frightened by a motor car and bolted. Both their horses were ponies which raced at Northolt and when Betty's horse saw the other one in front it took off after it. They raced side by side until the girls were able to pull them up and the groom caught up with them. The groom was annoyed because he was afraid of what the owners might have done if there had been an accident but Betty told him it was his fault for putting them up on a couple of racehorses.

I still kept in touch with Rob Passmore and we made up a foursome with him and a girlfriend. One of our outings was to Northolt to see the pony racing and when we were having lunch his current girlfriend started complaining about the food. He put on a schoolmaster's accent and told her, 'When one is a guest one does not complain to one's host about the food.' We all laughed but I think his remarks struck home. Betty joined the rifle club at Bevans. She had a good eye and a steady hand, becoming an excellent shot and beating the men, most of whom were in the Territorial Army Royal Engineers under the command of the manager, Colonel Brazier.

Our practice had a good connection with the film industry. My partner handled most of that work but I looked after some of the companies which were suffering from one of the periodic depressions which afflicted the industry. A casting director named Harvey came in to see me. In the course of our conversation he told me he had lost his job and asked whether one of the film companies for which I acted had a vacancy. I told him everybody was in the same boat but I could, as it happened, offer him temporary work until the film business picked up again. We had recently been appointed receivers and managers on behalf of the debenture holder of a laundry in Sidcup and I wanted somebody to take charge of it until we could sell it. He accepted the offer and managed the laundry under my supervision for six months until we were able to sell it to a national chain of laundries.

One distressing accident occurred whilst he was in charge. The clothes were washed in a long cylindrical colander driven by a belt at one end. The colander would be switched off and on by a lever which moved the belt over, but one man, thinking to save time, I suppose, kicked the belt over with his foot instead of using the lever, with the result that his foot was torn off.

The international tension with Germany continued to build

up and Rob had gone back to work in the aircraft industry with Fairey Aviation, leaving his father to continue running the business. He now had a regular girlfriend, Gwen. She and Betty became very good friends, both being interested in painting.

Neville Chamberlain made his visit to Hitler at Munich and came back with a piece of paper which he said guaranteed peace in our time but preparations for war continued. My partner was a lieutenant commander in the Royal Navy Reserve and he was called back to the Navy. He was certain that there would be war and I would be called up because I was young, which would mean the end of the practice. It was therefore agreed to dissolve the practice so that he could transfer his four fifths share to his brother-in-law, who had a well established practice outside London. I was left with the remaining one fifth of the clients, an office I could not afford and a shorthand typist whose salary I could not pay.

While I was deciding what to do Harvey came into the office. He was still unemployed and told me he was going to enlist in the army to make sure of getting into the regiment he wanted, perhaps the army film unit. He said I was bound to be called up and if I volunteered now I could get into the Army Pay Corps as an accountant officer. I was feeling at a low ebb, I had not reached a decision on my future, and knowing the way the army worked, I was certain that as I was an accountant I would be drafted into the infantry, so I agreed to go to Whitehall with him, mainly out of curiosity, without any definite intention of enlisting. When we got to the recruiting office, a sergeant with a red sash stood in the doorway. Harvey went up to him and said, 'We've come to enlist.' He stared at Harvey, then told him, 'Go away. We will send for you when we want you.'

Harvey was very downhearted but I was not bothered; it merely confirmed my impression of the army. We went for a drink and although I continued with my clients in the film industry I did not meet Harvey again. My future was settled by one of my clients, Mr Magowan, who had a company selling office machinery in the City. He offered me a room in the office he rented at Stationers Hall Court near St Pauls and accommodation for my shorthand typist with his clerks. He charged no rent but I helped him, of course, with advice on financial and other matters, which I was happy to do outside the annual audit.

91

The Government announced the formation of the Civil Air Guard, which was intended to train civilian pilots who would then be available to ferry planes for the RAF to operational stations from the manufacturers or between airfields. Amy Johnson was on one of these flights when she disappeared over the Thames Estuary. Neither her body nor any wreckage from her plane was ever found. I joined at the Maidstone Flying Club near West Malling. The cost of the instruction was half a crown an hour on Tiger Moth biplanes. With my leather flying helmet on, seated in the aeroplane, I looked like someone out of the film *Hells Angels*. The airfield was small, the planes having to come in over orchards and take off to clear woods at the other end of the runway. As I was working hard to build up my practice I could only spare an hour on Saturday mornings. Sometimes I was away and missed a week entirely and although I had done landings and take-offs with the instructor aboard I had not put in enough hours to go solo by the time war was declared and the Government closed down the scheme. The RAF took over the airfield and expanded West Malling to become one of the main fighter stations in the south east.

As I was too busy I could not spare the time to take a holiday in 1939 so Betty accompanied her elder sister on holiday to St Ives. When they arrived at the farm where they were to stay they were put in rooms over the pigsty but after protesting they were moved to a farmworker's cottage to be looked after by the farmworker's wife. They were there a week when they received a message from their mother to come home immediately. The rest of the family had gone on holiday to Hayling Island Civil Service holiday camp but their mother had to take father home when he became ill. The two girls went back to Hayling Island to care for the remainder of the family who stayed on there. On returning home Betty's elder sister married Fra Taylor, who was in the Metropolitan Police until the war started, when he was transferred to the Navy as a regulating petty officer.

I was best man at the wedding of Rob Passmore to Gwen. He volunteered for the RAF but was refused entry because of his work in the aircraft industry. However, his younger brother, Donald, became a pilot in Coastal Command and the youngest of the three brothers, Keith, was already a flying officer in the RAF, having been commissioned before the war as a regular officer. Donald and Keith both survived the war. Keith was

Rob and Gwen Passmore with Author and family at Jaywick

stationed in the Middle East before the war and served in Greece before being transferred with his squadron to Malaya. After the fall of Singapore the survivors of the squadron reached Java, where they borrowed a lifeboat from a ship with as many provisions as they could obtain and set sail for Australia. The voyage lasted six weeks, they reached northern Australia exhausted and emaciated. Keith returned to England via America and re-entered the war in North Africa and Europe. At the end of the war, after a spell at the staff college, he was sent as a wing commander on a goodwill mission to the USA. He travelled as a passenger from Prestwick on an RAF plane which was forced down into the sea by bad weather and icing, all the occupants being drowned. Some months later Keith's body was brought up in a fishing boat's nets and Rob identified a watch and other personal items as belonging to his brother.

When the war started my friend, Harry Turner, called to see

me at home. He was the chief engineer at the LCC and as he had been manager of a department at Woolwich Arsenal during the 1914-18 war he was seconded to the Ministry of Production and put in charge of three shell filling factories. The day to day running of these factories was the responsibility of three commercial companies; I think they were Unilever, J. Lyons and Marks & Spencer, but Harry had to organize his head office staff. He wanted me to do this and said that I would have a staff of 500 by the end of the war; he would see I would get one of the decorations the King would hand out when he visited the factories and I would not be called up for the armed forces. I was fed up with being told I would be called up after I had been in the RNVR, which dispensed with my services, and after applying for the Colonial Service, volunteering for the army and RAF and being turned down and finally having my training with the Civil Air Guard cut short. I thanked Harry for his offer but refused it. I told him that I would carry on with my practice and if the Government wanted me they would have to come and get me. Harry and I remained good friends; he gave me a nice set of sherry glasses for a wedding present when I married Betty.

Author building Anderson air raid shelter

I erected the Anderson air raid shelter in the garden with the help of Norman, Lydia's husband, and an anti-aircraft battery and camp was established by the army at the bottom of the lane about 200 yards away. These guns caused more distress to my mother than all the enemy bombing. When they opened up on German aircraft the noise was devastating and earsplitting; although she covered her ears in the shelter my mother's nerves were shattered to such an extent that she broke down and for the first time in my life I saw her cry. Bombs which were dropped nearby fell on soft soil, the force of the explosion making a large crater in the ground which muffled the sound of the explosion, but there was no way of avoiding the barrage from the guns during the day and at night, and except for the fact that we were not being shelled and all we suffered were broken windows, we might just as well have been in a bombardment on the western front in the 1914-18 war.

The Government ordered all vessels, small and large, to be registered in order to control their movements. I went to the Port of London Authority building on Tower Hill and as I waited the captain of a 10,000 ton cargo ship was giving particulars of his vessel to the official. When the captain collected his certificate, the man behind the desk said, 'What is the name of your ship, Captain?' I replied, 'Marietta' and he enquired, 'What is the tonnage?' I answered, 'It has no registered tonnage. It's a yacht.' He then said, 'What is the method of propulsion?' and I replied, 'It's a sailing dinghy.'

The official did not blink an eyelid as he finished completing the registration form and handed it to me, saying 'Here is your registration certificate, Captain. The number must be painted on the side of your yacht and you are not permitted to sail beyond the Nore.'

I thanked him and went out, feeling very pleased that I had received the same courtesy as the big ships' captains.

When Anthony Eden broadcast an appeal for men to join the Local Defence Volunteers I was one of the first from our village to enrol. We were issued with an armband, a rifle and ammunition. Our look-out post was on the top of Telegraph Hill overlooking the village, which we manned day and night, keeping watch for enemy paratroops. We captured two parachutists who turned out be be RAF pilots who had baled out when their planes were shot down. They were more

Betty bailing out dinghy *Marietta*

frightened of us than they were of the enemy; when we held them up at gun point they shouted, 'I'm British. RAF pilot', until we took them into headquarters to be identified.

An elderly employee of the people who owned the woods on Telegraph Hill came up to our post on several nights to see what we were doing, interfering with us and generally making a nuisance of himself. One of our members was a young man in his middle twenties called Bill Hill. His father was a Trinity House pilot, quite wealthy, and Bill had never had a regular job, living with his father, drinking and getting into all sorts of trouble. One night we heard old Ben making his way up through the woods and Bill said, 'I'll soon put the wind up that old sod so he won't come up here again'. He loaded his rifle and called out, 'Who goes there?' There was no reply and we heard Ben getting closer. Bill shouted again, 'Halt or I fire.' There was still no reply, so he fired his rifle in the air. Ben staggered the last few yards into our post white faced, and gasped, 'You knew it was me', to which Bill replied, 'You didn't answer my challenge. You're lucky not to be dead.' Ben never visited our post again.

Bill Hill enlisted in the RAF and was posted to Malaya in charge of a motor transport section. When the Japanese invaded he did not retreat to Singapore because he was cut off with his section behind the Japanese lines. He therefore drove north until he met up with General Joe (Vinegar) Stilwell, an American who commanded an army operating from China. Bill was posted as missing but if he was alive I knew he would turn up, and he did, a year later, in India, to rejoin his unit. The Local Defence Volunteers were formed into the Home Guard. I was given a commission in the Fourteenth Hoo Battalion Royal West Kent Regiment and appointed in command of Higham platoon.

We were on guard one night, watching a raid going on across the water in Essex. The enemy planes were bombing the oil refinery there and huge fires were burning where the storage tanks were hit, turning the low clouds to red as though it was the dawn of a summer morning. We heard the sound of a bomb coming down near us and saw the explosion near a bungalow on the lower road. One of my men said, 'That's where my grandparents live' and I sent him off with a squad to see what help they could give. The bomb had fallen on soft ground but the blast had caused the bungalow to collapse. Fortunately, as it was a single storey building, the elderly couple living there were not trapped under a lot of debris and we were able to get them out, badly shaken but not seriously injured. On another occasion, also at night, a quantity of fire bombs were dropped on the area. We saw a fire start at an isolated farm and alerted the fire brigade, but they were so busy dealing with fires elsewhere that they could not get to the farm until some time later. We went down to see what we could do. The farmhouse was not alight but the barns were burning and the farmer was trying to get his animals out. Several of my men were farm workers and with their assistance most of the stock were rescued from the buildings, but they were so frightened that they stampeded out into the farmyard and were in danger of seriously injuring themselves until they were rounded up and penned in. There was nothing we could do to save the hay barn.

One event occurred which changed the probable course of my life during the war. Mr Metcalf, my father's former employer, called to see me and asked whether I would take on the audit of his family shipping business because his auditor had died unexpectedly from a heart attack. I said I would be pleased to but pointed out to him that my resources were limited and I did not employ a large staff. He replied, 'If you are half the man your father was you are good enough for us.'

In addition to their own fleet Metcalfs managed ships on behalf of the Ministry of War Transport for Shipping and I was therefore appointed auditor to the Ministry, which meant that I could not be called up for active service. Metcalfs also owned a tanker company in Holland and when Germany invaded, the eldest son, Tom, was sent over to Holland to persuade the Dutch company to send their ships to England. The family were Catholics and when Tom was returning to his hotel after attending early morning mass he passed the British Embassy and saw the staff preparing to leave in two coaches. As he had registered at the embassy, taking the precaution when he arrived in Holland, he asked one of the staff whom he knew what was happening. The man told him they were leaving for the station to catch a train taking them to the coast, where there was a ship waiting to ferry them to England, because the Dutch could not hold out much longer against the Germans. Tom took a taxi back to his hotel, told the other English people what was happening and asked them to pack up and leave with him for the station. Nobody wanted to go; they offered a variety of excuses, one woman saying she had a hair appointment, and Tom drove to the station on his own, where he mingled with the embassy crowd and caught the train.

At the coast he boarded the ship and made his way to the galley, where he helped to prepare sandwiches for the passengers, including the Sadlers Wells Ballet Company and a group of German parachutists who had been captured. The ship was not attacked and when it arrived at Harwich a train was waiting to take them to London, but Tom was not allowed to join it. Bureaucracy had caught up with him; it was discovered that he was not one of the embassy staff so he had to make his own way home.

I was sorry to miss Dunkirk. I was away from home, otherwise I would have been able to join one of the Medway Yacht Club boats which went over. The old paddle steamer, *Royal Daffodil* from Rochester, took part and returned safely. Coming home from London I was caught in an air raid when the Germans dropped a stick of bombs on Tilbury Docks. The driver of our train stopped in a cutting at Northfleet because some of the bombs carried over to the Kent side where Bevans works were situated, destroying and damaging the workmen's cottages. I did not know at the time that Betty, who now worked at Bevans, was helping to get the children into the shelters and trying to comfort them while the raid was on.

I had to investigate and analyse a client's bank account for the last ten years to agree his income tax liability. I asked the bank to supply me with copies but they were unable to do so because they were short staffed and they said that I could inspect their ledgers if I agreed not to look at any other customers' accounts. I did not want to waste time examining other peoples accounts so I spent a week in the bank vaults, going over my client's records. The bank was situated in the East End, near the docks, and whilst the Germans were dropping their bombs up above I felt quite safe below, although the vaults were rather cold and I had to wear an overcoat to keep warm.

Magowan's building at Stationers Hall Court was damaged by fire bombs and we had to find other premises. I rented a small office in Fen Court off Fenchurch Street and Magowans moved to Wolverhampton, where they established a heavy engineering works making fabricated parts for ships, including bed plates for diesel engines. This meant I had to make frequent visits to Wolverhampton and all the time I was there I was not involved in an air raid; the bombing was concentrated on Coventry and the East Midlands.

I was staying at a hotel in the town when I was woken up one night by a terrific row outside the door of the bedroom next door. A woman had locked herself in the bedroom, although it had been booked by a man whose clothes were in the room. He was shouting, 'This is my room and my clothes are inside', while she shrieked, 'I am not coming out. I must have somewhere to stay the night'. Eventually he went downstairs and came back with the manager, who tried to unlock the door, but the woman kept the key in the lock inside the bedroom, which stopped him opening the door from outside. There was a lot more argument but the woman would not give way. The man pleaded with her to give him his toilet articles and pyjamas but she replied, 'That's only a trick to get me to open the door', and refused his request. Finally the man gave up and spent the night on a couch in the lounge.

Betty's father and the other Trinity House pilots were given commissions in the Royal Navy and Betty talked about joining the Wrens. The men from Bevans works who were in the Territorials had gone over to Calais to destroy the fuel dumps and stores before the Germans captured them and she wanted to become more involved in the war effort. That would have meant separation, perhaps for years, and as we always intended to marry I suggested we should marry immediately. I had no money, but I had my car, which I sold for £75. After paying the garage the £15 which I owed them I was left with £60 to prepare for married life. With the £60 we bought the wedding ring, a small oak dining room suite of sideboard, table, and four chairs, a sofa, two armchairs and a carpet for the lounge and a limed oak double bed with a wardrobe and dressing table to match. A client gave us a canteen of cutlery, Harry Turner sent a set of glasses, Betty's parents supplied the linen and she made the curtains from blackout material. One of Betty's boyfriends gave us a clock and we bought some crockery from the reject shop. We were married on Boxing Day 1940, as I could not spare any time away from the office. There was thick fog, which kept the bombers away. Betty's eldest brother, who was home on leave from the RAF, was my best man because most of my friends were in the forces and could not get leave. My mother would not come to the wedding but two of my sisters came and there was quite a gathering of Betty's relations. The reception was held at Betty's home, the family had pooled their coupons to provide a chocolate cake and we had a barrel of beer. My sister Gladys had found a house called Greenbank for us to rent on the outskirts of Strood from a family who had evacuated to the country. Our furniture had been delivered immediately after we bought it because the manufacturers wanted it to be taken away from their factory in London in case it was bombed, and although we only had enough to furnish three rooms that gave us a start.

There was a sequel to our wedding. Six months after the marriage we were informed by the vicar that the ceremony was not legal because the church had not been licensed. An old church had been pulled down to build the new one, and the authorities had forgotten to transfer the license. I had my leg pulled about that, some of my friends saying, 'Now's your chance to get out and regain your freedom,' but a special act was passed in Parliament, made retrospective to legalize the fifty or so marriages which had taken place whilst the church was unlicensed.

5

THE GOLDEN YEARS 1940-1970

It may sound strange to call the years between 1940 and 1970 the Golden Years when my practice had collapsed, I had no money, I was in debt to the bank for the loan I had borrowed to purchase my share of the partnership, I had to pay the interest on the mortgage for my mother's house and there was a war on. But I had married the girl I loved and who loved me; we were young and confident that we could support each other in facing the difficulties which lay ahead. As I had sold my car Betty cashed in a small life insurance which she had in order to buy me a bicycle, which I used to get to the village for Home Guard duties. I had never ridden one before but to her surprise I got straight on and rode down the road, only to fall off when I reached the corner out of sight.

Lower Higham consisted of old houses and a church on the edge of the marshes. The houses then straggled up the hill to Mid-Higham with a more modern church, as far as the main road called Upper Higham. I had between thirty and forty men in my platoon which I divided into three sections. The nucleus consisted of Local Defence Volunteers, the remainder being men who had been drafted into the Home Guard. I established my headquarters in a hut at the waterworks in Mid-Higham which we fitted out with bunks for the use of the men who would have to be on night duty. Each section manned the guard in turn for a week, the men not on duty being able to get some sleep because they had to go to work the next day. I usually saw the men on and off the guard each night and morning but when I was away this duty became the responsibility of the sergeant in charge of the section. We were armed with rifles which we kept at home, and in the stores we had hand grenades, a heavy machine gun, and what we called sticky bombs made of glass containing phosphorus which were intended to be thrown at tanks or enemy vehicles, breaking the glass and setting them alight. I had men who had served in the 1914-18 war and I was anxious to learn from their experience, one having been in the Rifle Brigade and another in the HAC.

They were entirely against manning the pill boxes which had been built in the countryside, calling them death traps and advocating the use of slit trenches. This coincided with my ideas, which visualized my platoon as a lightly armed mobile force to harass the enemy, hold them up as much as possible and send back details of their movements to headquarters, leaving the regular troops to man the pill boxes. My local men knew all the ways through the orchards, and woods, and the by-roads which our farm lorries could use. We therefore constructed slit trenches where the rising ground sloped up from the marsh and where there were likely landing grounds for parachutists further back. The farmers co-operated with us but one landowner was rather difficult until I pointed out that I was in command and he must allow us to do the work. We also constructed a firing range in an old disused quarry, where my men practised. They were used to shooting rabbits which rushed out of the corn when it was being cut and they were able to astonish the army with the accuracy of their shooting when we went to the army rifle range. We visited the Lodge Hill camp to practice grenade throwing and as the officer in charge I had to instruct my men. I had previously given them a demonstration with dummies on how to prime a grenade and also arranged for them to practice throwing the grenade on the cricket field, which came easily to most of the men. I took each section in turn, the men waiting in the trenches, which were shielded from the throwing bay by a corner made by the trenches being dug in zigzag fashion. I took the men one at a time into the throwing bay, saw they primed the grenade properly and held the lever in place when they pulled out the locking pin; then they threw the grenade with a high action to clear the parapet of the trench. The inevitable happened, as it always does in these cases. It was a winter's day and the men's fingers were cold, so it was no surprise when one of them let his grenade fall when he pulled the pin out. I stamped it into the mud at the bottom of the throwing bay and hustled him round the corner into the safety of the trench next door before it exploded.

Dad's Army is one of the funniest programmes on television and I even enjoy watching the repeats, but it has no resemblance to what really happened in the Home Guard. General Montgomery took over command of the south-east defences after Dunkirk and I am sure he would not have put up with the antics of Captain Mannering and his merry men. His first action was to move headquarters out of Tunbridge Wells and call a meeting of officers at the largest cinema in Maidstone. He started in the usual way by telling us to cough now because he wanted no interruption when he started his speech and went on to emphasize the importance of physical fitness, the need for training to become efficient and his confidence that if every man did his best we would hit the Germans for six and be sure to defeat them.

The Durham Light Infantry Regiment were drafted into our area to train us and as everything had to be done at the double it was rather hard on my older men. Jack Reeves, the sergeant who had served with the HAC in 1914-18 was leading a flank attack by his section on an enemy position when he halted and said to his men, 'Have a breather here'. Immediately one of the Durham Light Infantry instructors leapt out from behind a bush, waving his cane shouting, 'No bloody breather here! No bloody breather here!' And poor Reeves could only reply, 'I'm old enough to be your father.'

We had to join forces with a platoon from a neighbouring village and attack an enemy position on the top of a chalk quarry. The enemy were the Durham Light Infantry, who fired live machine gun tracer bullets over the tops of our heads and an officer threw cannon flashes at my feet to try and put me off whilst I was directing the attack. This was done to imitate battle conditions but it only annoyed me. Our men reached the top of the cliff and were deemed to have captured the enemy position after suffering heavy casualties, of which two were unfortunately actually real; one of my men had a broken arm and a sergeant in the other Home Guard platoon fractured his skull falling from the top of the cliff, dying on the way to the hospital. Our manoeuvres were staged at weekends, involving bivouacking on Saturday nights and marching to the camping ground at Light Infantry pace, carrying our full kit, which was very exhausting. My sergeant, who had served with the Rifle Brigade, coped with it well but I put Jack Reeves in charge of the transport section to give him a ride. I enjoyed the weekends because it reminded me of my boyhood days camping in the country and I was able to teach the army how to make themselves more comfortable. I told them to choose a bush or preferably a small hazel tree which had pliable branches and bend the branches down, cutting them partly through in the same way as laying a hedge so that the ends could be stuck in the ground. Tie a gas cape over the branches to keep the rain out, lay a ground sheet inside and there was a useful shelter for the night. It had one drawback for me. By the time I had seen all the men bedded down I was late getting to sleep and in the mornings I was last having my breakfast after the men. Now I know why officers needed a batman.

We had a field day with the army, who invaded our region with the support of armoured vehicles, which they were supposed to have landed. We were defending our area and I had sent out scouts to spy on the enemy movements. These reported that an armoured column was coming up the road towards us. I had in my platoon a young man of about nineteen years of age who had left school without being able to read or write. I was rather doubtful about enlisting him but he proved invaluable. He knew all the short cuts and byways through the surrounding countryside and could guide us anywhere by day or night. We prepared to ambush the enemy column and this young man hid himself in a heap of rubbish by the side of the road. An armoured car from one of the crack cavalry regiments came slowly down the road, the officer standing up in the hatch to look around, when my young man threw a clod of earth at the officer, hitting him in the face and spattering mud down the front of his tunic, at the same time as my other men bombarded the armoured car with bricks. The officer was so angry he could hardly speak but he managed to shout, 'What did you want to throw all that shit over me for?' I walked over to him with the umpire and said, 'That wasn't shit, that was a hand grenade and those bricks were sticky bombs'. The umpire produced his clipboard, wrote on it and then said to the officer, 'You are a casualty and your vehicle is out of action. You had better retire and get cleaned up.'

Our battalion was responsible for the defence of the Hoo peninsular, which lies between the rivers Thames and Medway.

We could muster over 500 men under the command of Colonel Morris Gill, a local businessman, and when we attended church service, led by our band, the Hoo silver band, who had won brass band concerts at the Crystal Palace, we looked a fine body of men. The headquarters of the battalion was on Windmill Hill, where we had our office staffed by an adjutant and a sergeant clerk from the army. We had regular meetings there to cope with all the paper work. There was an anti-aircraft battery and a searchlight unit stationed about half a mile away, and one evening when we were having a meeting there was a raid on and one of the bombers was caught in the searchlights. The colonel adjourned the meeting and everybody went outside to see the aircraft twisting and turning to escape the searchlights. I looked through the window, then returned to the office to continue with my paper work. Suddenly there was a roar from the aircraft engines as it dived and released all its bombs before making an escape. Our battalion clerk was killed and the second in command wounded.

After D Day, when everything was going well for the Allies and the threat of invasion was over, I asked the colonel if I could resign to give more time to my practice. He laughed and replied, 'No Brooky. I am afraid you can't resign in wartime, but if it will help you I will make you liaison officer to the ARP.'

I asked what my duties would be and he said, 'Just find out when they have an exercise on and where it is going to take place, then report back to me so that we can avoid them.'

I thanked him and after arrangements had been made for another officer to take over my platoon I ceased taking an active part in the Home Guard to devote all my time to my practice.

The main difficulty in running my practice was getting to my office in London and keeping staff. I had one clerk and a shorthand typist but when the air raids became too much the girl usually left and Betty had to fill the breach, usually typing my letters and accounts at home. When I was on Home Guard duty at night I went home as soon as it was light to have my breakfast and change out of uniform. I listened over night and in the morning to the radio reports on the state of the roads and railways after the previous day's or night's bombing and I then had to decide on the best way to get to London. If I travelled by rail I took a bus to Gravesend station and caught a train there because it had a choice of two routes; it could either go by the North Kent line or via the loop line through Sidcup. Often it was impossible for the train to complete the journey and then we had to change to a bus or coach to go the rest of the way. This meant that my office hours were very erratic; sometimes I arrived at ten o'clock and other times not until twelve and I had to leave early to make sure of getting home before the air raids started again. My alternative was to get a lift on one of the farm lorries taking produce to Covent Garden Market, which left at five o'clock in the morning. It took whichever route was open to get there, through the docks area which was a scene of complete devastation and the back streets of South East London. I could then arrange to be picked up about half past four in the afternoon for a lift home.

When I visited clients outside Central London I went by tube and on my way back I had to pick my way past people who had already made up their beds for the night on the platform. They made themselves comfortable with groups of friends or families and were able to buy refreshments which were brought round to them. They were safe in the subways, although a bomb did fall on the Bank underground station whilst the people were going down there for the night, causing very high casualties.

I usually had lunch in a small restaurant in the City and as I became well known there I was looked after by a waitress called Alice, who saved special items for me which were not on the menu. After my office was bombed and I did not go back to the restaurant for ten years, I walked in one day and sat at a convenient table. A waitress came to serve me and said, 'You are one of Alice's customers. Her tables are over there.' I changed tables and Alice greeted me as though I had only been away for a day.

One of my clients, John Collyear, had an engineering works at Wembley, where he manufactured winding gear and equipment for buses. When the war started smaller works were brought under the umbrella of large companies who passed on the Ministry contracts and supplied technical assistance. Collyears received contracts for the manufacture of bomb sights and camera mountings for the RAF through Kodak, and as Wembley was a target for enemy bombers Collyears were asked to build a shadow factory in the country to safeguard production. They chose a site at Towcester and I arranged for the finance for the building with a machine tool company by a mortgage on the factory. I stayed at a hotel in Aylesbury when I visited the factory and was very pleased to enjoy a few quiet nights away from the bombing. The works manager, Mr Courtney, was a keen fisherman, and at lunchtime I relaxed on the bank of the river while he tried to catch a few fish. I noticed he had lost the top joints from two of the fingers of his right hand and he said this was the sign of an engineer. He explained that apprentices working the guillotine, cutting metal in a factory, would put out of action the automatic guard on the machine, which pushed their hands out of the way when the cutter came down, in order to save time, with the result that they often lost the tops of their fingers. The contracts were all on a cost plus basis and it was important to get all the overheads included in the cost, including the time lost when employees went to the lavatory and their tea breaks. It was usual to have 'Music while you work' broadcast in the factories, which Mr Collyear could not bear, so he used to switch the radio off and then say it had broken down.

The machine tool company which provided the finance for building Collyears' shadow factory was started by the chairman of the company after he was demobbed from the army in 1919. He attended a sale of surplus army stores which included unopened boxes containing lorry headlamps. He opened one box and discovered that the headlamps also included the electric light bulbs; he bid for the whole consignment — none of the other dealers were interested — and he was able to buy all the headlamps at a knock down price. He joined the other dealers in the refreshment tent and one of them asked, 'What did you buy those headlamps for, Jack?' He replied, 'Have a look at them and see for yourself.'

The man opened one of the boxes, saw the electric light bulbs and said, 'How much do you want for them?'

There was a shortage of electric light bulbs immediately after the war and Jack resold all the lot there and then at a price which was sufficient to start him up in business. He became one of the largest dealers in secondhand plant and machinery in the country. He had a flair for dealing and could see where a profit could be made before other people even made up their minds on whether to deal or not. When Wembley Exhibition closed he bought the lavatories and sold them on site to the Slough Trading Estate, without having to remove them.

One transaction upset him. He was asked by a German company to take out all the plant from the Bow Chemical Company, which had gone into liquidation. When he enquired what he should do with the plant he was told, 'Smash it up', to avoid competition from any other chemical company. While he was driving me in his Rolls Royce to the station after a visit to Collyear's factory, he said to me, 'I wish I had your education' and I was quick to reply, 'If you had you'd be a poor accountant instead of a millionaire.'

One of my clients was a public works contractor and despite the fact that he had a lot of work on hand for the Government he was called up for the army. He could not get deferment but he was given long spells of compassionate leave to attend to his business instead of being released. He was enrolled in the Royal Engineers and as part of his training he was taken with other recruits to an RAF airfield, where an officer started to give them a talk on the drainage system there. My client was in the back row, chatting to the man beside him, when the officer called out, 'Why aren't you paying attention, Private Kent?' My client answered, 'I laid the drains in this airfield, sir' to which the officer replied, 'In that case you'd better take my place and tell us how you did it.'

In May 1941 the City suffered one of its worst air raids and my offices in Fen Court received a direct hit. Because of the devastation it was four days before I received permission from the police to inspect the ruins and when I got there all I found was a hole in the ground; the building and everything in it had been destroyed. The Government had established a scheme for war damage insurance and after registering my claim for the loss of my office furniture and equipment, which I valued at £60 as it had all been bought secondhand, I went to the GPO and arranged for all my post to be re-directed to the offices of my friend, Ferdinand Berringer, an accountant in practice at Bromley. I had an agreement with him whereby I could share his offices if my own were destroyed and I had also taken the precaution of duplicating all my clients' records and storing the copies at home. As it happened my young clerk, Robert Dawson, lived at Bromley and he was very happy with the new arrangement. He was one of the best young men I have had until he was called up for the Navy. He was so quick at his work that I used to double check it at first because I thought it could not have been finished correctly in such a short time.

I carried on my practice from Bromley until 1942, but I wanted to get back to the City as soon as possible and when the air raids became less frequent I rented an office on the fifth floor of Adelaide House at the north side of London Bridge, close to the Monument. Adelaide House was a large, substantial modern building, with the Customs and Excise occupying the ground floor, a restaurant in the basement and a garden with a putting green on the roof, which was later planted to grow vegetables. I still could not get a permanent shorthand typist and Betty came up to the office to work as travelling became easier.

We were at home one evening when we heard a sound like a noisy motor bike engine and when we looked out we saw what we thought was a small aeroplane with flames coming out of the back. As we watched the engine cut out and the object dived to the ground followed by a large explosion. The first of the flying bombs which were to plague the Home counties and London had arrived. The barrage balloons round London were moved out to the country to intercept them and RAF fighters were also able to shoot many of them down before they reached London. When the air raid warning sounded a watcher went up on the roof of our office to sound a klaxon if one of the bombs was coming in our direction. In the country there was no air raid warning and as I was walking home after visiting my mother, a lorry drew up beside me, when the engine of a flying bomb was heard, and the driver leaned out of his cab to enquire, 'Where is it going to come down, mate?' I said 'You're all right it's gone over' and he drove on quite happily. Everybody was becoming quite used to them.

Betty was in the office while I was out visiting a client when the air raid warning went. Our watcher on the roof saw the flying bomb coming over the river towards our building and as the engine cut out and the bomb started its downward course he sounded the klaxon and Betty dived under a table. The bomb hit Colonial Wharf next door, killing seven or eight men and unhappily our watcher on the roof was killed by the blast. All the glass in our office was shattered but fortunately Betty was not hurt and when I got back she had started clearing up the mess. She was pregnant with our first child at that time and although she was badly shaken she did not suffer any lasting ill effects from the bomb.

Our baby girl was born on 18 June 1942. I was away at the time but Betty rang for an ambulance, which took her to a maternity hospital established in a large country house at Speldhurst, near Tunbridge Wells. I had previously called into Foyle's secondhand bookshop in Charing Cross Road, where I had bought the books I needed to study for my examinations, and purchased a book containing a list of 1,000 names with their meanings. Betty had studied this and decided on Miranda, after a character in Shakespeare which denoted 'deserving of admiration' and Dorcas, described as 'with large dark eyes'. When Miranda was born her eyes were a brilliant violet but Betty knew that they would change to a dark colour. Miranda was a small baby. Whether this was due to Betty's work and experiences during the war I do not know but she was a lovely child with a perfect complexion like the bloom of a peach. I travelled from the Medway Towns to Tunbridge Wells by bus and walked out to Speldhurst. The flowers in the gardens round the house were a magnificent array of colour in the summer sun and a nurse showed me Miranda asleep in a pram on the lawn whilst she went away to call Betty. Betty looked so fresh and young as she came out into the garden dressed in a summer frock, radiant and proud but shy, wondering what I would think of the baby. I went to greet her, kissed her and just said, 'She's beautiful.' Betty returned home after a week. We had previously been to Sams second-hand store in Strood and bought a tin bath, a cot, a highchair, a pram and a small chest of drawers to hold the baby's clothes, so we were fully equipped.

As the baby was so small Betty had to take great care bathing and feeding her but sometimes I was allowed to help. As we all slept downstairs because of the air raids we had no problems looking after the baby at night, although Betty would get up to make sure she was still breathing.

A land mine destroyed the houses on the estate opposite us and when we looked across the road in the morning we could not at first understand why there was a large gap where houses had formerly stood. The man next door was hit by shrapnel as he made his way to the garden shelter but we only suffered from broken windows.

A litter of kittens was born at Christmas on the farm next to my mother's house and to save them from being drowned we took one. My mother had one and we gave Betty's mother two. We called our little tabby Noel, which later became Nolly, and my mother named hers Monty after Montgomery.

Under Betty's care and devoted attention baby Miranda thrived and put on weight, growing strong and active with a will of her own. During the daytime she was put outside in her pram, well wrapped up in all weathers. Nolly always tried to jump up into the pram to lie on top of the baby where it was warm and Betty was continually pushing him off, with the result that he hated her. He would hide under a chair until Betty came by and then dash out and attack her ankles, but he loved me. When I sat in a chair, reading, he would curl up round the back of my beck, occasionally nibbling my ear, and he always waited for me when I came home. Although I did not have regular hours, Nolly would go down the front garden and sit on the gatepost when I was not even in sight, the children would shout, 'Daddy's coming', and Betty would get the evening meal ready. He brought me mice I did not want and laid partridge eggs at my feet which I could not return, as I was unable to find the nest. One morning he sat on the balcony outside our bedroom about thirty feet up, gnashing his teeth at the sparrows twittering in the gutter above him. When one of the sparrows flew off Nolly launched himself from the balcony, catching the sparrow in mid-air and landing safely on his feet in a flower bed below. Nolly was a great hunter but this proved his undoing. He liked to cross the road to reach a sandy bank in the woods opposite to catch rabbits, and he was hit by a motor car and killed. Miranda buried him in the garden.

Betty would not take the baby on a bus for fear of infection and walked into the town, pushing the pram, to reach the clinic and to do the shopping. When I was at home we spent fine afternoons in the country or sitting on the bank of the river opposite Shorts aeroplane works, watching the giant flying boats take off and land on the water.

The birth of the baby brought a lessening of the hostility of my mother. We took Miranda to see her; she loved her first grandchild, who could do no wrong in her eyes, and the child was allowed to do anything she wanted, scattering her toys and the contents of Grandmother's work basket over the floor. It also provided relief for us because we could have the occasional night off to visit the cinema. I was able to get a shorthand typist for the office, so Betty was able to concentrate on being a wife and mother.

My first year in practice on my own after my marriage had resulted in a net profit of £130 after paying my expenses, including interest on my mother's mortgage and the charge of my bank loan. I gave Betty £2 per week for housekeeping and had 10s. for myself. £2 per week to keep a family seems a small amount but food was rationed and Betty was able to save 10s. out of her £2.

Mr Metcalf, who had appointed me as auditor to his shipping companies, died and his eldest son, Tom, became managing director of the company. We became firm friends and worked closely together to expand the business when I became a non-executive director of the company. In the preparations for the invasion for Normandy the captains and crews of merchant ships were given cash by the Ministry of War Transport as an encouragement to sign what were known as 'V' articles to man the ships taking part in the invasion. Months later a request landed on my desk from the Ministry, asking me to send in accounts for each ship, showing how the money had been spent and asking for repayment of any balance remaining. The captain and crews had thought the money was a gift, spending it without keeping any records. I had to interview the captains when the ships came into port and after recalling the captains' memories and a lot of heart searching on my part I was able to report that all the money was accounted for by expenses, but no records or receipts were available as they had been destroyed or lost in the invasion.

V2 bombs now took the place of V1 flying bombs and descended on the country like thunderbolts from the wrath of God or the Devil, depending on which way you looked at it. They came down without any warning and with far greater force; they could not be seen, unlike flying bombs which might be avoided; no air raid warnings were sounded and as the bombing was indiscriminate it was no use taking shelter unless you were prepared to spend all your time there. Consequently one had to carry on with one's normal life and hope for the best. Some bombs dropped near our house, one in the next road, destroying a block of houses and damaging a restaurant, where all the soot blew down the chimney and smothered the proprietress.

Our second child was born on 27 February 1945, in

Gravesend Hospital near Betty's parents' house. As I walked up the Avenue her father came down on his way to the pier to report for duty and shouted when he caught sight of me, 'It's a boy!' Everybody was delighted because he was the first grandson, but my mother said, 'I shan't like him as much as Miranda.' Betty looked up her book of names and decided on David, meaning 'Beloved one', which pleased me because it was my father's name; but because it was my father's name we had to include Sidney after Betty's father and finally, to balance it up, we added Sherard, which means 'Of splendid valour' from the Anglo-Saxon. This went well with the surname of Brooks, old English for 'Dweller by the stream'. As Betty's friends, brothers and sisters had children we passed the book round, so if any of them do not like their names they have me to blame for buying the book.

After the launching pads were captured the V2s ceased and the family who owned the house we rented wanted to come back and reoccupy their home. I therefore called on all the local estate agents to see what was on offer. A four bedroomed house on a small private estate next to Gads Hill, Dickens' old house in Higham, attracted me but the asking price was too high. I could not find anywhere I liked from the other agents so I went back to the first people to tell them I would buy the house near Gads Hill, but they said the price had gone up. I said it was too much and continued my search for something else without success. Finally, I went back again and agreed to buy the house. I raised another loan at the bank and we moved into the first house we owned, appropriately called 'Dingley Dell' at Copperfield Crescent, Gads Hill.

The war in Europe ended and we celebrated VE night with Rob and Gwen Passmore and the crowds singing, dancing, and drinking in the town. I was able to engage more staff but also spend more time sharing in the love and happiness of my wife and children. When David was asked as a small child what he was going to do when he grew up he replied, 'I'm going to be an "incountant" so that my Daddy can have more holidays'. As movement in the invasion area of the south-east coast was still restricted I was able to buy a small seaside bungalow at Jaywick, near Clacton, very cheaply, because we lived in the restricted area. Betty's mother and youngest sister, Glenys, opened up the bungalow and made it ready for us to join them there.

The family spent the whole of the first three summers at Jaywick after the war. I caught a train from London to Clacton on Friday nights and walked to Jaywick, leaving early on Monday mornings, about five o'clock, to catch a train back to the office, until I bought a Ford eight horsepower car when I obtained a petrol allowance for the journey to and from home. Betty and the children spent most of their time on the beach, David learned to walk, and I looked forward to the weekends playing with the children and occasionally visiting the theatre in Clacton with Betty. When Jaywick became busy with holidaymakers we decided to make a move. I would have been satisfied to get my money back on the bungalow but Betty put up a 'For Sale' sign on the garden gate and so many people were interested in buying it that she sold it for twice the price we had paid for it.

Betty's mother came down at the end of the summer to help clear up and we drove back home in my little eight horsepower car, loaded down with the family sitting on piles of blankets and a chest of drawers full of clothes tied on the back with rope. We stopped on a hill overlooking Tilbury to admire the view. It happened to be outside an army camp and the guard were called out to close the entrance in case we tried to get in. They were afraid we were squatters because several army camps had been taken over by homeless families. When we were within a hundred yards of Betty's mother's house in Gravesend, the springs on the car finally collapsed under the strain. I was glad not to have to make the journey to Jaywick any more.

The car ferry from Gravesend to Tilbury was very busy on Friday evenings with weekend traffic and sometimes delayed me for hours before I could drive on. One evening a steam roller had been taken across just before I got there but when it reached the other side it could not be taken off because the tide was low and the weight of the steam roller caused the ferry to list to one side below the level of the quay. I passed the time waiting for high tide by buying a pint of shrimps and brown bread and butter with a cup of tea from a shop near the ferry entrance and eating my evening meal. Gravesend shrimps had a reputation as the best you could buy.

We decided to purchase another bungalow at Greatstone, where we had spent our days before the war. It was called Lingalonga — we always seemed to buy places with a funny name — and was situated on the coast road at the back of the sand dunes which ran along the seaside until it reached Dungeness, then turned inland to Lydd. Apart from the coastguard lookout and house there were no other buildings between us and Dungeness at that time. Greatstone was approached by an avenue of trees from New Romney to Littlestone, which consisted of a large hotel called Popes Hotel and a row of Victorian houses. Before the war families waiting to embark on the ferry for France at Folkestone stayed the night at Popes Hotel and their chauffeurs or servants were accommodated in one of the houses.

Whilst I was helping to get the bungalow ready I put my hand through the glass of one of the windows and cut the veins in my wrist. The blood spurted out like a fountain and I was rapidly losing strength before Betty tied a tourniquet on my arm and tightened it up with a poker, whilst the children danced about singing, 'Daddy's cut his wrist, Daddy's cut his wrist'. As we had more room in our bungalow at Greatstone we had taken our maid, Doreen, with us and she rushed over to one of the nearby houses to telephone for the doctor but she was gasping so much that it was some time before she could get a message through to him. Betty continued to loosen and tighten the tourniquet, remembering her Girl Guide first aid training, until the doctor came and sewed the wound up with seven or eight stitches. As he left he said to Betty, 'Well done Mrs Brooks, but there is just one tip, don't put cotton wool on an open wound'.

Doreen was a nice girl and quite a character. During the war she was directed into a factory and learnt to work the overhead crane carrying supplies to the machines in the engineering department. Her husband worked there and from her perch in the roof she saw him paying attention to a girl at one of the lathes. Doreen ran her crane directly overhead and then dropped the iron castings it was carrying, weighing about a ton, at his feet. He nearly fainted with the shock and when he recovered he shouted up to Doreen, 'What did you want to do that for?' And she called back, 'That's just to show you I've got my eye on you'.

The beaches and sand dunes at Greatstone were deserted, except for relics of the war, including a four engined bomber which just failed to make land before being forced down on

116

returning from a raid, a part of the floating breakwater from the Mulberry harbour at Normandy, which had broken adrift, and a large drum that still had pipeline from *Pluto*, intended to carry oil supplies across the Channel, wound round it. The Italian prisoners of war working on adjacent farms spent part of their lunch hour resting on the beach watching the children playing with Betty, who looked marvellous in a white two piece bathing costume against the golden brown of her skin. Betty took the children shopping in New Romney but if she wanted to go into Hythe they caught the New Romney Hythe and Dymchurch light railway train which ran along the field at the bottom of our garden. The engines were exact copies of expresses in service on the main lines, hauling freight as well as passengers and mounting light anti-aircraft guns during the war. They were named after well known characters but the children's favourite was the one called Dr Syn, after the leader of the smugglers in Russell Thorndyke's book about Dymchurch and Romney Marsh. There was no official stop at the bottom of our garden but we just waved to the engine driver and he picked us up. We gave him a packet of cigarettes and asked him to drop us off at our garden on the way back.

I bought a new car, driving down on Friday night and back early on Monday morning as I did at Jaywick, seeing the birds up at dawn, the night owls which had not yet returned to their nests, and breathing the fresh exhilarating air across the marshes. We spent another three years at Greatstone until Betty said she was tired of living away all the summer and would prefer to spend her summer holidays in a hotel and be waited on. I sold the bungalow but I was not such a good salesman as Betty and I managed to make a loss on it.

When my youngest sister, Barbara, was demobbed from the WAAF she asked if I would help her to get her own hairdressing business, for which she was fully qualified, having spent seven years training as an apprentice. I found a business in the Medway Towns and arranged for her to buy it with a loan from the bank, which I guaranteed. She was hard working and successful but after two years the landlord who owned the premises said that he wanted to sell them and would not renew the lease. I therefore bought the shop so that my sister could remain in occupation and continue her business. Two years later her husband telephoned me to say they wanted to buy the shop

Author, Betty and baby David at Greatstone

and he would give me what I had paid for it. I told Betty about the conversation and she said, 'You've done enough for your family, it's time you thought more about me and the children'. I therefore went to an estate agent and asked him to agree a fair price for the property with my sister and her husband, who subsequently bought it. That set my mother against me again, saying I was wicked and if my father had been alive he would have been ashamed of me.

I gradually built up my practice to employ twelve staff with two qualified accountants, each in charge of a team of four clerks, and two secretaries. I limited the practice to this size in order to be able to supervise and control it and maintain the high standards of work which I set. In my forty years in the profession I did not once have any allegation of misconduct or negligence brought against me, although claims for damages were instituted against several of the large firms, especially those with international branches. I did not advertise and I did not cut fees. If I was asked to take on work previously carried out by another accountant I always asked him if he had any objection and whether there was any reason why I should not act for the client, in case he had resigned because of some misconduct by the client; then I would not accept the appointment.

I was able to offer a full range of services to my clients, preparing and auditing accounts, dealing with the tax authorities, forming companies, establishing partnerships, acting as receivers and managers, conducting liquidations, bankruptcies and executorships, but what I liked most was helping clients to build up successful businesses.

I had a wide variety of clients — shipping, engineering, manufacturing, wholesalers, retailers, importers and exporters, lawyers, doctors, dentists, stockbrokers, Lloyds underwriters, farmers, builders, property developers, film and theatrical producers and artists and writers. I was offered full directorships in companies but I would not compromise on my independence. I accepted some non-executive directorships but without a salary; instead I charged a fee at my normal rate for the time I spent as a director. I was not interested in amassing a fortune. I was content to make a good life for myself and my family with something left over for the charities I supported.

I arranged my work so that I had time to spend on holidays with my wife and children and I was happy as I helped my clients to grow and prosper. I kept in close contact with all of them, small or large. I always visited them to explain in detail their accounts and balance sheet and advise them where expenses had exceeded budget or where receipts had fallen short, so that their profits could be increased and balance sheet strengthened. In appropriate cases I established a system of records whereby the financial figures were tied in with the costings and stock control and monthly management accounts could then be produced.

All this work was included in our audit fee. Nowadays accountancy firms have set up management accountancy departments for which they charge an extra fee, but I did all this type of work for clients as part of my service.

My clients sometimes added an extra hundred or so guineas to the fee I had charged them in appreciation of the work I had done. Some businesses operated as family groups or loose type of partnership and in such cases I advised them to form companies which helped to define the interests of the various parties, install financial discipline, open up possibilities for rewarding managers, also saving tax and death duties. My close contact with clients involved me in personal matters outside routine accountancy. The chairman of a firm of precision engineers told me that his son, the managing director, had bought a racing car which he drove in races at Brands Hatch and other meetings. He thought that this was too dangerous a sport for his son with his responsibility to the company to indulge in and asked me to have a word with him.

I had a talk with the son, pointing out the problems which would arise if he were injured or killed and the distress he was causing his father, with the result that he stopped motor racing. But some months later his father telephoned me to say that his son had bought himself a private plane and taken up flying.

The machine tool merchants who had financed Mr Collyear in building his shadow factory at Towcester during the war started putting pressure on him to obtain control of the company. I supported Mr Collyear, who was my client, and matters came to a head when they demanded a board meeting and threatened physical violence if I was there. I attended the meeting, which was held in my office, and produced sufficient shares to prevent Mr Collyear losing control, whereupon one of the other people threatened to throw me out of the window, which was five storeys up from the ground. In reply I pointed out, 'The office is air conditioned and we have double glazing which prevents the window from being opened.'

This quietened them down and I put a proposition to them whereby the shadow factory would be transferred to them and the mortgage cancelled, and in return they surrendered their shares in the company to Mr Collyear and granted the company a long lease on the factory, which they accepted.

During the audit of one of my client's accounts I discovered that one of the directors had purchased goods in the company's name which he retained as his personal possessions. I attended the board meeting at which my report was discussed and it was resolved that the director involved should be dismissed without compensation. As I left the meeting this man was waiting for me outside. He came up to me in a threatening manner and said, 'I know you walk over London Bridge to catch your train home and I'll be waiting for you one evening to throw you over.'

I replied, 'In that case I'll catch a train from Charing Cross.'

Whether he meant what he said I do not know, although he could be a violent man, but he did not carry out his threat. My clients knew that they could rely on me but it meant that the difficult decisions were passed on to me to carry out. In one case I had to ask a managing director to resign because the results of the business he ran were not satisfactory and he stormed out of the meeting, accusing me of being a hit man, but I always tried to be fair and I arranged a golden handshake for him.

I attended the board meeting of a company of which I was a non-executive director, sitting next to the managing director, who was acting as chairman for the meeting. An argument broke out between two of the directors who sat immediately opposite us and this developed into personal abuse, having nothing to do with the business we were supposed to be discussing. The chairman was quite incapable of keeping order and I had to intervene to separate the two who were arguing. The wife of one of them telephoned the chairman and asked him what had happened at the meeting to cause her husband to be so distressed when he arrived home. He told her that he had seen nothing nor heard anything untoward at the meeting and as she could get no information from him she said, 'I'll ask Reuben what happened, he won't be afraid to tell me.' When the wife got in touch with me I explained that both myself and the chairman were sitting opposite the two directors when the row started between them and that her husband had been provoked by personal remarks involving her which made him lose his temper.

My efforts to be fair in my dealings with everybody sometimes involved me in their private affairs. A client employed his two sons to run a business for him and, like many parents, paid them a shall salary with the promise that they should have the business eventually when he died. His widow went to solicitors to make a will and, whether it was in accordance with her instructions or not, the will provided for the business to be sold and the proceeds distributed between all the members of the family. I asked my client to let me see the will and I was surprised when I read it. I pointed out to her that her husband had promised the two sons that they would have the business when she died and that they had relied on his promise when they worked for practically nothing. As a result of my intervention a new will was drawn up, leaving the business to the two sons and the residue of the estate to be divided among the family. None of the beneficiaries knew what I had done.

If the interests of one client clashed with that of another for whom I acted I resigned from one of them. I audited the accounts of two clients who both had similar businesses but in different parts of the country. One of them opened up in the other's territory and I found I was advising one client how to compete with the other. I kept the audit of my oldest client and resigned from the second and larger one, despite being offered a substantial increase in my fee if I would remain, but I had to explain that I had too much work on and neither client knew I had acted for the other.

As with most professions it is very important in accountancy to be able to handle people as well as understand a balance sheet. Many of my clients were self made men who built up their businesses from nothing with my advice and help in raising money for them and arranging their tax affairs, so that most of the profits could be ploughed back. One of my clients started an engineering business with one lathe in a stable and after twenty years was employing 300 or 400 men. He had all the most up to date plant and machinery and owned his own factories, one of which accommodated a row of large machines costing hundreds of thousands of pounds, which he referred to as Park Lane. He was an absolute autocrat in the running of his business, having nothing to do with trade unions or works councils. I was in his office when his secretary came in and said one of the workmen wished to speak to him. He told her to show the man in and when he appeared my client enquired, 'Why can't you see the foreman?' The man replied that he wanted to speak to my client who then said, 'Before you say anything, Bill, just remember I don't have to employ you and you don't have to work for me. Now what do you want?' The man replied, 'I think the foreman can handle it' and disappeared rapidly out of the office. We were walking round the factory when he saw a workman rolling a cigarette. He asked the man, 'How many of those do you smoke a day?' The man replied, 'Ten or a dozen' and was told, 'Well don't roll them in my time. Do it in your own.' My client paid good wages and expected a high standard of work and efficiency in return. If he caught men packing up ready to leave at the end of the day he called out, 'Either work or clock off. Don't hang about.'

I had to cross the Medway to get to his works and when the river was in flood I drove to the bridge at Wateringbury. The water was washing across the road on the bridge and I thought I could get across, but I had forgotten that the bridge was lower in the middle, with the result that my car came to a stop in midstream and the water flowed through the car. I put my feet up on the seat and saw a lorry approach the bridge from the opposite direction and stop when the driver saw the water. I opened the window and shouted 'Help', when to my surprise and relief, the lorry driver got out, put on a pair of thigh length waders and came towards me with a length of rope, which he tied to the front of the car, then went back and fastened the other end to the lorry. He backed off and towed my car to dry land and continued pulling it while I put it in gear to get a flying start. When he stopped to retrieve his rope I offered him £1 which he did not want to accept, but when I said, 'It's worth £5 to me' he took it.

Most contracts boil down to negotiations on finance before they are finalized, whether they involve millions or thousands of pounds and the finance directors or accountants are the people who very often have the final word in bringing deals to a successful conclusion. This was so in my case, whether I was acting as a director or as an adviser. I found it very hard going when business men from the Midlands came down to London and I had to attend the client's meetings with them. We continued working over lunch and on into the afternoon until evening and then they had to be entertained. They wanted to go out on the town and make a night of it. They were hard drinkers, always starting off with a double Scotch, never a single, with dinner at one of the best hotels and a visit to a night club until three or four o'clock in the morning. I had to drink with them and keep sober but by the time we had returned them to their hotel I was exhausted and I used to go to the Turkish Baths in Russell Square followed by a massage, with a bed for the night, to be woken up in the morning with tea and toast in time to get to the office by nine o'clock.

When the Germans came to town they were still full of energy after hours of bargaining and wanted to spend the evening dancing, so we found them some partners at a club and I was able to slip away and telephone Betty to pick me up in the car about two o'clock in the morning. I was the auditor for a British company owned by a German firm and I prepared management accounts each month to send to Germany. When we had a meeting in London the president of the German company said he had not received my monthly accounts but I confirmed to him that they had been posted. He immediately telephoned head office and although he spoke in German I realized he was telling the person at the other end off by the sound of his voice. I asked the managing director of the British company what was happening and he explained that as my reports were marked 'Private and Confidential' the president's secretary had locked them up in the safe and allowed nobody to see them. Kurt Hofer, the director of the British company, was a German and he got the worst of both worlds. When he visited his English customers he was greeted with, 'Here comes that bloody German again' and when he went to head office they said, 'Here's that damn Englishman', because he had married an English girl and dressed and behaved like an Englishman, after having lived many years in England.

I went to Munich to visit the factory which the president had re-established there by going over the border into East Germany with a few of his former employees to smuggle back the plant and machinery which had been taken over by the Communists after the war. He had a fine house with heavy oak furniture and sombre paintings to match which made the rooms rather dark. At the factory the next morning the managers stood outside the doors of their offices, clicked their heels as the president walked by and greeted him, 'Good morning Herr President' (in German of course). I went with Kurt into the beer cellar where Hitler established his Nazi party. The 'oompah oompah' band was playing and the girls were hurrying through the tables with large steins of beer for the customers, who were singing and banging on the tables in time with the band. As we went out Kurt looked at them and said, 'They are a lot of American tourists. I don't think there are many Germans here.' By the doorway there is a plaque commemorating the date when the Nazis surged out of the beer cellar shouting for revolution and the police opened fire, wounding Goering. I drove home with Eric Abrahams, the sales director, in his car and we stopped for the night in Nuremberg where the Nazi rallies had been held. After dinner in the evening we had a walk round the town and called into a wine bar for a drink before returning to our hotel. We were overcharged and when the bill had been adjusted Eric paid it on his Diners Club card. I do not know whether they were annoyed because we queried the bill or whether they saw Eric's name was Abrahams when he signed it, but as we got to the door we were attacked by two burly thugs. The wine bar was on the first floor of the building. I was taken by surprise, knocked down the stairs and kept on rolling until I reached the bottom, in case one of the thugs put the boot in. We were bruised but not badly hurt.

I also audited the accounts of the subsidiary of an American company. The Americans directors flew into Heathrow at ten o'clock at night and I met them with the managing director, sales director, and production manager of the subsidiary company at one of the airport hotels where we had booked rooms for them. Coffee and sandwiches were brought up and we got down to business straight away. I produced the financial report on the trading results to date, the managing director outlined his plans for the future, the sales director presented his budget for the coming year and the production manager explained how his output would link up with the projected sales. Discussion on the plans went on all night until eventually the chairman of the American parent company gave his decision: 'Increase your sales figures by ten per cent for next year.'

I explained that would mean raising the bank overdraft to cover the cost of additional materials, the managing director said he would need more factory space and office staff, the sales director pointed out that his budget had been based on a market survey, coupled with reports from his travellers, and the production manager said that his men would have to work overtime at double rates. To sum up, all this would mean higher bank interest, an increase in head office staff, extra production costs and no certainty that they could all be met by extra sales. The Chairman decided, 'I am sure you will be able to manage it,' then looked at his watch and said, 'We've just got time for breakfast before we catch our plane out.'

The film industry revived after the war and my clients started making pictures again, one which was very successful, about a submarine trapped on the sea bed with John Mills, Nigel Patrick and Richard Attenborough portraying an ordinary seaman suffering from claustrophobia, afraid to use the escape chamber to get out when the submarine was unable to surface. I attended the trade shows on these occasions, watching with some amusement the back slapping, and mutual congratulations which went on. Everybody seemed to live in a world of fantasy. When I had lunch with them at the Connaught Hotel or The Ivy, which was the favourite restaurant for show business people and a 'must' for every aspiring actor or actress to be seen there, a newcomer would halt at the entrance, have a quick look round to see who was there and put on his or her film face and personality before coming into the room.

J. Arthur Rank asked me to investigate the accounts and costings of a film they were financing for an independent producer. As soon as the film company received the finance to make the film, the producer, director and star drew their fees up front, leaving insufficient funds to complete the film within the budget. I reported that there was no prospect of finishing the film without the injection of further substantial funds and advised that the production should be stopped. J. Arthur Rank followed my advice, putting the shots which had been taken on location into their film library for possible future use and the producer told me, 'You are only an accountant, but I was creating art', to which I replied, 'You can't produce art without money and you've spent it all.'

Some films were made with finance advanced by underwriters at Lloyds, who charged the film company substantial premiums for insuring the production against delays due to stars or directors falling ill, third party claims, fire, accidents and so on. They were faced with demands for more money to complete the films and as they became more frequent the underwriters instructed William C. Crocker, a well known lawyer in the City to investigate these claims. Crocker asked me to see him with his accountants, and enquired what my experience had been in dealing with similar cases. I told him that I had discovered no wrong doing but that the money had been spent legitimately without regard to expense because of inefficiency and lack of financial control. I also found it difficult to collect my fees, so I refused to act for any more film companies or actors, although I retained membership of the Green Room Club and the Players Theatre, where I could see a show and get a drink and something to eat if I had to wait for my train at Charing Cross. I did in fact help to finance two plays by William Douglas-Home, who was a very successful playwright, with plays running in the West End, but they both failed although they had well known actors in the cast.

I had a very good friend at Lloyds, David Green, an underwriter and underwriting agent to whom I introduced four clients to become underwriters in the syndicate he managed, in which I also had an interest. He gave a dinner and dance every year, usually at Quaglinos, to which Betty and I were invited. He left the choice of band to his secretary who chose Tommy Kinsman, the 'Debs Delight', and the artist for the cabaret, including Dave Allen, who was starting his career at that time and later became very popular. When I bought Hook House I approached a building society for a mortgage and they appointed a local firm of estate agents to make a valuation. This firm were not used to valuing country house estates and advised the building society against lending me the money I required. I contacted David Green and he arranged a mortgage for me at six per cent without any trouble.

I chose my staff from young men who had obtained the necessary A levels to enter university but preferred to go straight into accountancy. They had an ambition to succeed and as they had the necessary A Levels they were exempt from the preliminary examination of the Institute of Chartered Accountants and could be articled for five years after six months' probation, which I always insisted on. I did not charge a premium for the articles because I wanted to give any young man the chance to succeed if he was prepared to work hard. My clerks were taken through a course of training which I had devised, covering all the different types of work we were doing, and as this was so varied they had no difficulty in passing their examinations and becoming competent accountants by the time they completed their articles.

One of them, Andrew Lis, took first prize at the final examination of the Institute in Taxation and he received several offers of employment from the large firms, finally deciding to join Arthur Anderson & Co. His father was an officer in the Polish Air Force who escaped with his family after the fall of Poland during the war and joined the Polish squadron of the RAF. Andrew married one of my secretaries. Betty and I attended his wedding, and met the members of his family, including relations from America, Canada and other countries where they had fled because of the war. His father and mother were particularly pleased to meet us and to have the opportunity of thanking me for the help I had given Andrew.

Owing to the success I had in training my articled clerks, I was telephoned one day by the secretary of the Institute, who explained that the Aga Khan was establishing scholarships for a small number of boys of his religion from East Africa to come to England and train as accountants. The secretary suggested that in view of our record, would I be prepared to take on one of these students? I agreed to do so and the boy did very well, passing his examinations and qualifying at the end of his articles, but he did not get back to East Africa. He married an English girl and accepted an appointment in Canada.

During my years in practice I had three disappointments with articled clerks. One boy, whose father was a regular RAF officer, came to me with the makings of a good accountant. He was one of my best clerks, very good at the practical work in the office, and I had every confidence that he would pass his intermediate examination, but to my astonishment he failed. I rang the secretary of the institute and asked him why, and he told me that in the opinion of the examiners he had deliberately tried to fail. I called the boy in to see me and asked him, 'Why did you deliberately fail your examination?' He did not attempt to deny it and explained that his father had insisted on his becoming an accountant, but he wished to join the RAF. I was very annoyed and told him, 'We have spent the last two years training you, wasting our time. You have taken the place of a boy who would have liked to have the opportunity of articles with us, and you have let us down.'

The boy was genuinely sorry for what he had done and asked me to try and persuade his father to allow him to join the RAF. I said, 'I am going to cancel your articles in any case but I don't know how successful I will be with your father.' His father came to see me, I explained the boy's feelings, and told him that it was no use forcing his son into a career he did not want to follow and I was going to cancel the articles, so there was no prospect for the boy in the accountancy profession. The articles were cancelled and the boy joined the RAF. Sometime later he came in to see me, looking very smart in his flying officer's uniform with his wings up, told me he was serving in a fighter squadron and thanked me for what I had done for him.

My students came back to let me know how they were getting on and to discuss any problems they were having in their new work. Not all of them continued in accountancy practices. Some went into industry, one becoming a director of Tesco.

The secretary of the Institute again rang me and asked if I would take on the son of a major general in the Pakistan army. I agreed and he came to me on the usual six months trial. He was a young man of twenty and was very mature for his age. He had been having a good time in London and I soon realized that he had no interest in becoming a chartered accountant. All he wanted was an excuse to stay in London, but I told him that he would not be suitable and that I wanted him to leave. He pleaded with me to allow him to stay, otherwise, if he went back to Pakistan, his father would make him join the army. However, I insisted he left. A day or two later I received a telephone call from the Pakistan Embassy to say that the military attache would like to come and see me. A smartly dressed officer arrived and explained that he had been sent by the major general to ascertain the reasons for his son's dismissal, in particular whether he had misbehaved himself or done anything wrong. I told the officer that the young man had done nothing wrong, he had behaved properly, but he just was not suitable to become a chartered accountant and should seek a career elsewhere. The attache seemed very relieved and said he would send a favourable report to the major general.

I had always refused to take on undergraduates, but when my son got his degree and left Durham University he said he wished to join me. I told him that it might be better if he trained with a larger firm and came into my practice later, but he said he preferred to join me immediately. I therefore articled him to me. Whilst he had been at university I gave him the same allowance as the other students who were grant aided and when he joined me I treated him in the same way as my other clerks in the office. He was very good at the practical work and got

129

on well with the clients, but after several years' study at school and university he found it difficult to get down to studying again. I arranged for him to have extra tuition to help him pass his examination and everybody in the office expected him to be successful. After the examination I asked him how he had got on and he said he had not taken it. We were a very close family and I knew my son well. He had arrived at the same stage as I had been after spending three years in my first employment, when I had an easy life and I could have been prepared to coast along unless I made a move. He was the boss's son, had the use of a car and a yacht with lots of friends and a good life. The only difference was, I made my own move but I must make the decision for him. I knew from experience that David could take care of himself and strike out on his own, but it would ruin my plans for the future. I had not taken partners into my practice because my idea was that David should take it over when he qualified and I could then retire and run my farm. I had all this in mind when I said to him, 'When would you like to leave? Would the end of the month be suitable?'

I think David was rather shaken but he kept his composure and replied, 'Yes, that will be all right, Dad.' It was a bitter blow for me but it was the right decision for David as it brought him face to face with the realities of life and he made a successful career in another profession. It made no difference to our love for each other. He dined out on the story of how his father sacked him and we both saw the joke when I explained that I started at the bottom and worked my way up, whereas, he had started at the top and worked his way down.

When David was five years old he attended a 'dame' school in Rochester called the Chestnuts, run by an elderly lady named Miss Snowden-Smith, where the discipline was strict but administered with kindness. This suited David because he was a kind and considerate boy, although he reacted strongly against anybody who tried to push him around. He spent four happy years there as a day boy until he was old enough to go to a preparatory boarding school called the New Beacon in Sevenoaks.

It was usual to have tea with the headmaster and his wife when the new boys started at the school and Betty prepared herself for the ordeal of parting by going to her doctor, who prescribed a tranquilliser for her. There were several little boys with their parents or nannies when we arrived but not many fathers. Some of the children were tearful but the others, including David, seemed to take it in their stride, although they were quiet and subdued. Betty was composed, and chatted to the headmaster and his wife, Mr and Mrs Pratten, and the owner of the school, Captain Norman — whom we had met on a previous visit — until it was time to leave David in the care of Matron and drive home. The boys were not allowed to be taken out for a fortnight to give them time to settle in. My advice to David was to work hard and play hard and take part in all the school activities; in this way he would help himself, have the cooperation of the masters and get on well with the other boys. He followed my advice and enjoyed all his time at school and university. He was in the top three in his form and played in the first teams at rugby and cricket. As David was so good at cricket I had put his name down for Tonbridge, a first class cricketing school, but we had also entered him for Cheltenham because Miranda was due to go to Cheltenham Ladies College and we thought that it would be a good idea for them to be in the same town when they were away from home. They could keep in touch with each other and we could visit both of them at the same time.

We drove to Cheltenham in the winter to make the final arrangements at both schools but Betty was not happy with either of them. There was a laundry basket filled with crusts in the dining room of the boys school which they were allowed to eat if they were hungry and she thought that if they had to eat crusts the feeding arrangements could not be adequate for growing boys. Nor did she like the repressive atmosphere at the girls' school so we decided against both of them. Fog began to come down as we started for home and gradually thickened as we neared London, which we had to cross from West to East to reach home. The fog was the last and the worst of the thick yellow smog which descended on London in a thick choking mass, causing an estimated total of 4,000 deaths. It was possible to proceed at a walking pace through the streets, illuminated by lamps and shop windows, but when these were out of range it was practically impossible. We came to a roundabout in Eltham and could not see where to go, when a man stepped off the pavement and said, 'I live here. I'll guide you round. Follow me'. He went ahead but we came up against a bus with the conductor walking in front and he came back and explained,

'I'm lost. You'd better follow the bus.'

We turned round and did so until the bus gave up and Betty got out to guide us. She walked and I drove the car close behind to keep her in sight, but she fell over in the road and I nearly ran her down. We were close to her mother's house in Gravesend and I decided, 'That's it. We won't try to go any further. We'll have to ask your mother to put us up for the night.' We knocked at the door and she welcomed us in. We had a meal and went straight to bed, utterly exhausted. When I went out to the car the next morning for the drive home, I found all the chromium parts were coloured bright yellow, caused by the sulphur in the smog.

David passed the entrance examination for Tonbridge and to his great delight he became a boarder in Parkside, where the housemaster was John Knott, the Kent county cricketer. Following the comparative comfort of the New Beacon, David's study at Tonbridge was Spartan to put it mildly but Betty, helped by her mother as usual, set to and made it more comfortable by plastering the walls, putting up curtains, providing a reading lamp and mending the chairs. After an initial period, when David was involved in a campaign by the 'Novi', as the new boys were called, against oppression from the older boys, he settled in and in due course batted number one for the school, obtaining his colours for cricket and rugby, becoming a member of the shooting eight and a sergeant in the school Cadet Corps.

During the holidays Betty took him to the cricket school at Clapham, run by Alf Gover, the old Surrey player, who said that David was a natural allrounder and could be good at both batting and bowling. In the annual match against Clifton at Lords he was fielding on the boundary and the opposing batsman hit a high ball which was dropping in midfield when David ran in at top speed from the boundary and flung himself at full length to catch the ball in one hand, inches from the ground. It would have been nice to report that this won the match but it did not. The game was drawn, although as we left the ground an old gentleman wearing an MCC tie stopped us, and said to David, 'That was one of the finest catches I have seen in the many years I have been watching cricket at Lords', which was appreciation indeed.

When he left Tonbridge David went to Durham University at Hatfield College, where he obtained his Bachelor of Arts

David batting against Clifton at Lords

degree. He continued with his cricket and rugby and grew a beard to take part in the college dramatics. The cricket team came down to play some matches in the south and we entertained them at home. They called the district below a line drawn from the Severn to the Wash the Gin and Jaguar belt, but they were not disappointed when we gave them beer instead of gin and did not have a Jaguar in the garage.

We went up to Durham for the ceremony when David received his Bachelor of Arts degree. We stayed at the County Hotel and when the hall porter showed us to our room he took us out on to the balcony and proudly told us, 'This is where Harold Wilson made his speech at the Durham Miners gala.'

David was at the stage undergraduates go through when they profess that money means nothing to them (provided they have enough) and they want no show, so he did not allow us to buy his cap and gown but preferred to hire one. He introduced us to his friends and I was quite surprised at the number who came from the south of England, although most of them came from the north.

When David left my office he took a job with Captain Watts,

who had a yacht chandlers business in Albermarle Street, while he decided on his future. Captain Watts was a master mariner who had an international reputation and taught navigation to the junior officers of the Royal Navy at Greenwich during the war. Yachtsmen from all over the world who came to the UK to cruise or race consulted him and purchased their gear from his shop, which led to some amusing incidents.

The staff changed frequently because they were usually young men who wanted temporary employment until the sailing season started, and one day the telephone rang and a voice said, 'The Prime Minister here.' The clerk who took the call thought another member of the staff was playing a joke on him and said, 'Stop fooling about. what do you want?' The voice replied, 'I am Edward Heath.' It was just after he became prime minister. On another occasion a man came into the shop to order some equipment and the employee asked, 'What name is it, Sir?' to receive the reply, 'Olaf'. The clerk then enquired, 'Where shall we send the goods, Mr Olaf?' to be told, 'Just address them to King Olaf, Norway, that will find me.'

David made himself very useful in the business, with the experience he had gained in my office he re-organized the stock room and helped to run Captain Watts' stand at the Earls Court Boat Show. He gave David a £50 bonus which David spent on a skiing holiday. Captain Watts published *Reeds Nautical Almanac*, annually costing two guineas at that time. David pointed out that half the information in the Almanac was repeated each year and only the new details needed to be printed, which could then be sold for one guinea. Captain Watts soon poured cold water on that idea.

David decided to become a schoolteacher and entered the University of Western Ontaria in Canada, where he gained the degree of Bachelor of Education, commencing his teaching career at Huron High School, Exeter, Ontario. He married his girlfriend, Jane Maynard, whose family lived in the next village, Ticehurst, to our house in Wadhurst and they subsequently had a family of three boys. I lent them my motor caravan for their honeymoon to visit Jane's relations in the West Country before returning to Canada.

David fitted out a twenty-five foot yacht. I sent him equipment from one of my clients and bought him a life raft and auxiliary engine together with the Admiralty charts and sailing

134

Author, son David and wife Jane fitting out yacht in Canada
ready for Atlantic Crossing

135

instructions for crossing the North Altantic, which I obtained
from Captain Watts. He sailed from New York with his wife
Jane, who was experienced, having crewed on my yacht in
England, and her brother Jonathan, who had never sailed before.
They arrived at Falmouth a month later, after sailing 3,000 miles
and David remained in England a year, teaching at Tenterden
school; but Huron High School wanted him back, so he sold
his boat and returned to Canada. He went on from Huron High
School to teach at Upper Canada College, a well known private
school in Toronto founded by Major General Sir John Colborne
in January 1830, with masters brought out from England, a
tradition which has been continued since that date.

Sir John Colborne was born in 1798, joined the army at
sixteen, campaigned with Sir John Moore's Light Brigade in
Spain and distinguished himself in the battles of the Peninsular
War under Wellington. At the Battle of Waterloo he was in
command of the famous fifty-second regiment on the right of
the line. The French infantry always attacked in column and
were opposed by the British in line which was the direct opposite
of the tactics they used in naval battles, where the French
anchored their ship in lines to receive the English warships,
which sailed in two columns to break into the middle of the
French defences; the French ships anchored at each end of the
line could only look on helplessly as the British ships defeated
them one by one. When Napoleon launched his Imperial Guard
in a last desperate attempt to break the British line at Waterloo
Sir John Colborne wheeled the entire fifty-second regiment,
without any orders from Wellington, to catch the French column
in the flank with such devastating effect that the enemy reeled
back absolutely shattered, and Wellington ordered the rest of
his troops to advance, completing the defeat of Napoleon's army.

David became a housemaster at Upper Canada College and
in addition to teaching English coached the cricket team, taking
them on tour to play in Bermuda, Babarados and the public
schools in the south of England. He obtained the further degree
of Master of Education and when two schools in Victoria, British
Columbia, Norfolk House School for Girls and Glenlyon Boys
School amalgamated, David was appointed headmaster of the
combined schools. To mark his success we bought him his
Durham University cap and gown which he refused to have
when he graduated.

136

Miranda started her education at Gads Hill School which was Charles Dickens' old house, close to where we lived. As she went through the gates carrying her satchel she turned to Betty and David, who were watching her go, and called out, 'I shall be thinking of you' before disappearing out of sight. She left the infants' class at Gads Hill to continue her education at Throwley House School which was also near, while we obtained details of a suitable boarding school after we had decided against Cheltenham Ladies College.

Before the war Bexhill had as many as seventy-five boarding schools in the town, mainly for girls, and after the war there were still over fifty to choose from. Betty chose Charters Towers School, because she liked the atmosphere and the headmistress, Miss McGarry; it was also at the seaside and within easy reach of our house. Miranda soon settled in and made friends with the other girls, who came with us on days out to Eastbourne. She won a cup for horseriding, acted in the school play, joined the Girl Guides and enjoyed cricket until one of the girls was hurt and Miss McGarry stopped them playing. The senior students were taught ballroom dancing by Victor Sylvestor's sister and once a year the boys from Charterhouse public school were invited to a dance which the school gave for them at the Sackville Hotel. Beauty specialists came to the school to advise on make up and the girls were also given lessons on deportment and how to dress for different occasions. Miranda was taken ill with appendicitis and Miss McGarry made all the arrangements for her to be taken into hospital at Bexhill for the operation to remove her appendix.

When Miranda and David started school they caught the usual childish ailments, which Betty nursed at home by natural means, plenty of liquids, and cleansing diet of fruit but no drugs. I was kept away from them, as I never had an illness as a child. Miranda slipped on a polished floor when she was young and broke her arm, which was set at the local hospital, but it was not mending properly and she had to go back to the hospital for it to be re-set. When they placed her on the operating table she shouted, 'Not again,' jumped off and ran round the room until she was caught by the doctors. David also broke his arm at the elbow by falling off his bicycle when I was teaching him to ride.

The children were very fortunate because a client, Mr Gare,

Miranda, summer holiday, aged 18, Cattolica, Italy, 1960

had a large sports and toys shop at Dartford, adjoining the Ancient Inn where Wat Tyler lodged on his way to London, and when his new stock came in they were able to try out everything and buy their bicycles.

Before taking over the management of the family business Mr Gare had been first officer on one of the Shell-Mex oil tankers. He volunteered for the army when the war broke out and was posted to the Eighth Army in North Africa. During the campaign he was asked, 'You know something about oil don't you?' When he replied that he did he was told, 'Take a squad and repair those jerricans, we're running short.' On the invasion of Italy somebody must have looked at his record again, because he was given command of a small unit to track down and uncover hidden dumps of Italian oil. He found them in all sorts of unlikely places, including golf courses and blocked up tunnels, but when he opened up one abandoned railway tunnel he was horrified to find the bodies of men, women and children who had been entombed there after they had been murdered.

As the army advanced up the Italian coast he was asked to inspect the oil installations which had been damaged when the ports were shelled or bombed. He made a complete inventory of what was needed to get them back in working order again, sent it to America and within a month shiploads of new equipment arrived to enable him to arrange for the work to be done. Despite his request to be released and return to England and his family business, he was retained in Italy for two years after the war ended, working on the re-establishment of their oil installations. Mr Gare's son was a keen motorist and Mr Gare bought him a Lotus Elan sports car for a birthday present. The son wanted to race it on the Continent so he took it over by air and when he arrived the car was driven off the aeroplane while he waited on the tarmac. The airline employee drove the car off the ramp from the aeroplane at full speed to show off his driving skill, lost control, hit the side of the airport building, wrecking the brand new car, then scrambled out and ran off.

When she left school Miranda attended Miss Judson's Secretarial College in London, recommended by David Green who lectured there on the history and working of Lloyds. Miranda became a secretary to a partner in one of the largest firms of solicitors in the City, who had a house at Wadhurst where she and her friends sometimes used his swimming pool. She and David lived in flats in London, but came home at weekends, usually going back on Sunday night. But on one occasion Betty persuaded them to stay overnight and catch an early train on Monday morning. That Sunday night the train on which they usually travelled was derailed at Sidcup with heavy casualties, including the deaths of David's and Miranda's friends.

English secretaries were considered a status symbol by executives in America and Miranda, with three other girls, decided to go to Canada. They sailed on the *Empress of Canada* from Liverpool and were met by one of the girl's fathers, who had arranged accommodation for them. They soon obtained work in Toronto and rented their own flat. Miranda had a happy time there as secretary to a legal firm, sailing on Lake Ontario, and becoming a member of the baseball team, where her experience at cricket came in useful. One of the girls married, another left the flat and Miranda, with her remaining friend, decided to try Vancouver. To save the fare they delivered a car from Toronto to Vancouver, stopping on the way at Calgary to see the Stampede.

Miranda became personal assistant to the partner in another law firm but she was not so happy in Vancouver as she had been in Toronto and she thought she would like to come back to England and perhaps run her own business. Betty missed her children tremendously, always hoping they would return to live in England, and she was very disappointed when David decided to return to Canada after staying for a year, when he sailed his boat over. I was not surprised, therefore, when Betty said I must immediately find a business for Miranda.

My daughter had a good business training at Miss Judson's, which she had developed in her subsequent employment, showing she had initiative working in Canada, and with my help there was no reason why she should not be successful running her own business. She had clothes sense and had sailed as my crew for years, meeting the yachtsmen at the various regattas we attended. Bearing all this in mind I found and bought a shop selling yachting and beach clothes on the coast at Shoreham in Sussex, called Seagear. It was the middle shop in a row of three with a café on one side and a bookmakers on the other, owned by one landlord who wanted to sell all three properties, which I also arranged to buy. After giving in her notice and settling her affairs in Canada, Miranda flew home and took over the shop. She lived at home and I bought her a Renault car to get to and from the business, which she ran successfully with help from Betty and two assistants.

I went with Betty and Miranda to clothes shows at hotels where manufacturers displayed their new creations, to keep a check on the finances and watch the models showing off the latest in bikinis. We also put on a fashion show in aid of a local hospital, with two ballet students to model the teenage beachwear, the assistants wearing the slightly more mature clothes and David and Stuart — Miranda's husband — the men's clothes. I gave the commentary, written by Miranda, the husband of one of the assistants provided the music, and the whole show was organized by Betty and Miranda. Betty was supposed to wear some of the clothes but unfortunately she tripped over in the shop, broke her elbow and had her arm in a sling.

Stuart, Miranda, Fiona and Melissa

Miranda was introduced to Stuart McKay by a mutual friend and they became engaged. They were married at All Saints Church at Waldron, our parish church, by the rector. Miranda I were rather late getting there because the driver of our car took a wrong turning. A friend of Stuart recorded the ceremony and one of David's friends from Canada, an opera singer who was fulfilling an engagement in Europe, sang beautifully during the signing of the register. The reception was held on the lawn in front of our house. It was spring, the weather was warm and sunny, the rhododendrons and azaleas were in full bloom, and everybody enjoyed themselves, some relations staying long after the bride and bridegroom had left.

Stuart worked for British European Airways until they were taken over by British Airways, when he left and joined British Aerospace. He founded and ran the de Havilland Moth Club, whose members owned and flew these biplanes built before and during the war, used extensively as trainers by the RAF. I trained on one during my short time in the Civil Air Guard and there were still hundreds in existence after the war. Stuart owned three of this type in various stages of construction, one with the fuselage in the garden and the wings and engine in the living room of his house at Maidenhead, until Miranda rebelled and said the house was like an aircraft hanger and they must be removed.

Miranda continued to run the business at Shoreham, driving down from Maidenhead each day, until the first of her two little girls was born, and Betty took over. We left £20 in the till over night as a float for the assistant who opened up in the morning, and one day it was missing. We called the police. There was no sign of a break-in, but Betty found some marks on the trap door leading to the loft, and told the police she was sure that was the way the burglar had entered. She also suggested that one policeman should stay in the stockroom and arrest the burglar when he came down from the loft, but this method was too simple for the police, who installed hidden cameras trained on the cash register and connected to an alarm in the police station. The same night the alarm rang and four policemen raced over the footbridge across the river to get to the shop, knocking over a boy cycling on the footbridge against the law — who was told, 'This is your lucky night son, we can't stop', and arriving at the shop just in time to arrest the burglar before he got away. The man was charged, given bail by the magistrates, and disappeared.

It was not our intention to run the shop permanently and Betty had a closing down sale of all the stock, after David and Miranda had what they wanted for themselves and their families. I let the shop, but unfortunately the man who bought it died and his widow gave up the lease, while the bookmaker went out of business, leaving only the café paying rent. I therefore sold all three shops.

After we sold the bungalow at Greatstone on Betty's insistence on staying in a hotel in future, I booked a holiday for the following summer at a hotel in Babbacombe near Torquay. I had decided that the children should get to know their own country before going abroad and I chose the West Country because we had previously had our holidays in Jaywick on the

East Coast and Greatstone on the South East. We decided on seaside resorts because all the family liked the sea and were fond of swimming. Our usual programme was to spend our time on the beach in the morning, then explore the surrounding villages after lunch, and Dartmoor, where David fell into the water at Watersmeet; but we enjoyed a Devonshire cream tea at an isolated farmhouse. The cream was put on the table in a large vegetable dish to help ourselves, with plenty of scones and jam.

On the way down we took the A31, which is a fast straight road after leaving Alton. The traffic was fairly heavy, the cars in front stopped and I pulled up behind them. As we sat waiting for the traffic to start up again we heard the roar of a powerful motorbike coming up behind us, followed by the shrill squealing of brakes. We could do nothing but brace ourselves for the tremendous bang as the motorcycle hit us, catapulting the driver over the top of our car to land in front of the bonnet, while his passenger was thrown off into the middle of the road alongside. I had a heavy Standard Vanguard and all our cases were packed in the boot. The rear panel was pushed in and the cases crushed but the children, who were sitting in the back seats, were not injured. The passenger on the motor cycle had a leg cut open to the bone but Betty bound it up and attended to the injured riders while I called an ambulance. The hospital informed us that there were no more serious injuries, we learned later that they were on their honeymoon.

The following summer we went to North Wales, staying at Golgarth Abbey, the former home of Lewis Carroll, where he wrote *Alice in Wonderland*. The hotel was situated at the base of the Little Orme near Llandudno. It was a marvellous summer with a heatwave the whole fortnight and when we went to see the Swallow Falls they were practically dried up, which was rather disappointing, but the views from Snowdon and our trip over the Menai bridge to Anglesey made up for it. The next summer we went to Scarborough, staying at the Royal Hotel owned by the family of the actor Charles Laughton. The weather that year was terrible; it rained every day and when we went to the beach for our morning swim we had to slide down a bank through mud to get to the water. However, we made the most of it, exploring the moors and ruined abbeys and taking the children to a show in the evenings.

The weather decided me that it was now time to go abroad

and our next holiday was to Heist on the Belgian coast, a small resort near Knocke le Zoute, the large seaside town favoured by British holidaymakers. It was the year of the Brussels Exhibition, which we visited. It was not as large as the Wembley Exhibition before the war but in addition to the colonial pavilions there were displays of scientific achievements by various countries, including a Russian show which the guards did not seem to wish the visitors to inspect too closely. Betty had her first experience there of having to go through the men's lavatory to reach the ladies, but after some hesitation she was guided by David.

Holiday flights had been started from Gatwick Aerodrome and as it was within easy reach of our home, we decided to go by air to Bordighera on the Italian Riviera. We landed at Nice and continued by coach to our hotel, driving through Monte Carlo. Gatwick was a small aerodrome at that time. It had not then been developed, there were no crowds, parking was easy, it had a nice restaurant, but all the flights were at night with the result that when we arrived at our destination about two or three o'clock in the morning, we had to wait for our bedrooms to be vacated and cleaned. After the flight we were so tired that we slept the first day until the evening and on one occasion when it was time to go down to dinner, Betty could not wake David up, despite repeated knockings on his bedroom door. We could not get into the room because it was locked on the inside and it could not be opened from the outside because the key was still in the lock. By this time Betty was sure something dreadful must have happened and she insisted on the staff bursting open the door. When they got inside they found David still fast asleep in bed, oblivious to all the noise which had been going on outside.

I like Italy because of the music. Everybody wants to sing, whether they are good at it or not. The municipal orchestra played in the gardens fronting our hotel and in the cafés there was always a small band or somebody with a violin or accordion playing and singing operatic or light classical music.

In the evenings crowds gathered to listen but it was always possible to get a table because as the number of customers increased the proprietor extended the room for the newcomers over the pavement on to the road until the street was completely blocked and the police did not seem to mind. We had a day in Menton on the French Riviera to see the flowers and took a trip up the mountains where every villager seemed to make his own wine and insisted on us trying it. We had another night flight to Cattolica on the Adriatic Coast and visited Rimini to see the Roman mosaics and the small republic of San Marino, where we were surprised to find an English tea shop run by two elderly English ladies.

The next year we flew to Lloret de Mar on the Costa Brava in Spain. We stayed in a hotel there instead of Tossa, which was the favourite tourist resort and very overcrowded, although we spent a day there sightseeing. I enjoyed watching the Spanish dancing but the music did not attract me so much as that of Italy. We had to go and see a bullfight in Barcelona to find out what it was like. We occupied the more expensive seats on the shady side of the arena and when the toreadors, picadors, banderilleros and matadors came in with the band playing it was very colourful and exciting as the crowd shouted and cheered. The bull was let in and stood bewildered until the banderilleros rushed over and threw their darts into its neck before running for cover behind the wooden partition at the side of the arena. The picadors on horseback then appeared to dig their spears into the bull to weaken its shoulder muscles, whilst it tried to retaliate by goring the horses, which were protected by heavy padding. The bull was bleeding badly from its wounds and a matador came in to finish it off with his sword, but when he was acknowledging the applause of the crowd the bull rushed at him and tossed him into the air. A group of attendants drove the bull off while four men carried the wounded matador out above their heads. Another matador came in and despatched the bull with one thrust of his sword. The programme stated that there were six bulls to be fought that afternoon, but we had seen enough and left.

For our next holiday to Italy we went by car and on the way through France stopped at the Golden Lion in Rheims. We went out to dinner at an open air restaurant and in order to celebrate the start of our holiday I ordered a bottle of champagne with melon to start, lobsters to follow and strawberries and cream to finish the meal with coffee and liqueurs. We were watched with interest by the other diners as we ate our meal and when the waiter brought my bill to the table everybody turned to look at me. I studied it with great composure, paid the waiter from my wallet, handed him a tip, said goodnight to the watching diners and left. Little did they know that as we continued on our journey we saved the bread rolls and butter for breakfast, bought a bottle of wine and some cheese at the grocers and had a picnic lunch each day.

I had a new car, a Sunbeam Talbot Alpine Sports Saloon in chocolate and cream, which was ideal for motoring in the mountains. When I take a car abroad I always have it specially cleaned and polished to create a good impression and be admired by the local people, who do not seem to have much opportunity to see a British car well presented. The Sunbeam Talbot negotiated the hairpin bends up the St Bernard pass with ease until we stopped at the summit to visit the monastery and St Bernard dogs. The monks lived in squalor, the lavatories were a health hazard, but the dogs lived in luxury, the puppies lying in their comfortable quarters with infra-red heaters keeping them warm. We left the car on the outskirts of Venice and took a ferry to the Lido where we were to stay. We spent the morning on the beach; after lunch we visited the city and islands by the ferry, which ran at regular intervals, having tea in St Marks Square and dinner in a different restaurant each evening.

It would take a guide book to describe all the wonderful buildings, statues and paintings in Venice and it is one of the few places I have visited which has come up to all my expectations and not disappointed me. St Marks Church has a magnificent facade, in the centre of which are four Grecian horses in bronze and inside beautifully sculptured tombs of former doges of Venice with paintings by Tintoretto, Bellini and other artists of the period. The Doge's Palace is a wonderful building with a marvellous golden staircase leading to several halls and the private compartments of the doges, containing more paintings by Tintoretto, Bellini and Tiepolo with fireplaces by Lombardo. We hired a gondola, rowed by two gondoliers, to tour the Grand Canal and see the palaces lining each bank, gliding slowly along under the Realto Bridge and the Bridge of Sighs by which prisoners were taken to the dungeons, before we returned to the landing place. The cost was £10 to us but as we stepped ashore a man waiting there with his wife asked the gondoliers how much they charged and one of them, recognizing an American accent, promptly said it was £25 which the man paid.

We left Venice after a week and drove on to Florence, where I had booked a hotel near the Ponte Vecchio, stopping on the way to climb to the top of the leaning tower of Pisa and visit the cathedral and baptistry. There was so much to see in Florence that it was just as well that it was not at the seaside, and I can only mention a few amongst the many sculptures and paintings on display: Michelangelo's sculpture of the Pieta in the cathedral and tombs in the Medici Chapels, the paintings in the Uffizi Gallery and Pitti Palace by Giotto, Uccello, Botticelli, Correggio, Raphael, Michelangelo, Leonardo da Vinci, Tintoretto, Titian and Caravaggio, the museums of San Marco, containing the work of Fra Angelico and Michelangelo's sculpture, David, in the gallery of the Academy. At the end of each day I was mentally and physically exhausted by so much sight seeing but Betty seemed to thrive on it.

After a week we left Florence to drive north, taking a different route home through Switzerland, Luxembourg and Belgium. We shared the driving. I told Miranda to follow a bus in one town to get through the traffic, which she did so well that we ended up in the bus station. David had the difficult part driving through Brussels, following another motorist who was showing us the way at top speed. Belgian motorists did not have to pass a driving test and if they were involved in an accident in France the French police always assumed they were at fault and charged them.

We flew to Ibiza by the first flight to land there. Previously it was necessary to fly to Barcelona and finish the journey to the island by boat. The aerodrome consisted of just one building for the customs and immigration authorities. We stayed in a modern hotel at the seaside village of San Antonia a few miles from the town of Ibiza with its harbour, and white houses in the cobbled streets, rising to the old quarter surrounded by the city walls. It is picturesque but with no outstanding buildings apart from the cathedral and look-out on top of the hill. We spent our time on the beach swimming, sunbathing, and water-skiing, sometimes taking a boat trip round the coast to other villages, and in the evening there were Spanish dancers at the local night club. One day was designated Tourist Day, when all drinks were free in the hotel. Free drinks are always a danger to British people, who do not seem to know when they have had enough, and I always steer clear of these occasions abroad.

When we went to Cyprus David was unable to come with us. It was foggy over the island; we were unable to land and had to fly on to Tel Aviv in Israel. When we came down the steps from the aeroplane we were surrounded by armed guards because Golda Meir, the prime minister was due there. We spent the night in the airport buildings and flew on to Cyprus the next day. When we landed we were told to line up and be inoculated against typhoid, but I refused and showed them our international certificates confirming that we had had the necessary injections against typhoid before leaving England. They would not accept them and I would not give in to the authorities, although they called the police to threaten me with all sorts of penalties. By this time all the other passengers had gone and I said we would take the next plane home unless they released us. The police agreed to let us go provided that I reported to the police station every day, but I never did and I heard nothing further from them.

This was only one of several disputes I have had in foreign countries and in England when people have tried to push me around. I was staying with Betty at a hotel in Gerlos, skiing in Austria. We had booked full board at the hotel but when we were skiing we had a snack in the mountains and did not go down for lunch. At dinner I was served with the lunch menu and told that I must eat that because I had not come in to lunch. I told the waitress to take the food away but she came back with it again and explained that the proprietor said I must eat it. At that I really got annoyed. I stood up, banged on the table and said, 'I have not been told what to eat since I was a boy. Go and tell the proprietor to come here.' He sent his wife over instead with a bottle of wine to calm me down and although I did not speak German and she did not speak English we shared a glass of wine and I got my dinner.

When Betty and I flew to the Bahamas the plane landed at Kennedy Airport in New York to refuel. We had to leave the plane while this was being done and the Americans made us go through customs and immigration. We were detained and told that we must be vaccinated against smallpox. I had not been warned by the travel agent that we would stop in New York and I was not prepared for it, otherwise I would have been vaccinated before we left England. I explained to the official that we had both been vaccinated many times before, that there

148

had been only one isolated case of smallpox in England, and that we were not prepared to be vaccinated again and spoil our holiday. He insisted that as we had come to America we had to comply with their laws, but I told him I did not want to come to America and I did not intend to stay there. He went out and brought in three men in white coats who enquired, 'Are you the ones to be vaccinated?' I replied, 'No we are not', which started an argument between the men in the white coats and the official. By this time more than an hour had passed and one of the aeroplane crew came in and said, 'We are ready to go now. You must get aboard.' The official said to us, 'Off you go' and we went. I expect he was glad to see the back of us.

On the return flight a fortnight later we again stopped at Kennedy Airport and went through customs and immigration. I spotted the same official, so I went up to him and said, 'Now we've had our holiday we don't mind being vaccinated'. He replied , 'There's no smallpox in the Bahamas. We don't want to vaccinate you'.

When we arrived back at Heathrow a woman attendant pointed to a small room and said, 'Please wait in there.' I looked in and saw several coloured people wearing labels, sitting on benches round the room. I asked, 'What's all this about?' and she replied, 'There's smallpox in the Bahamas and you must be vaccinated', I replied, 'There's no smallpox in the Bahamas and I am not waiting in there.'

We went to the immigration desk, and the woman chased after us and said, 'Don't let these people through.' I told the man at the desk, 'We are British subjects. We have valid passports and you can't stop us'. He looked at the passports and said, 'You are quite right. I don't want to stop you.'

As we collected our luggage the woman came up to us again and said, 'If you feel ill you must see a doctor', I told her, 'If we feel ill we always call in a doctor.' The next morning the local medical officer of health came to our house and explained that he had been informed that we might be suffering from smallpox but Betty was able to assure him that we were quite healthy.

We stayed at a hotel on Cyprus in Famagusta near the port and Othello's Tower which was occupied by Turks. It was before the Turkish Army invaded the island, but there was tension between the Greek and Turkish populations and United Nations

Swedish soldiers were stationed in our hotel. No Greek taxi driver was prepared to go into the Turkish quarter and I therefore hired a car to explore the island. The capital, Nicosia, was divided between the two communities but we were welcomed in both parts. The north of the island, which was controlled by the Turks, was badly run down with dilapidated buildings and roads needing repair, but it was the most picturesque. There was a fine harbour and castle at Kyrenia with a museum containing a 3000 BC cargo boat. We visited St Hilarion Castle, perched high up on a rock, looking like an illustration from a fairy tale book, which was filmed by Walt Disney and where Richard the Lionheart spent his honeymoon. It was very hot in the sun and it was a relief to walk through the cloisters of Bellapais Abbey and the cool leafy gardens. We drove up to the Troodos mountains and down to the sea at Salamis where French archaeologists had uncovered the ruins of the ancient city and the goddess Aphrodite was supposed to have risen from the waves.

We always bought a souvenir to remind us of our holidays, not something made up for tourists but a good painting, sculpture or pottery. Betty is a talented painter, having had one man exhibitions of her work and pictures accepted by the Royal Academy, although they were not hung due to lack of space. We therefore visited the studio of a local man whose works were in collections in Europe and America, and after great deliberation Betty chose a dramatic painting of a woman standing in the ruins of her house, which had been destroyed by an air raid.

When we went to Morocco we flew to Gibraltar and after exploring the Rock and visiting the apes we took a boat across the Straits of Tangier, where we stayed in a hotel run by a Dutch family. At that time the town was a free port with a lively atmosphere, good shops, bars and hotels, but it still had a native quarter in the casbah, separate from the other part of the town, behind walls, with an entrance through gates which could be closed by large wooden doors. I visited the casbah every day to have my morning coffee, exploring the narrow streets with their small shops displaying leather work, brass ornaments, metal pots and pans, clothes, shoes, fruit, vegetables and sweetmeats, and watched the snake charmers, jugglers and water sellers. At first I was pestered by small boys asking for money, but as I became well known the traders drove them away. When we swam in the sea we changed on the beach and Betty looked after our clothes until she went in. The natives saw this and came up to ask Betty to mind their garments because she was English and they knew the clothes would be safe with her, so she ended up sitting on the beach surrounded by a circle of little heaps of clothing. We met Grace and Leonard Mostyn, who were staying at the Riff Hotel, became friends and still keep in touch with them. They were very good company and we spent a lot of time together. We were sitting at a table on the beach having a coffee, when a youth of about sixteen years of age snatched Grace's bag from the table and ran off with it along the beach. Grace immediately gave chase and as she was catching him up he threw the bag away but Grace continued after him, caught him, flung him on the ground and gave him some good hard slaps to teach him a lesson. Leonard could stay up half the night dancing and never seemed to get tired. We were at a night club watching two belly dancers, very pretty blonde girls with good figures, when Betty went to the ladies room after they had finished their act. As she opened the door a voice shouted in a strong northern accent, 'Close that bloody door'. It was the two girls who were changing their clothes and they both came from Lancashire.

The King of Morocco was to pray at the mosque in the casbah before going on a journey and I went into a small run down hotel in the square to ask the proprietor if I could rent a room from which to see the procession. We went upstairs to a bedroom with an old brass bedstead, a cracked wash basin and some rickety chairs, which overlooked the entrance to the mosque and I agreed the price to be paid for renting it for three hours. Betty said the room would do and warned the children, 'Don't sit on that bed. You don't know who's slept in it.' The proprietor said, 'You pay me now'. I counted out the necessary dinars and gave them to him but he looked at the money and exclaimed, 'I want twice'. I reminded him that I had paid the amount we agreed, but he said, 'Agreed for you but not for me.' I took the money back, turned to the family, said, 'We're going', and we all trooped out and started going downstairs.

By that time we could hear the clash of cymbals and the cries of the crowd as the procession came nearer but as we reached the door a voice called out from the top of the stairs, 'Mister,

Mister, you come back'. We went up the stairs again, I paid the agreed price and we were waiting for the procession when there was a knock on the door. The proprietor appeared again, in his slippers with the toes turned up, dressed in his white cotton gown, and a young woman wrapped in the traditional black clothes they all wore. He asked, 'You let my brother's wife watch?' I invited her to come in and told the man, 'We don't want anybody else'. Then he handed me a key with a flourish and said, 'You lock the door'. When the young woman took off her outer clothes she revealed that she had a baby with her which she laid on the bed and Betty was soon asking her about the baby, partly in English aided by sign language.

The King rode into the square on a white Arabian horse with a group of priests preceding him and a troop of soldiers behind. The horse was richly decorated and the colourful robes of the priests with the full dress uniforms of the soldiers together made a perfect setting for the King as he dismounted and followed the priests into the mosque. The wooden gates were closed while the King was in the casbah and were not re-opened until he left.

We took a trip into the mountains to see the Riff villages where we were warned not to take photographs, and we also visited the souk at Tetuan in the Spanish part of Morocco, which retained more of its native atmosphere than Tangier. We returned by boat to Gibraltar and flew back to England.

I had clients in Jersey and visited the Channel Islands frequently, sometimes with Betty, and on one occasion we took the children on holiday to the Bouley Bay Hotel. We were due to fly from Gatwick, but we were informed that the Channel Islands were fogbound and that an aeroplane from Italy had crashed in Jersey trying to land the previous day, killing everybody on board. Most of the intending passengers left to catch a boat at Weymouth, but we decided to stay and wait for the fog to lift. It was not until the evening that an announcement was made, informing us that although it was still foggy in Jersey the pilot was going to make the trip because he lived there and wanted to get home, but if the fog was still too thick to land he would divert to Dinard in France. We boarded the aeroplane and as we approached the Channel Islands the fog thickened, swirling past the windows and blocking out the light. The pilot gradually came down until he was within 500 feet of the airport, and was on the point of deciding to fly on to Dinard when a hole appeared in the fog below revealing the landing ground, and he dived straight in to bring the aeroplane down safely. We were very thankful but I thought afterwards how silly I had been to risk the lives of all the family just to save a day getting there. The airport facilities were closed, the mechanic who should have met us at the airport with a car had gone home, because he thought there was no possibility of any aircraft arriving and I had to ring the garage to order another car. The fog cleared the next day, the sun shone, it was fine and warm, we enjoyed our holiday and had an uneventful flight home.

We booked a Mediterranean cruise on the *Reina del Mar*, a Union Castle line ship of about 20,000 tons, but David could not come with us. It was quite calm crossing the Bay of Biscay and we were able to join in all the deck games. I defeated the expert in the shuffleboard competition, and everybody was pleased to see the champion dethroned. Our first port of call was Malta, where we anchored in Valetta harbour with its massive fortifications built by the Knights of St John, and small picturesque streets.

We drove to the centre of the island to visit Medina, a walled city with fine old aristocratic mansions but an eerie deserted atmosphere. Our next stop was scheduled for Alexandria and Cairo with a trip to see the Pyramids but this had to be cancelled because war had broken out between Israel and Egypt and the ship was diverted to Istanbul. We sailed through the Dardenelles into the Bosphorus and when I was telling the boatman of our yacht club, who was an ex-navy man about it, he asked whether we had noticed the ruins of a fort on the shore of the Dardenelles. When I told him I had he said, 'I was in the raiding party when we destroyed it in 1915'.

There were so many interesting sights to see that we did not mind missing Cairo. The Blue Mosque was a magnificent building although it seemed very bare inside compared with an English cathedral, because there were no pews or chairs, the worshippers all kneeling on prayer rugs. We had to take off our shoes to put on slippers and go inside and all the attendants rushed to help Miranda change. The Topkapi Museum, situated in what used to be the sultan's harem where his wives lived, contained the most amazing collection of precious stones and jewelled ornaments, which had been amassed by previous sultans over the years, including a throne encrusted with diamonds, rubies and sapphires. The souk in Istanbul was very large and contained a higher proportion of shops selling expensive items of carpets, jewellery, shoes and clothes than any of the other markets we had seen. We purchased a prayer rug to take home for David and whilst we were drinking coffee and discussing prices with the proprietor, his son was trying to persuade Miranda to stay in Istanbul at his flat with a car for her personal use. After leaving Turkey we sailed for Greece, arriving at Piraeus, the port of Athens.

We walked up the Acropolis to obtain a bird's eye view of the city and see the Parthenon, the Doric temple regarded as the finest example of classical Greek architecture. We saw the temple of Apollo, visited Corinth and Mycenae to see Agamemnon's tomb and the Lion Gate, but Delphi was too far to go.

Our final port of call was Naples. The bay used to be praised for its beauty and charm, giving rise to the saying 'See Naples and die'. But present day sailors now say 'Smell Naples and die' because of the industry and pollution there. However, the Sorrento peninsular which juts out south of Naples has fortunately preserved its scenic beauty, with spectacular rugged cliffs where the coastal road winds round hairpin bends past steep terraces of vines and citrus groves above the villages of multi-coloured houses built into the hillside. The resorts of Sorrento and Positano have very small beaches; the one at Sorrento is only accessible by lift. Amalfi has a beautiful setting but it was crowded with holidaymakers and we preferred to spend more time visiting the ruins of Pompeii, a Roman city which suffered one of the worst volcanic eruptions in history. A plume of steam still rises from the crater of Mount Vesuvius, a reminder that it may still erupt any day. The remains of Roman villas, bath houses, soldiers' barracks, public buildings and theatres are marvellously preserved with temples, beautiful mosaics and frescoes. The remains include kitchen pots, marble shop counters and other items, giving an insight into everyday life of ancient times. One villa which had been the home of two young men was kept locked, guarded by a policeman who only allowed men inside to see the wall drawings and decorations.

We visited Rome, passing Monte Cassino on the way, where a statue of Christ has been erected on the hill, and inspected more Roman remains, including the Coliseum, before spending time sightseeing in the modern part of the city. We had no further stops on the voyage home, enjoying a fancy dress party and dances in the evening as well as the usual deck pastimes during the day, until we reached England.

While the children were young we took them to the pantomime at the Palladium and Bertram Mills Circus at Olympia during the Christmas holidays. We always had lunch at the Trocadero, an excellent family restaurant where the band played; the waiters remembered their customers and the children were given presents. Well known theatrical people frequented it; Robert Morley was there with his family one day and ate his lunch with one hand while signing autographs with the other. I had a client who was a director of West Ham Football Club and when he entered the restaurant the band always greeted him with West Ham's supporters' song, *I'm forever blowing bubbles*.

As they grew older Miranda and David came with us to the theatre, including that of Stratford-upon-Avon to see the historical plays of Shakespeare which commemorated the 400th anniversary of his birth. A play we particularly enjoyed was *Salad Days* by Sandy Wilson, a musical put on by the Footlights at Cambridge and transferred to London. It was unpretentious but had several catchy tunes, including our favourite, *We said we'd never look back*, which we adopted as our motto, enjoying new places and experiences instead of dwelling on the past and what might have been.

This decision helped me to sever my connections in the City when I retired. The public perception of big business lunches and entertainment is all wrong. They are not parties for friends, they are meetings between people with mutual interests who are able to do business with each other just the same as relationships between countries, where Germany has now taken the place of Great Britain with America. I was lunching in the City with a client when a man came in and approached people at the bar with whom he had transacted business in the past. He had always been welcomed and entertained before but he had retired, and after nodding to him his former associates took no further notice of him. He was so distressed that my client said to me, 'We've had no business with him but we can't let him stand there on his own, ask him to join us for lunch'. I invited him over. He lunched with us before going back home and we did not see him in the City again. After retiring I went back only twice, on both occasions to attend the funerals of former clients.

We were very happy living at Gads Hill. It was a small private estate of about twenty houses, there were other children for Miranda and David to play with and we got on well with our neighbours. Betty left the brake off when she parked the car outside our house, it ran backwards and knocked down the garden wall of one of the other houses, but the owners were more concerned to comfort Betty than to trouble about the hole in their wall and our neighbour arranged a special dinner party to take my mind off the damage to my car. I was secretary of the Road Fund to maintain the private road on the estate, and as a good accountant I accumulated a reserve against future expenditure. At the annual meeting all the members voted to spend the money on a night out in London and, although I was against it, I made arrangements for dinner at a West End hotel, followed by a visit to the theatre.

Betty and I saw several of the American musical shows, *My Fair Lady*, *South Pacific*, *Carousel* and *Kiss Me Kate* at the Coliseum, when Mr Churchill came in to see the show and all the audience stood up and cheered him.

Betty at work

When the children went away to boarding school, Betty was able to spend more time at her painting, attending the Medway College of Art, followed by Sir John Cass College in London and Tunbridge Wells Art School, She had one man shows and group exhibitions at Tunbridge Wells, the East Kent Art Society, Canterbury, the Royal Society of Oil Painters, London, Sussex Artists at Brighton and Wealden Artists in Sussex. She has work in private collections in England, Canada and Europe and in the Kent Education Centre.

As my practice increased our social life had to expand to keep pace with it. We visited the Chelsea Flower Show and were entertained in a private box at Royal Ascot each year. Immediately after the war the boxes did not have facilities for preparing food and we had lunch and tea at a private table in the Garden Restaurant overlooking the band and placed our bets at the totalizators on the way to the paddock or with one of the bookmakers on the course. The wooden stand in which the private boxes were situated was replaced by a modern concrete building, the new boxes had their own arrangements for providing meals and the tote had offices in the stand, making it unnecessary to go outside to place bets. We did not like this so much, although it was more convenient, because we preferred to walk about and see the well known people who attended the races. We always went down to the paddock to see the horses parade when the Queen had one running, and a line was made for her and the royal party to pass by. The Queen and Princess Margaret were walking together, smiling and saying good afternoon, while the men raised their hats and the ladies, including Betty, curtsied; but when they had gone Betty found her purse had been opened and her money stolen by one of the pickpockets who frequented the racecourse. We were always driven to Ascot in a Bentley which was parked in the front car park facing the entrance to the racecourse, which was full of Rolls Royce and Bentley cars. If it was a warm summer evening we sometimes had a launch to take us on the river to Skindles for dinner, otherwise we went back to London for a meal. When my client asked his wife what wine we should have she always replied, 'Well, we have been drinking champagne all day and we'd better not change now.'

I was given two tickets for the Royal Academy private view by clients who had paintings exhibited there and when I could not go Betty invited a young man whom we knew, just down from Cambridge, to accompany her there. He wore morning dress for this occasion and insisted on her wearing a hat and gloves because he said they were there to be seen. He always laughed when she told him that I could not go because I was at a meeting with one of his uncles. He was a perfect escort, meeting her with flowers for a buttonhole and taking her to one of the best restaurants for lunch.

I was also given two tickets for the Centre Court at Wimbledon each year, when the tennis was all amateur and the great Australian players were at their peak. I bought two tickets for Number One Court for Miranda and David and we changed over tickets when we met for our tea of strawberries and cream. We had a private launch to see the Boat Race and the Queen's return on the royal yacht *Britannia* when she came back from her world cruise. We attended the Spithead Review of the Royal Navy. The commander giving the commentary on it for the BBC had too much to drink and as the ships were illuminated could only repeat, 'The fleet's lit up. The fleet's lit up'. We were also at Lords during the year Edrich and Compton both reached 3,000 runs for Middlesex.

After the war it was impossible to get a berth for building a new ship in England and the shipping company of which I was a director had one built in Germany at Bremen. It was the custom to limit the guests at the launch to the directors and their wives and to invite business associates to the trials later on. We flew to Germany on a Vickers Viscount four engined aircraft which was the latest type in service at that time. We stayed at a hotel in Bremen and also visited Hamburg, where we saw the devastation caused by the bombing raids during the war. The day after the launch we were entertained by the shipbuilders at lunch in the Ratskeller in Bremen. I was on one table with the daughter of our host and Betty was on another table with the son-in-law, who was paying her a lot of attention. We returned to the shipbuilder's house on the outskirts of the town for dinner and spent the evening there, during which time the son-in-law invited Betty to see the gardens attached to the house and tell her how much he admired her. Our host's wife was a formidable lady, large, blonde, with a commanding presence. She hated the Americans. When they arrived during the war the colonel in charge of the troops said that he was taking over the house as his headquarters. She told him she was not getting out, that he had no authority to give her orders and defied him to do his worst. He said to her, 'Lady, if you don't get out in two hours I will billet my coloured soldiers in the house and you will be lucky if you escape being raped.' She left the house and never forgave the Americans, despite the help they gave to Germany after the war.

We were with the German family until past midnight but they were so pleased to entertain us they would not take a hint that we were exhausted and wanted to get back to our hotel, until we all sang 'Show me the way to go home, I'm tired and I want to go to bed.' They saw the joke and laughed and ordered the cars to drive us to our hotel. When the American aeroplane arrived from Frankfurt for London, the cabin staff said there was not enough room for us but the captain came through to find out the reason for the hold up and said to Betty, 'You can sit on my knee'. Seats were immediately found for all of us.

Other ships were built at Burnt Island in Scotland. We stayed at the North British Hotel in Edinburgh, where Betty had the opportunity to visit the National Art Exhibition. It is the tradition for ships to be launched by a lady and if one of my client's ships had been chartered when it entered service, it was usual to invite the wife of one of the directors of the charterers to officiate at the launching, otherwise a member of the family did so. It was also traditional for the lady launching the ship to receive a present, usually jewellery, from the shipbuilders, which was charged to the shipowners. The director whose wife was invited to launch the ship asked his board's permission for his wife to accept the present, and this was usually granted, except in the case of a multi-national oil company, where it was refused.

Several ships were built in Holland, where they were launched sideways into one of the canals. The apprentices at the shipyard stayed aboard and as the ship was not ballasted it heeled over at a frightening angle when it entered the water. After one of the boys was killed this custom was stopped, but the water displaced by the ship overflowed the canal flooding the workers' cottages on the opposite bank and they continued to line up outside the offices to receive their compensation money.

We lived in a hotel in Amsterdam while we were in Holland and toured the canals in the city. Betty visited the art exhibitions with my client, including the marvellous paintings in the Rijkmuseum by Rembrandt, Vermeer, Steen, and other members of the Dutch school.

Betty was liked by all my clients, which was a great help to me, and she was able to deal with any awkward questions by explaining that I did not discuss client's business affairs with her.

After the ship was fitted out it had to undergo trials before being accept by the owners. In addition to the owner's marine and engine superintendents, captain and crew, technicians testing the radio, radar and navigation instruments, there were the underwriters, charterers, shipbrokers and the representatives of other companies interested in employing the ship. It was usual after the trials, when the ship returned to port, for the shipbuilder to entertain all the party to a dinner, at which he expressed his thanks for receiving the order to build the ship and his confidence that it would give excellent service for many years. In reply the owner thanked the shipbuilders for the fine work that had been put into the ship, said he was sure that it would be a very useful addition to his fleet, and was pleased to accept it.

The Dutch were fair in their business dealings, but they drove a hard bargain and always insisted on contracts being carried out to the letter. There is a saying that 'In business the fault of the Dutch is in giving too little and asking too much' and I had an example of this when one of the ships built in Holland could not complete its trials because of bad weather. When we all returned to the hotel I found that no preparations had been made for the usual dinner and the manager explained it had been cancelled. I found the shipbuilder and asked him, 'Why have you cancelled the dinner?' He replied, 'The trials have not taken place. The ship has not been accepted so there is no dinner'. I told him, 'When the weather clears tomorrow we can have the trials and there is no reason why the dinner should not take place. You can't have much confidence in your ship if you are not prepared to have the dinner beforehand.' But I could not shift him. I saw the hotel manager, organized a dinner and had it put on the owner's bill. The ship carried out its trials the next morning, our party were booked on a flight back to London in the afternoon and had to leave.

My clients purchased a fishing vessel and I went up to Lowestoft for the trials. The night before we met in a hotel with the captain and crew and the usual officials and after dinner the talk was of fishing with plenty of advice to the skipper. The following morning it was blowing a gale but the captain was used to North Sea gales and he took the trawler out. When we cleared the harbour it was not long before the brave fellows who had lectured the skipper on how to fish began to go down with sea sickness. We carried on out to sea and shot the trawl where the captain thought there was a chance to catch a few fish and after four or five hours he hove to and started to haul in the nets. There was a big swell running, the trawler rolled from side to side and the steward took the opportunity to bring round ham sandwiches and beer, which finished off most of the remaining passengers, who went below to lie down. I was on deck to see the catch, which was very small. The engineer came up from below and selected the crabs he wanted in accordance with the custom on trawlers and we returned to port. When we arrived and tied up alongside, everybody was presented with a bag of prime fish, which miraculously appeared from below, to take home.

My good friend, Mr Magowan, who had provided me with an office at the beginning of the war, died, leaving two small grandsons, and I was appointed in his will to manage his companies until the boys became of age and were capable of running the businesses. There were three enterprises established in Wolverhampton, one heavy engineering works, another making small tools and the third supplying office machinery. I had a manager for each business but, although I could retain control through monthly management accounts, it involved frequent visits to the works at Wolverhampton. However, I was able to keep them running successfully until I handed them over to the grandsons.

I was approached by a client who had invested his money in a small engineering company because the managing director wanted more capital to develop the business, but the client preferred to withdraw his money and close it down. I asked the managing director to prepare a plan setting out his objectives, the cost involved and his profit projections. After investigating the figures I reported that the managing director should be supported in his plans and the client, far from withdrawing his money, should increase his investment to allow the company to expand. This he refused to do and I undertook to find the additional capital and pay him out. Another client agreed to

161

put in the necessary funds, the original investor withdrew his money and I re-organized the company, allotting some shares to the managing director, giving him an additional incentive to make a success of the business. However, the new investor made it a condition that I should become chairman of the company to look after his investment and I agreed to become non-executive chairman. This involved me in more travelling abroad with the managing director, who was an engineer and keen motorist.

The company produced machines for the cable industry, involving the appointment of agents in Europe, with whom I had to be concerned. Having made one call in the south of France we decided to cross the Pyrenees into Spain through Andorra, but the weather changed and we were fortunate to get up the mountains by driving behind a snowplough. When we arrived at the town the snowplough stopped, as that was as far as it went, and we were faced with the difficult descent into Spain. It was dangerous at the start but the road ran south and the snow gradually cleared, until we finished the journey in warm sunlight.

When we attended the International Machine Tool Exhibition in Milan the agent booked us into a hotel on Lake Como, which was a welcome relief after the crowds at the exhibition, although the traffic jams were terrible getting in and out of Milan. Before making the journey home we had a day to spare. The managing director decided to play a round of golf with the agent in the morning, and we had a trip on the lake in the afternoon. It was necessary to travel in a lift to the top of the mountain overlooking the lake to get to the golf club, which was marvellously situated, with splendid views of the surrounding countryside from that height. There were no other players on the course and I borrowed some clubs to go round with them. We had a very good lunch in the clubhouse and I took the opportunity of inspecting the library, which consisted of a wide range of English books on golfing history and famous personalities. The portraits round the walls were all of Englishmen and Scotsmen who had been presidents of the club and I found out that the club had in fact been founded by Scotsmen.

On our way back from Italy we stopped for the night at a hotel in the Black Forest in Germany. While we were having dinner in the restaurant there was a party which looked like an army reunion going on at the next table and when he heard us speaking English the man at the head of the table, presumably an ex-officer, came over to us and asked whether we would join them. I said we thought his men might be embarrassed by our presence. He then brought a bottle of wine to our table and sat down to drink the wine with us. He told us he had been a major in the panzer regiment but although he was in the invasion of France he had not come up against the British, having subsequently been transferred to the Russian front. He said the Germans liked the English and it was a tragedy that we had not joined with them to destroy Communism, which was the real enemy. I had heard this many times before and we did not argue with him, being content to listen to the stories of the campaigns in which he had been engaged. When we left I thanked him for the wine and remarked, 'You seem the sort of man who could look after himself', and he laughed and replied, 'Yes. I was a good soldier'.

There was so much talk in the City about the possibility of a capital gains tax that I contacted all my clients to arrange for them to realize their capital profits before the act bringing in the capital gains tax was passed in 1965. I sold the factory belonging to the company of which I was chairman to an insurance company and distributed the proceeds to the shareholders as a capital bonus, at the same time leasing back the factory. All the other cases were not so easy but I was able to put through waterproof transactions for most clients. The client who had invested in the company where I was chairman became involved with the editor of a woman's magazine; his personal affairs were in such a tangle that he could see no way out and he committed suicide. His widow wanted to realize his investment in the company and I therefore sold it to a public company after arranging suitable safeguards for the managing director.

During the war I did not have time to keep up my sports activities and I did not renew my subscriptions to the clubs after the war but looked instead for something which the family could also enjoy. I therefore joined the Bolebrooke Beagles and the Ski Club of Great Britain to keep fit in the winter. I kept up with the huntsman in charge of the hounds but Betty stayed with the master, who gave instructions to the huntsman.

A hare has its own territory and when it is hunted usually

runs in a circle to return to the place from which it started. I probably covered ten to fifteen miles in a day with the hounds, but Betty walked round with the master when he took the hounds to a different draw, after they had lost or killed the first hare. We did not kill many hares, usually only one or two in a day, sometimes none, because of the reduction in the hare population caused by the destruction of their natural habitat by intensive cultivation of the land and by shooting. Betty picked mushrooms on the marshes and we both enjoyed the fresh air and exercise but the children were not very keen to join in after a trial run. They were, however, anxious to come skiing but I decided that Betty and I should try it first. I had always wanted to explore the mountains because the space and feeling of freedom away from the crowds was very similar to waking up at dawn on board a yacht in a quiet anchorage, to see the sun rise with only the cries of the sea birds to break the stillness.

I booked a holiday with Cook's Initiation Party to Kandesteg. We bought our clothes from Lilleywhites, black baggy trousers, anoraks and what seemed like army boots. Skiing had not become a fashionable sport at that time, there were no package tours by air, and we travelled by train under the care of Cook's uniformed guide, who met us at Victoria to escort us all the way. We slept in couchettes, six bunks to a compartment, and soon got to know the rest of the party, which was evenly divided between girls and men aged between twenty-five and thirty-five. As I was forty I was the oldest and there were only two married couples. We were in holiday mood and when we arrived at Basle on the Swiss border about five o'clock in the morning, where we were to stop for an hour, everybody decided to get off to have croissants and coffee in the station restaurant. The customers eating an early breakfast inside looked up with astonishment to see a group of people enter, dressed in pyjamas and dressing gowns, but when they realized we were English they just shrugged their shoulders and went on eating. We returned to the platform after half an hour but to our dismay there was no train standing where we had left it. After checking to make sure that we had come back to the correct platform, I went in search of the station master and enquired in my best French, '*Pardon monsieur, où est la voiture numéro vingt-deux, s'il vous plaît?*' He took me by the arm, led me to a platform on the other side of the station, pointed to a train standing there and said,

'*Voilà*'. It was our train, which had been shunted from the French side to the Swiss, and I went back to the rest of our party to tell them the good news.

We were met on the station at Kandersteg by Mr Trog, the owner of the hotel at which we were staying, with his porters to carry our luggage and Nesta, Cook's representative. As we were not able to have a honeymoon when we were married, due to the war, I had booked the Honeymoon Suite at the hotel, which had its own private bathroom. None of the other bedrooms had private baths; the guests had to pay to use bathrooms, which were kept locked in charge of attendants. We were allowed to take abroad only £25 to spend and the other members of our party asked whether they could use our private bathroom to save their money. Consequently, although I had intended our holiday to be a delayed honeymoon, we had a constant stream of friends queuing up in our bedroom to use our bath. In the morning our ski instructors were waiting outside the hotel after breakfast and we were taken to the ski shop to obtain our skis and sticks. The length of the skis was judged by extending one hand as high as possible above the head and measuring the distance from the tip of the fingers to the ground. There was no such thing as short skis and the boots had to be fixed as tightly as possible to the skis by leather straps to make sure they would not move or come off. Nowadays safety bindings are used to make sure that the skis do come off in a fall.

Nesta divided us into classes, the girls in Bernard's class, a happy jolly Frenchman who carried their skis and anoraks and exclaimed 'Hoopla' when he picked them up after a fall, while the men had Adolf, a rather dour German Swiss of about my age who was a local councillor and a mountain guide. My age at school, where I was always younger than the average in my class, was an advantage, but at skiing when I was older, it was a distinct disadvantage. Adolf started it by saying to me when our class came to a difficult part of the run, 'You go first, sir' which I did. He then turned to the rest of the class, who were holding back, and exclaimed, 'Look! He is an old man. If he can do it so can you.'

We enjoyed our skiing although it was hard on the knees and ankles. There was only one casualty; a girl in Betty's class broke her leg when she was skiing without Bernard.

We organized tailing parties to the other hotels in the village, seated on toboggans pulled by a horse-drawn sleigh in a long line and took part in all the social activities at our hotel. There were dances after dinner and a fancy dress party, Betty and Marge, who joined in all our fun, dressed in bath towels with a clothes line fastened round their necks, joining them together, on which they hung their undies, and received the prize of a bottle of champagne to the applause of the soldiers who were having a night out at the hotel. I went as an abominable snowman, dressed in my longjohns and ski boots but I did not win a prize.

On the last day of skiing Adolf planned a tour in the mountains but by that time most of our class were tired out and only one of them came with me and Adolf. We took the cable car to the top and skied over to the Gemmi pass, stopping to eat our lunch, while Adolf pointed out the chamois on the mountainside. This was what I had come to Switzerland for, to enjoy the solitude and beauty of the mountains. It was a long run down from the Gemmi pass and when I slipped over the edge on a narrow path Adolf had to drag me up by my skis, which was agony for my knees, but we arrived safely back at our hotel in time for dinner. On the final evening we were presented with our Swiss bronze medals and to mark the occasion Betty had written a song bringing in the names of our party, the ski instructors, Nesta and Mr Trog, which Betty, Marge, myself and Michael Hawkes sang to the tune of Widdicombe Fair. Michael had rowed in the Oxford boat which sank during the Boat Race; he had a very fine voice and was in the choir at St Martins in the Fields, so he sang the verses while Betty, Marge and I joined in the chorus. We practised beforehand with the band and had a couple of gins to boost our confidence and face the audience in the restaurant, who gave us quite an ovation at the end of our performance.

When we left the following morning Mr Trog escorted us to the station, asked Betty for a copy of her song and said, 'You were the happy ones. Will you tell Mr Cook how much you enjoyed staying at my hotel?' We promised to do so and on the way home we all arranged to keep in touch and join Cook's Continuation Party at the Palace Hotel in Murren the next year. We left behind the other married couple, the husband explaining that although his wife had joined in all our activities she was in fact suffering from leukaemia and was not expected to live more than a few months. He wanted to give her as long a holiday as possible, but owing to the currency restrictions he had used up their allowance and our party therefore gave him all the foreign money we had left, which he promised to repay to us in sterling when he arrived home. We received a cheque later with a letter thanking us for our help and enclosing a copy of the obituary notice of his wife's death, from which we discovered she was a nurse who had devoted her time to nursing the terminally ill patients at the local hospital.

The following year we travelled by boat and train to Switzerland, as usual sleeping in a couchette. After about an hour a lady came into our compartment and asked Betty if I could sleep in her compartment which adjoined ours. She explained that she was on her own and that the attendant had made up all the bunks in the expectation that there would be more travellers to join the train and she was afraid that they would be occupied by strange men. There was no room for her in our compartment as all the bunks were taken. Betty said, 'We will both join you', we packed our bags and occupied two of the bunks next door.

We joined Cook's Continuation party at the Palace Hotel, Murren. Nesta was again Cooks representative there with several of Cook's Initiation Party from the previous year. Murren is reached by a funicular railway, there is no road and no car traffic and consequently no noise. It was the winter home of Sir Arnold Lunn, the father of British skiing and inventor of the slalom. Most of the skiing was on the Schiltgrat but we also made excursions to Wengen and Scheidegg for a run down the Mannlichen to Grindelwald. Field Marshal Montgomery, who was head of NATO at that time, was staying at the Palace Hotel to support the British Army ski team in their race against Air Marshal Tedders Royal Air Force team from Wengen. The girls dressed up in their party frocks, hoping to dance with the young soldiers after dinner, but the team were all sent to bed at half past nine.

In honour of Viscount Montgomery and knowing his interest in physical fitness, the hotel had arranged for a gymnastic team to give a display. The team stayed in the hotel and after dinner one of them asked Betty to dance. As they danced he called her an English rose, whispered she was simpatico and asked her to meet him later. She thought he was a dreadful man and when he came up for the next dance I told him Betty was dancing with me. We managed to keep him at bay for the rest of the evening but the next morning he followed Betty about the hotel, trying to catch her alone.

Viscount Montgomery, who was entering a lift in the foyer, invited Betty to join him and as the member of the gymnastic team hurried across to get into the lift Montgomery asked the attendant to close the doors and shut the man out. Fortunately, the team left later that day but our friends called Betty 'the English rose' for the rest of the holiday. Although we belonged to the Ski Club of Great Britain we did not compete in the races they organized because we preferred longer runs instead of speed trips down the pistes. The club representatives asked whether we would make the effort to join a special race they were organizing and we said we would get one of our party to compete. We persuaded Gordon Binns, who had skied in the Cambridge University team to enter, and he won the race, greatly to the surprise of the Ski Club members when they presented him with the trophy, a silver spoon.

Miranda and David were now old enough to learn to ski and we went back to Murren with them for their first season. In order to encourage them Betty and the children entered for the Murren two star test, which they passed, and I took the three star, as I had passed the two star test the year before. In order to make sure of passing I did not brake on the way down and afterwards my ski instructor said, 'That was not skiing. That was dicing with death'. As we had a skiing holiday every winter, the children quickly outpaced myself and Betty, they both gained the Ski Club bronze medal with me and David obtained the silver medal, but he did not try for the gold and Miranda concentrated on style instead of speed. I booked the holidays at resorts over 6,000 feet. We always had plenty of snow and good skiing so my memories are of the different incidents which distinguished them.

We visited Andermatt at Christmas and the New Year where the Navy Ski Club had their base. As we were living at Gads Hill on the outskirts of the Medway Towns we knew Chatham well and David became very friendly with the daughter of the admiral in charge of Chatham Dockyard. The promotions in the navy list were published on the first of January and there were great celebrations over the New Year holidays. I went on

Betty being presented with the cup for winning the shooting competition at Andermatt

a mountain tour with Michael Pret Roose, the Ski Club representative, and as we started down from the top an avalanche on the other side cut us off from our route home. We skied down the next valley, arriving at an inn where we obtained beds for the night and the next day caught a train up to Andermatt. We had not been able to get through to our friends to let them know that we were safe and there was great relief when we arrived back. Michael kept a yacht in Brittany to sail during the summer and spent the winter at his chalet in Andermatt. He became president of the Ski Club of Great Britain and was an expert skier with great experience of the mountains, but he was caught with his wife and son in an avalanche above Andermatt and they were all killed.

The Swiss are great shooting enthusiasts, which is encouraged by the Government, and the annual shooting competition was held while we were there. Betty won the ladies contest, Miranda was third. Betty received the cup, and they were both presented with large Swiss rolls and kisses by the mayor. David and I won nothing in the men's contest, although David had been in the shooting eight at Tonbridge. We returned to Andermatt the following year and Betty again won the shooting contest, but we did not go back the third year in case she won, because she would then have to keep the cup and we did not want the trouble

Betty swanking with no hands at Courcheval

of getting it through customs. We donated a cup to the White Hare Ski Club for a toboggan race to be held annually on New Year's Day.

Pontresina was very enjoyable because we were able to ski over to Celerina and St Moritz, see the Cresta Run, take the lift up to the Daviolezza Hut which is just under 10,000 feet high, admire the view there with Audrey Hepburn and ski down.

Author skiing

The skiing at Lech in Austria was organized by officials who controlled the ski school. Betty, Miranda and a girl from Holland were together in a class when the teacher wanted to get Miranda away from Betty and suggested Betty should transfer to a different class. All three joined another instructor instead and they were asked by one of the officials whether the first man was no good, but Betty said they merely decided on a change, although whenever they passed him the three always laughed, greatly to his embarrassment and the amusement of the other ski instructors.

Lech had some very fine high altitude runs with magnificent views and one particularly steep descent, which had to be negotiated as the quickest way to get down to the village. When we hesitated on the edge of the plateau overlooking the valley the instructor said to me, 'You go first'. I started off and got a quarter of the way down before I lost control and fell the rest of the way to the bottom. When I fall, I always follow the advice of my former gym master at school to relax, let yourself go and do not try to fight it, otherwise you will break something. The sight of my sticks and skis flying and my body turning over and over on the way down must have seemed dreadful to the watchers above, because the ski teacher launched himself off the top, lost his balance and landed in the snow beside me with no prospect of being able to rejoin the class huddled together on the mountain. Fortunately, we were not hurt and another instructor arrived at the top with his group to guide the class a longer and easier way back to the village.

We attended church on Sundays and if there was no English church in the resort a local church was usually made available for a Church of England clergyman to take an early morning service, but in Lech this was not possible. An army padre had brought a group of young army officers to Lech for a skiing holiday and he turned the lounge of the hotel into a temporary church to conduct a service which we attended. There was a church in Andermatt where a Church of England priest conducted services and while we were there a new clergyman arrived to take over. On the first Sunday in the middle of the communion service he found that the chalice had been locked away and he had not got the key. He could not stop the service while he hurried back to his hotel to find the key or get a cup and we therefore had to drink the communion wine out of the bottle. One man who was also a clergyman left the church, but we stayed because the priest conducted the service in a reverent manner, and the way in which the wine had to be drunk did not alter the meaning of it.

When we were at Wengen an avalanche crashed down the mountain, demolishing trees and bringing down rocks before coming to a stop on the ice rink. One of the waitresses in our hotel was skating at the time but she saw the mass of snow and broken trees coming down and was able to skate to the side and escape injury. When we visited St Anton we shared a table in the dining room with Paul from Durham, who was a chartered accountant employed by the Coal Board and John, who came from Glasgow. Paul had a caravan in Scotland, which they used when skiing there; they were very experienced and good skiers. One girl who arrived at the hotel whilst we were there went out on the first morning to post a letter home, slipped on the hotel steps, broke her leg and spent her holiday in hospital. There was no entertainment in the hotel but John had brought his own supply of whisky, which we drank whilst we watched a guest demonstrating that he could hypnotize people in another party of friends. We went out to other hotels, including one which had a band and a very good zither player; at the time the Harry Lime theme was very popular. Cook's courier was supposed to collect us by car at the end of the holiday but she telephoned the hotel to say that it would not be possible because the roads were blocked by snow and we would have to make our own way to the airport. We managed to catch a local train which connected with the main line and get a taxi to the airport just in time to board our plane. I sent a claim to Cooks for the amount I had paid out and they sent me a cheque for £5 'as a goodwill gesture'. I sent the cheque back and said I would sue them for the full amount unless they paid up, which they did, but I never booked with Cooks again.

Travelling in winter, we naturally experienced bad weather which sometimes made it difficult to get home. One train was iced up. We could not get a hot drink, there was no heating and it was diverted to Boulogne because Calais, where we were supposed to board our boat, was frozen in. We landed at Folkestone and I had to collect my car from Dover, where I had left it. The weather in England was just as bad as that on the Continent, and as I drove slowly home on the icy roads we were met by cars competing in the Monte Carlo rally, coming at us full speed with their headlights blazing, relying on the grip of their studded tyres.

Something always cropped up to make train journeys more interesting. One train slipped the rear section in Switzerland whilst the front half continued at full speed on to Austria. The front section included the dining car, and two girls travelling with their parents in the next compartment to ours were late going into breakfast when the train parted. They careered off to Austria in their dressing gowns, leaving their distracted parents behind. They packed their belongings, rushed outside the station, hired a car and set off to chase the train to its next stop.

I drove one of the new Austin A30s with front wheel drive to Seefeld when we skied there, and it surprised the Germans when we were able to negotiate the icy snow covered roads, whilst their Volkeswagen Beetles with rear engine drive slipped and slithered about. We stayed in a luxury hotel which had been converted from an old monastery and there was a tea dance each afternoon. We were sitting listening to the band when a handsome well dressed man of about forty-five approached our table with the obvious intention of asking Betty to dance. A sudden reminder of her experience at Murren with the gymnast from Berne overcame her and Betty stood up in a panic and rushed from the room. The German, who spoke perfect English, asked 'Has you wife been taken ill?' I managed to reply, 'Yes, she has not been very well' and he said, 'I trust that she will soon be recovered'. But I am sure he was not deceived by my explanation.

I had another illustration of the way in which German employees keep strictly to the rules or instructions given to them and will not vary them. I had to pay a deposit to the concierge on two bath robes which we wanted for the swimming pool. As I settled our account with the concierge when we were leaving, I said, 'Deduct the deposit on the bath robes and I will pay the balance.' He replied, 'I cannot do that, sir. You must pay the account and I must pay you the deposit.' I paid the account and he solemnly handed back my deposit.

Zermatt had the flavour of a mountaineering village in the true Alpine tradition, with a museum commemorating Whymper's great climb of the Matterhorn. The Gornergrat mountain railway goes to over 11,000 feet and provides splendid long runs down to the village, while the chairlift up to Sunegga and the cable cars to the foot of the Matterhorn rise to over 8,000 feet for long and short runs. All the top stations have superb views of many of Switzerland's highest mountains but owing to heavy snowfalls the Theodule Pass down to Breuil-Cervinia in Italy was closed when we were there. There are plenty of tea rooms, restaurants and bars with dancing and entertainments in the hotels. Access to Zermatt is by rail so there are no motor cars in the village. There was an outbreak of typhoid whilst we were there, caused by contamination of the water supply during work being carried out in the mountains. One of the workmen was found to be a carrier of the germ. We were not affected because we drank the beer in the railway station buffet, which Betty said was the best she had ever tasted, and we had wine in the hotel.

Betty always resisted falling but although safety bindings had been introduced the first models were not reliable and consequently, if they did not open, something had to break.

We enjoyed the skiing at Davos, particularly the run down to Klosters, where we caught a train back, but in the second week Betty had a fall and broke her ankle. We were staying at the Grand and Belvedere Hotel which was the best place to be if you were injured; the staff were kind and attentive, the doctor called every day with ice packs to reduce the swelling in the ankle, and when it was put in plaster Betty could come to the cinema with us and watch the dancing in the night club after dinner.

I booked a hotel at Courcheval in the French Alps, one of the three resorts forming the Three Valleys Concept, the others being Meribel-les-Allues and St Martin de Belleville, which provided access to a wide variety of ski-runs. At the end of the first week the proprietor of the hotel said he would have to change Miranda's room because he had a group of investment analysts coming for a conference. The alternative room he offered was small and pokey. Betty said it was not suitable and an argument developed which was not helped by the fact that the proprietor pretended he did not understand English and Betty could not speak French. We enlisted the help of the captain of the French-Canadian Ski Team, who was staying at the hotel, to translate, but the proprietor still insisted Miranda must move, so I settled the matter by telling him we would leave. I booked accommodation in another hotel and came back with a taxi to take our luggage. As we left all the staff assembled on the front steps to say goodbye; they were sorry to see us leave, Miranda and David had become great favourites with them. Unfortunately, during the second week Betty had a fall and broke a bone in her knee. It was put in plaster for the journey home and Betty was visited by our family doctor. He was one of the old school and immediately arranged to have the knee x-rayed to make sure it was set properly, saying, 'You can't trust the Frogs'.

As the children were living in Canada I went with Betty to Val d'Isère, a true Alpine village in the French Alps, reached by road through tunnels and avalanche galleries. The next morning we put on our skis; Betty was ready before I was and set off on the drag lift for the first run. The lift stopped just short of the top and to prevent herself slipping backwards, Betty took the strain on her legs. The safety bindings did not open and she broke both bones in her right leg. She was taken down to the clinic in the village on the 'Blood Wagon' and after first aid treatment transferred by ambulance to Bourg St Maurice, the main town in the area. She had a private room at the hospital. We were covered by insurance, and I took her in a French phrase book so that she could converse with the doctors and staff.

There were two good main skiing areas in Val d'Isère but my skiing was limited because I went by bus every afternoon to visit Betty in Bourg St Maurice. I made several friends in the hotel and one evening the travel representative gave us a drinks party after dinner. Our group consisted of myself and two other Englishmen, two Irishmen from Belfast, two Australians and three American air force officers. The wine flowed freely, we told jokes against each other. I was referred to as the Ancient Brit, the other two Englishmen as Wingeing Pommes, the Australians as Abos, the Belfast men as Irish Gits, and the Americans as Colonials. It was all good humoured, although I do not think the Americans appreciated being called Colonials. When the girl from the travel agency visited Betty she said she was horrified at the size of the wine bill and did not know how she was going to justify it to her employers. The wife of the consultant at the hospital had a baby daughter and he celebrated the birth in true French fashion by supplying champagne for all the staff and patients. Betty saved some for me when I visited her in the afternoon. At the end of the fortnight's holiday Betty was taken by ambulance to the airport, where I met her with our travel representative.

The staff at the airport were very officious and at first refused to allow Betty to be taken in a wheelchair straight onto the aircraft. A blazing row developed between our representative and the official in charge but she got her way and Betty was allowed through. I asked the ambulance driver what the man had remarked at the end of the argument, and he told me he said, 'She's no lady'. After the scene at the airport it was a great relief for Betty to be carried aboard the British Airways plane and made comfortable on a row of seats; it was like coming home. An ambulance was waiting for us when we arrived at Heathrow, we called to see Betty's mother in Hampton on the way home to have a cup of tea, and when we arrived at our home the ambulance men carried a bed downstairs for Betty to sleep in. A specialist from Eastbourne hospital, who had a private practice locally, took over her treatment, but it was many weeks before she was able to walk. Betty did not ski again and I went on holiday to Verbier with two friends, an Englishman and a German.

They were both good skiers, we did not got to ski school and we usually arrived on the slopes about eleven o'clock. The ski school assembled outside our hotel and every morning, as they waited for their instructors, my German friend went out onto his bedroom balcony overlooking the ski school in his dressing gown and gave a speech to them on skiing and how they should behave. The first morning everybody looked up in astonishment, but on subsequent mornings they looked forward to his speech and cheered when he appeared on the balcony. We started skiing rather late in the morning but we were on the slopes all day and as I had visited Verbier before with my family there was no difficulty in picking out the runs, which sweep down at all sorts of angles from the top of the huge amphitheatre area, forming an arc as a background to Verbier.

After skiing we usually spent sometime in a sauna and finished off by diving into the icy pool, fed by a spring from the mountains. Our English friend wore glasses and forgot to remove them when he dived in. They fell off and landed somewhere at the bottom of the pool. He jumped in repeatedly before he found them, ended up blue with the cold and had to return to the sauna to warm up again. One evening we had a fondue party with three Americans and we all had rather a lot to drink before they returned to their hotel at midnight. We decided to visit the night club and our Englishman went to the bar to order the drinks. I was standing with my back to the bar when I heard the sound of smashing glass. I turned round and found he was seizing the ashtrays and throwing them at the bottles of wine, which stood on a shelf at the back of the bar, like a row of soldiers. They were only three feet away so he could not miss

177

and the two barmen were in a panic, running to and fro, not knowing whether to save the bottles, dodge the flying ash trays, or tackle our friend. I got hold of him, together with my German companion. We tried to get him outside but he clung to the bar and shouted, 'Are there any old Stoneyhurst boys here?' He had been at Stoneyhurst public school run by the Jesuits in the north of England, and the headmaster was a priest who subsequently became Cardinal Hume, in control of the Catholic Church in England.

The band stopped playing, put down their instruments, pushed their way through the crowd and came towards us, but at that moment, when the situation looked like becoming desperate, to my astonishment two young men came forward and said, 'We were at Stoneyhurst. We'll give you a hand'. With their help we were able to hustle our friend outside and get away. When we got back to our hotel he wrote a notice which read, 'Rally here tonight at eight o'clock for a raid on the night club' and put it up on the hotel announcements board. But after we had got him to bed I tore it down.

* * *

After the war I kept up my membership of the Medway Yacht Club but I did not renew my subscriptions to the other sports clubs; I looked instead for something new. I joined a gliding club at Maidstone. We were given two gliders by Lord Rothermere and established ourselves at Detling on the North Downs above Maidstone, which was an ideal launching spot for the gliders. However, we were notified by the Air Ministry that we were in a direct flying path to London Airport and would have to move. The club therefore transferred to a site near Herne Bay, but as this was further than I wanted to travel I resigned my membership.

The Medway Yacht Club was founded in 1880 at Rochester and in the summer of 1898 the eyes of the yachting world were focussed on the River Medway. The Australian yachtsman, Mark Foy, commodore of the Sidney Flying Squadron, had brought his reputedly unbeatable boat, *Irex*, over to England and issued a challenge to match her against any comparable English vessel. The Medway Yacht Club was quick to respond.

In one month they designed built and equipped a boat which they named *The Maid of Kent* to meet the *Irex* in a series of five races on the Medway and they nominated as skipper Mrs Wyllie, the wife of the well known marine artist, W.L. Wyllie, A.R.A., who was commodore of the Medway Yacht Club. *Irex* was no match for Mrs Wyllie and the *Maid*, the English boat gaining three successive victories, all by convincing margins, rendering it unnecessary to complete the series of five.

When the war ended I attended a meeting at the Kings Head Hotel in Rochester with Rob Passmore and a dozen other friends interested in sailing, to decide on our future programme. The Medway Yacht Club was established above Rochester Bridge, but we wanted to have direct access to the sea without the necessity of negotiating the bridge. We therefore decided on a site at Lower Upnor where the Government had built a jetty and laid down a concrete hard as an embarkation point in preparation for the landings in Normandy. We also agreed to purchase a fleet of six eighteen foot National dinghies, a new design by Uffa Fox, to be built by Anderson Perkins and Rigden at Whitstable. We arranged for the use of the land at Upnor with the landowner, who was known to us, for a nominal rent of 1s. a year and we laid moorings for the boats off the hard. Rob Passmore supplied a hut for the race officer and another for making tea, we erected posts to mark the starting line with two miniature cannons and put Pop Parsons, who had served in the RAF on aircraft carriers, in charge.

We were now ready and awaited the arrival of our new boats. The cost of each boat was £350 and those who could not afford the full amount shared with a friend. I joined with Mike Wood and we each paid £175, which was all I could afford.

Mike had a commission in the Royal West Kents after leaving Tonbridge School, and when he was wounded during the invasion of Italy he was sent home and after recovering, was posted to an officers training camp as an instructor. A friend who was trained at the camp said he was one of the best instructors, but also the untidiest. He would take the early morning parade dressed in a greatcoat with one or two buttons missing, and would severely reprimand any man who had a button undone. Mike was outspoken; he did not worry if he offended anybody, but we got on well together. When he sailed our boat I crewed for him and when I sailed he came with me and Betty or Rob Passmore. On one occasion when I was not with him he had as crew Michael Chavasse, the Bishop of Rochester's son, who had served with him in North Africa, although Michael had not sailed before. They were trying to made headway against the tide with little or no wind to get to the finishing line. This is a frustrating business at the best of times, and with an inexperienced crew the continual tacking to and fro tries everybody's patience, which was always in short supply so far as Mike was concerned. In the end he could stand it no longer and he shouted to Michael, 'You're no bloody good in the boat. We'd do better without you.' Michael replied, 'All right, I'll go then' and promptly jumped overboard and swam ashore. Mike eventually finished the race but as he ended one man short he was disqualified.

Mike's family had a sheep farm in Patagonia. They always reminded me of the 'Brains Trust', a radio programme where the three members answered questions sent in by listeners. They were very entertaining. Bob Boothby always knew some important person and started to reply by saying, 'When I saw Lord or Sir so and so'. Commander Campbell had travelled the world and usually said, 'When I was in Patagonia ...'. While Professor Joad, the philosopher, cautiously replied, 'It all depends on what you mean by ...'. This delightful programme was in great contrast to its successor, 'Any Questions?' where the members are politicians or party members, who are only interested in trying to score points off their opponents.

The racing was very keen in the eighteen foot Nationals and as they were all built as a class it was always very close. Jim Kenny, an Irishman, was over the line at the start of the race and did not return when he was recalled. At the finish he was ahead but he did not receive any acknowledgement from Pop Parsons on the line because he had been disqualified. He let out a stream of oaths at the top of his voice, demanding to know why he had not got a gun. A crowd of spectators had watched the race and as Jim came ashore he stumbled on the hard and went down on his knees right at the feet of his parish priest. I thought at first he was going to ask for absolution for his sins. I had Vic Costanzo, an Italian, as crew with Betty when we were out in rough weather, beating against a strong wind with the waves breaking over the bows, causing us to ship a lot of water. the only way to get it out was with a hand baler which Vic was using, but as the water kept coming in he screamed, 'We're going to sink,' threw the baler overboard and started taking his oilskins off. Betty shouted at him, 'Pull yourself together, Vic, and bale the water out with your hat', which they both did until we were able to reach calmer waters under the lee of the land. We had a very full social life together, usually having tea when we came ashore and later going into the town for a meal in the evening. We had our first annual dinner at the Leather Bottle in Cobham, when Rob Passmore, in his speech, made a plea for 'cleats for sheets', because, although our dinghies were much larger, they were rigged in the same manner as the smaller boats, where nothing was made fast in case a sudden squall capsized them.

The second year we hired the banqueting room at the town hall in Chatham, which was large enough for Mike Wood and David Clarabut, our class captain, to install a fully rigged dinghy. The evening ended with Mike borrowing a large tray from a waiter, going to the top of the magnificent staircase leading to the council chamber and launching himself off, flying across the pavement and landing in the middle of the road. Fortunately there was no traffic about, as it was after one o'clock in the morning.

We sailed against the Whitstable Yacht Club at their regatta and they visited us. They had a large class of eighteen foot Nationals and we were great rivals. David Clarabut's uncle, who had been my colonel when I was in the Home Guard during the war, asked us whether we would like to take his yacht *Cyrilla*, a West Coast One design, to Burnham and race her during Burnham Week Regatta, as he was unable to spare the time and the boat was entered for all the races. We were glad to have the opportunity and made up a crew with David as skipper, myself and Mike Wood, and we also took along with us a young lad aged about fifteen called John Furlong. David had been a pilot in the Fleet Air Arm during the war and worked in the family shipping business.

We left Upnor at the top of the tide to carry the ebb down the Medway and up the east coast, to catch the flood tide at the mouth of the Crouch for the run up to Burnham. The navigation is not difficult because the channels between the sand banks are well marked, and provided the East Cant Buoy is picked up after crossing the Thames estuary, followed by the West Oaze Buoy and the remaining Oaze Buoys to the Barrow Buoys in turn, these will mark the channel to the Whitaker Buoy and the entrance to the River Crouch. In fine weather it is a pleasant sail and provides an opportunity to see the many seabirds on the mud flats and the seals basking on the sand banks, which are uncovered as the tide leaves them. We sailed hard all the week and came in first every day. We could not beat our handicap and never received a prize but we enjoyed the social life attending the dinners and parties in the clubs. We were astonished when young John drank whisky and smoked cigars. He explained that he went to a boarding school where all the pupils were allowed to do what they liked and his parents encouraged this at home.

David always insisted on winding up the evening with port and singing 'Cigarettes and whisky and wild wild women, they drive you crazy, they drive you insane' before we turned in. We had rented a caravan in the field at the back of the Royal Corinthian Yacht Club, as the boat had no sleeping accommodation. Despite his education, or perhaps because of it, John grew up to be a fine young man. He bought a boat of his own and married a very nice girl.

We sailed *Cyrilla* back to Upnor and told David's uncle how we had got on. He had already seen the results in the paper and was not surprised that we had not been able to win the cup.

The following year we sailed our eighteen foot Nationals to compete at Burnham Week Regatta with the boats from Whitstable and I continued to attend Burnham Week each year with the various boats I owned until I gave up sailing. The three yacht clubs at Burnham, the Crouch, the Royal Burnham, and the Royal Corinthian, combined to run Burnham Week and the yachtsmen competing in the races were made honorary members of all three clubs. There was a tremendous social life, with cocktail parties and dinner dances every evening, ending with dancing until past midnight in the night club. It was an early start to the morning races and my crew would sometimes arrive on board bleary eyed after a hard night, wearing oilskins over their pyjamas, but they soon recovered in the fresh air, combined with the hard physical work of crewing a racing boat. As Betty was always one of the crew I booked a room for us at the White Hart Hotel on the quayside. This was the best hotel, although the top floor, where Rob Passmore had his room, leaked when it rained and the beer cellars were flooded at high tide, but the food was excellent and the hotel was always full.

When we did not stay at the White Hart we rented rooms at a doctor's house in the village which he left in charge of his housekeeper. He had two large dogs which slept on the bedroom landing. When we returned late at night they refused to allow us to reach our bedroom and we had to call out the housekeeper to control them. We also stayed at the Anchor Hotel on the quay, where the bedrooms were worse than those at the White Hart. The mattresses had such large depressions in the middle that we had to sleep on them in a sitting position. When we took the cover off the cheese board it revealed a blob of green mould which had once been cheese, but the cooked breakfasts were very good. The two front bedrooms had bay windows overlooking the river and one night when we were in bed we heard voices outside and the sound of somebody climbing up to the windows. There was a whisper of, 'I'm right behind you, boy' and we recognized the voice of one of our friends, Ray Sarrant, who had probably missed us when we left the night club. We kept quiet, they reached the bay window of the other bedroom next to us, occupied by David Clarabut and his wife, and when they discovered their mistake they beat a hasty retreat.

In 1950 Wilmot Price, the commodore of the Medway Yacht Club, reminded us that we were all members of the Medway Yacht Club and it would be a pity if we established another club at Upnor. He said that if we transferred our interest in the site at Upnor and the moorings to the club it would erect a club house with showers and changing rooms and transfer its main activities from Rochester to Upnor. This we agreed to do. We gave up our independence and the club established itself at Upnor, becoming the largest yacht club on the Medway, as well as the oldest.

Betty won the Ladies Race in the eighteen foot Nationals and when I bought a small dinghy called a Duckling, she taught the children how to sail. Betty's interest was in racing. When we had to make a passage to Burnham or Cowes or West Mersea she brought the car round with our gear and personal belongings and then joined us on the boat. Tom Weekes, one of the best helmsmen in the club, bought a small day cruiser designed in Norway called a Dragon which was very fast and seaworthy, ideal for racing. The Dragons were adopted as an international racing class and the club decided to promote them on the Medway. Max Hamilton, who became commodore after Wilmot Price, bought an old Dragon called *Hai Lung* in order to popularize the class and asked me to sail it up to Burnham and compete in the regatta. I took Rob Passmore as a crew and left the boat on one of Prior's moorings opposite their boatyard. Betty came up and drove us home and we all went back the following weekend for the start of racing.

As we rowed out to *Hai Lung* the owners of the other yachts moored nearby looked at us without saying a word and we understood why when we reached our boat. A hole had been smashed in the side of *Hai Lung* just above the waterline and when we asked what had happened, the men on the other yachts explained that a sailing barge leaving Prior's yard had hit *Hai Lung* and the fluke of the anchor hanging from the bows of the barge had penetrated the side of our boat. It looked as though we should be out of racing but the boatyards provided a magnificent service for yachts in regattas, repairing damage, fitting new masts, patching torn sails, to keep the boats racing and Priors towed *Hai Lung* to their yard, worked all day Sunday repairing the damage, and had us ready for the first race on Monday morning. I telephoned Max Hamilton to tell him the name of the barge which had hit *Hai Lung*, and its owners, so that he could claim on them.

We had a good week's racing in company with Tom Weekes. We did not win any prizes but we learnt how to sail a Dragon and joined in all the parties with our friends from the Medway who were visiting the regatta. Betty took the car home at the end of the week and I prepared to sail *Hai Lung* back with Rob. The wind had got up and it looked like being a rough ride to the Medway but we both had to be at work on Monday and we reefed well down and set sail.

As soon as we got out of the River Crouch we met the full force of the wind, which whipped up the waves, bringing cascades of water over the bows and into the boat as we tried to make headway against them. The boat was old and took in water. I nursed it along, while Rob had to spend all his time on hands and knees, pumping the water out. When we arrived at Upnor he was so stiff that he could not stand upright. However, I liked sailing the Dragon so much that I resolved

Author's Dragon class yacht *Askalon*

to buy one. I sold my share of the eighteen foot National dinghy and bought a Dragon named *Askalon* at Cowes, costing £750. Our friends in the eighteen foot National class also bought Dragons and the club went on to build up one of the biggest Dragon fleets in the whole country. The international Dragon class presented a Dragon named *Bluebottle* to the Queen and Prince Philip as a wedding present and the yacht came to the Medway to sail against our boats. Lieutenant Commander Graham Mann who skippered *Bluebottle* did not know the Medway and finished fourth in the first race, but the next day Tom Weekes sailed her and came in first. The regular crew on *Bluebottle* was a young man named Clive Smith, who spent most of his time sailing away from home. This depressed him and he committed suicide by shooting himself with a shotgun.

185

Author's house. Hook House estate Wadhurst, Sussex,
compulsorily purchased to create reservoir

I sold our house at Gads Hill and bought the Hook House
estate at Cousley Wood near Wadhurst. At one moment I had
no house because I had sold Gads Hill and there was a delay
in completing the purchase of Hook House, owing to a
disagreement between the husband and wife who owned it; the
next moment I had two houses, when a problem arose regarding
the sale of Gads Hill after the purchase of Hook House was
completed. However, the difficulty holding up the sale of Gads
Hill was cleared up and we moved into Hook House. The estate
consisted of the main house, surrounded by its own land of 130
acres, bounded by a small river, and the home farm with the
farmhouse, farm worker's cottage and farm buildings, which
was let to a tenant farmer, whilst I retained control of the woods.

Hook House was approached by a long drive to a courtyard,
surrounded by the stable for four horses and the garage for three

or four cars, over which was accommodation for the staff. The house had a panelled dining room, a very large drawing room with an inglenook fireplace, a study and a housekeeper's room, in addition to the usual domestic offices of kitchen, larder, dairy and outside boiler house for hot water and central heating. A wide staircase led up from the stone flagged hall to a galleried landing with five bedrooms and the bathrooms. All the rooms had oak floors and oak beams and the ironwork for which Sussex is noted. The industry in the county was famous in the Middle Ages, when the iron was smelted with wood from the forests which covered Sussex and supplied the oak for building the ships of the navy, as well as the cannon.

There was a large, cool wine cellar. Water came from a stream running through filter beds, which was replaced by mains water before we moved in, and electricity was supplied by two Lister diesel engines which were automatically switched on from a bank of batteries when current was required in the house or on the farm. After moving in, I contacted the electricity board to arrange for mains electricity to be brought to the area. They quoted me a price of £650 and I got in touch with the neighbouring farms and houses to enquire whether they wanted electricity and would share the expense. Everybody replied no, but when I went ahead on my own and paid all the cost they applied to the electricity board to be connected to the mains supply. I told the board that I expected a refund on the amount I had paid but they replied that it was their duty as a statutory body to connect people free of charge when electricity was available in the area.

Mrs Sylvia Eldridge, whose family owned Ladymeads, a farm adjoining ours, called to help us when we moved in and was a good friend the whole time we were at Hook House. Since her husband sold Ladymeads and they moved to Suffolk to be near their daughter, we have kept in touch and visited each other when we have been on holiday.

As we had a larger house we were able to give dinner parties and dances to entertain my clients as well as our friends. Sylvia decorated the house on those occasions with flowers from her own garden and also from the people living in the cottages who wanted to help. There was plenty of room to dance Scottish reels and Roger de Coverly; Miranda knew all the set pieces from her dancing lessons at Charters Towers school. We had large gatherings at Christmas when Betty's family came to stay for the holiday. I arranged a shooting party for Boxing Day. My farmer had left some wheat standing near the edge of the woods to encourage the pheasants to remain and we were able to give every family a brace of birds to take home at the end of the holiday. Betty's father, in common with most seafaring men, liked the country and always enjoyed his holidays with us. In winter we could be rather isolated when there were heavy snowfalls. If we were going on a skiing holiday we left our car on the top road and took our luggage up to it on a sleigh.

We were disturbed by the noise of car rallies at night, organized by motor clubs from the towns. We therefore arranged for a watch to be kept and when the cars left the main road to enter the country lanes near us one of the farmers would bring out a combine harvester or similar machine and drive slowly along to a field some distance away. There was no room for the cars to pass and they abandoned their rally, giving the farm workers a chance to have some sleep before they had to get up to do the early morning milking.

I surprised Sylvia when I told her I had found a carving on a tree in our woods of a heart intertwined with her initials and those of her husband, Wilf. She came from Cornwall but she worked in the Land Army at Hook House during the war and Wilf must have carved the initials when they were courting.

My mother had always suffered from high blood pressure and when the veins broke at the back of her eyes they destroyed the nerves, leaving her totally blind. I took her to an eye specialist in Harley Street but he said that as the nerves were dead nothing could be done to restore her sight. I engaged a housekeeper to live in and take care of my mother but she could not become reconciled to losing her sight and she did not like another woman running her house. She therefore asked to live with my youngest sister, Barbara. Her home was sold and the furniture given to Barbara and her husband, who were able to furnish their empty rooms. Barbara's hairdressing business was attached to the house. She had a competent staff and could give attention to Mother, who lived happily there within the limits of her disability. Living at Hook House we were some distance away, but we called to see her at weekends on our way home from the yacht club. When I had my mother's house built I thought my parents would be able to spend their retirement there, but the early death of my father and my mother's blindness had destroyed my plans, which was a great disappointment to me because I had hoped in this way to repay some of the sacrifices they had made, enabling me to become a chartered accountant.

My mother wanted to make a will, leaving her estate, consisting of the money from the sale of her house, to me or my children, but I said this would be unfair to my sisters and she did not leave a will when she died. There was not much money left and when I administered the estate I did not take my share but divided it equally between my sisters. It may seem strange but I cannot bring myself to benefit from the death of someone I love and when the nurse at my mother's bedside offered me my mother's rings, I could not take them and asked them to be given to my sisters.

I continued my racing with *Askalon*. With such a large fleet of Dragons on the Medway competition was fierce but it was good training when we had to race against the other boats at the regatta we visited. At Southend Regatta there was such a gale blowing that the Trinity House ship *Patricia*, on station there, had to leave and return to London. David Clarabut and I were the only two Dragons to complete the race — the rest ran for shelter into the Medway — but it was too rough for us to get ashore to collect our prizes. It was very dangerous at Burnham when one of the crew from a cruiser was lost overboard and drowned at the start of the first race. All the races were cancelled that day and the rest of the week because the weather was so bad. The Dragon class were getting fed up, as there was no sailing, and the race committee said they would lay on a race for us on Friday, although the weather was so bad that it would not be official and we would have to take part in it on our own responsibility. Six of us started, one was wrecked on the Buxey sands, another was swamped and sank, the crew being picked up by a following Dragon, and four finished, including *Askalon*.

Several new owners without any experience of racing bought cruisers after the war, although they attended the regattas. One man had a fine new yacht called *Lassiette* at Burnham. He had hired a man from one of the boatyards as helmsman but he and his wife did not know how to sail. Four of us thought we would have a day off and we arranged to crew for him. We had a good start, set the spinnaker with a following wind and were soon out in front of the fleet. As we approached the outer mark of the race, which had to be rounded to beat back up the river to Burnham, the owner's wife came up from below and called, 'Lunch is ready. You must come and eat it before it gets cold.' We explained that we must wait until we had taken down the spinnaker, rounded the mark and set the sails to beat back up the river, but the owner would have none of it and said, 'Let the helmsman handle it, my wife will be very annoyed if you don't come.' We abandoned the helmsman to his fate and trooped below. We had a three course lunch with two types of wine, followed by coffee and liqueurs. Two hours later, when we reappeared on deck, the poor helmsman was trying to go to windward with the spinnaker up and drifting rapidly backwards. We took the spinnaker down, hoisted the Genoa and got the yacht back on course, finally finishing last. We had a few more drinks before going ashore, the owner was very happy, and we had difficulty explaining to our friends that we had been 'Oshun Rayshin'.

An American named Ray Sarrant sailed his Dragon *Mustang* from Burnham to the Medway, where he joined our yacht club. He was a wealthy man, half French and half Greek, with the confidence and energy of an American coupled with French charm, which was very attractive to the ladies. He was fun to be with, we all liked him, and I know he was very fond of Betty and enjoyed being with us. He came to our parties and we went to his daughter's wedding, where we met his wife and the members of his family who had arrived from America. His wife was not interested in sailing but she was certainly interested in meeting Betty.

He came to supper one evening after racing and he and I finished a bottle of vodka between us. He told us that when he left he drove a short way up the road into the woods and went to sleep in his car. He explained to his wife what had happened when he arrived home the next day, and said that for the first time in his married life when he had a real excuse for staying out all night, his wife would not believe him.

He had an interesting business, travelling all over the world to discover sources of new perfumes, distilling them for use in cosmetics, lotions, scent and toiletries, which he supplied to companies such as Revlon. After a dinner dance at the Royal Corinthian had finished Ray went off with Betty and I took my partner, a girl called Wendy, to the night club to continue dancing and afterwards saw her to the ladies dormitory where she was sleeping. She had to catch an early morning train to London, and I offered to drive her to the station. I called for her at the dormitory about six o'clock and when we came out we saw Colonel Reed who owned a Dragon called *Chameleon*, and the buzz soon went round that I had been seen going into Wendy's room at midnight and coming out at six o'clock in the morning, having spent the night with her. Colonel Reed said to Betty, 'Brooky is a fine man. I am sure he wouldn't do anything to hurt you', and when our other friends started offering sympathy to her she wondered what it was all about. When she found out she had a good laugh and told them I had spent the night in bed with her.

Burnham Regatta was held at the end of August to mark the end of the sailing season and sometimes the autumn gales started early. We were racing *Askalon* hard with full sails up when the mast broke. Most people, when describing a broken mast, say it comes crashing down on the deck, but this is not what happens. The mast slowly subsides, held up by the wind in the sails, which act as a kind of parachute, and there was no danger of myself or Rob and Betty being hurt. We managed to get the sails off as they were thrashing about in the wind and likely to tear themselves to pieces, lash the broken mast to the deck, let go the anchor and sit back until we were towed in by a cruiser. When we arrived back at our moorings I asked the boatyard to make me up a new mast, let me know when it was ready and I would come up and sail *Askalon* back to the Medway. I had a telephone call from the yard to say they had an offer of £500 for *Askalon* from an American who wanted to ship it out to San Diego. I was all ready for a change and I therefore accepted the offer.

The *Arethusa*, one of the last windjammers still afloat, owned by the Shaftesbury Homes and used as a training ship for boys who wished to go to sea, was towed to the Medway and anchored off Upnor. David Clarabut and Mike Wood organized the first summer ball to be held aboard the ship. They engaged a top London band for dancing on the after deck, the ship was dressed overall with coloured lights, there was a full moon and it was a warm evening, which allowed the ladies to show off their ball gowns, adding colour to a gay, romantic occasion. The club took over the running of the summer ball on the *Arethusa* in the following years until the ship was sold to a museum in America, which restored her original rig as a four masted barque and her former name, *Peking*.

While I was considering what to do next after selling *Askalon*, David told me a new member had joined the club and bought a Dragon and asked me whether I would help him sail it. I said I would be pleased to do so, and he introduced me to Arnold Lindley who had bought *Voodoo*, a newer boat than *Askalon*. Arnold had started work as an engineering apprentice with the General Electric Company and had worked his way up through the company to run the whole of their South African organization. When Sir Leslie Gamage retired Arnold was called back to England to become chairman of GEC. He purchased a successful business called Sobell, which was being run by Arnold Weinstock, whom he introduced into the GEC management team. The reorganization of the company inevitably resulted in large redundancies in the work force, which must have distressed Arnold, who I knew was a kind considerate man, always ready to help others. He was asked to see a minister in the Labour Government; he thought he was going to be hauled over the coals because of the large number of redundancies he had created during the reorganization of the GEC, but instead he was requested to set up the Engineering Training Board and was knighted for his services to industry, becoming Sir Arnold Lindley, but still the same man we knew and liked. He was asked to solve the trouble with the Cunard Liner QE2 turbine blades and he was just as happy dealing with any problems which arose when we were rigging *Voodoo*. If anything had to be forced into place he said, 'We'll give it a bit of Scotch science' and hit it with a large hammer.

We raced *Voodoo* with the Dragons on the Medway and at Burnham. I wore my oldest clothes for sailing and when I was waiting for Arnold to pick me up at Gravesend Car Ferry to cross over to Tilbury on the way to Burnham, the attendant said to me, 'Are you waiting for a Ford Cortina, mate?' I replied, 'No, I'm waiting for a Rolls Royce.' He looked me up and down then said, 'I was trying to help you,' and walked back to the ticket office. Arnold arrived with his Rolls Royce which had a personal number plate, ALL 1, and as the attendant gave us our tickets he poked his head inside the car and enquired, 'What is it then? One for all or all for one?' So he got in the last word.

Arnold would have made a good helmsman but his business commitments did not allow him enough time to get in sufficient practice. Rob Passmore moved on to crew with the cruisers but Miranda and David were now old enough to join us on *Voodoo*. They were very keen on racing, David trimming and tuning the sails, whilst Miranda and Betty managed the spinnaker, which is a difficult sail to handle but essential when running before the wind and racing hard. They enjoyed the social activities of the clubs, particularly Burnham, where David was lured away from us by the captain of the Royal Burnham Dragon class, to crew on his prize winning boat *Black Adder*; this was a long time before the TV character was created by Rowan Atkinson. One evening Miranda was being entertained at dinner on the commodore of the Royal Corinthian Club's table and we were dining with our friends on a table nearby. We were all drinking champagne but they were only drinking table wine and we kept toasting them just to show Miranda what she was missing.

The commodore of the Royal Corinthian was a judge and brother of Orde Wingate, the general commanding the British force called Chindits which operated behind the Japanese lines in Burma. General Wingate was killed when his aeroplane crashed on landing in the forest.

Eventually I found I was sailing *Voodoo* all the time because Arnold could not manage to join us and I did not think it was fair that I should have the use of his boat while he paid all the expenses and I told Arnold it was time I got another boat of my own. *Voodoo* was sold and Arnold moved from London to Yorkshire to be midway between England and Scotland, where he also had business interests. We have not seen much of each other since he left but we have kept in touch with him and Lady Lindley.

My sister Lydia's husband, Norman, was taken ill and I paid for both of them to go on holiday to Bournemouth for a month, hoping that the sunshine and seabreezes would help him to recover. Although he improved for a time Norman's health gradually deteriorated and he was taken to hospital, where it was discovered he had cancer from which he subsequently died. He had not been able to save any money during his lifetime, when wages were low, and Lydia had no resources to keep up the payments for the mortgage on their house. I therefore bought the house and after paying off the mortgage there was a small balance left which was not, however, sufficient to provide for all Lydia's requirements. I arranged for her to live in the house rent free, paid all the maintenance, insurance and upkeep and made her periodical gifts to relieve her of any money troubles. She also had a small income from the balance on the sale of the house which I had invested for her. She was a very good bridge player and won the cup with her partner in the Medway Towns competition. She was chairwoman of the local branch in the women's section of the Conservative Party and was active in collecting for charity, particularly cancer research. Unfortunately she had a stroke which affected her left side, and made it difficult for her to walk. I had a lavatory built downstairs, her bed was moved to the ground floor and a home help came in every day to clean the house and look after her. I kept in touch with the Social Services Department and they decided that Lydia should be moved to a residential nursing home where she would have attention at night. I contacted the local branch of Abbeyfield Homes so that she could have her friends visit her, but they had no vacancies. The Social Services Department recommended two or three other homes, which we visited, and Lydia decided on one at Herne Bay, but she had only been there five months before she was taken ill and died of cancer. She had previously told me that she wished to make a will leaving everything to me, but knowing her love for children I suggested she should give legacies to her three nieces and nephew instead, which she did; £500 to each of them absorbed most of her money, she gave the furniture to me and a small amount of money left over that I gave to Betty. The nursing home sent me a bill for five months' residence and nursing care which I had to pay because the Social Services Department said that a patient had to stay for six months before they paid, otherwise the residential homes would be turned into geriatric hospitals. I paid for the funeral and gave the furniture to David to furnish a house if he returned to England but he decided to stay in Canada and sold it. A month after Lydia died the Abbeyfield Homes had a vacancy for her but it was too late.

My eldest sister, Minnie, also died after a short illness. She lived in Hastings but we did not see so much of her as we did of the other members of my family. She was active up to the time she died, very independent, and managed her own affairs.

After I stopped sailing *Voodoo* I decided to buy a racing cruiser and order a Twister class yacht designed by Kim Holman to be built by Uphams yard at Brixham. It was twenty-five feet overall with accommodation for a crew of four. Betty chose all the fittings for the cabins and named the boat *Meris*, which means 'of the sea'. It was late being completed but after running trials we accepted it and I paid the cost of £2,500. The next day I set sail with Miranda and David while Betty drove the car back to Weymouth, which we intended to be our first stop because we wanted to get used to the boat before continuing on to the Medway. I had filed our route with the coastguards at Brixham and they would notify the coastguards at Weymouth to expect our arrival. The wind dropped light, we could not carry our favourable tide all the way and when we had not arrived by midnight at the Royal Hotel where Betty had booked a room, she went down to the harbour and asked the coastguard whether we had been sighted. He said we had been seen rounding the Shambles, a group of rocks off the shore, and that we should make the harbour within the hour. Betty was waiting for us when we tied up at the quay. We had supper in her room, I stayed at the hotel and Miranda and David went back to sleep on board. The following morning we had a conference. The wind had changed direction with hardly any strength, and it was a question of whether we could get David back in time for the start of his university term, and Miranda's holiday was coming to an end. We decided to drive home and I telephoned a client who organized yacht deliveries to arrange for *Meris* to be sailed to Upnor, where we greeted her four days later.

The Cruiser class in the Medway Yacht Club expanded rapidly and races were organized in conjunction with the Royal Engineers Yacht Club and the Royal Naval sailing Association. I also joined the East Anglian Offshore Racing Association based at West Mersea, taking part in their races. The Medway Yacht Club had extended their regatta from four days to a whole week and we therefore had a very full summer programme.

Sir Francis Drake's father, the Reverend Edmund Drake, was instituted vicar of Upchurch near Gillingham on the Medway in 1560 when young Drake was about seven years old and he must have learnt how to sail a boat as a boy on the Medway off Gillingham and Chatham. Nelson was twelve when he joined his uncle's ship, the *Raisonable*, at Chatham to start his career in the Royal Navy; *HMS Victory* was built at Chatham and launched in 1765, becoming Nelson's flagship in 1803. Chatham and the River Medway have therefore had a long and honourable connection with the Royal Navy but this was interrupted in June 1667, when a Dutch fleet under the command of Admiral de Ruyter, captured Sheerness at the entrance to the Medway, sailed up the river and attacked the English naval ships, burning three and capturing a fourth.

A cannon ball which had been fired by the Dutch against Upnor Castle was dredged up from the river, suitably mounted, and presented to the Royal Netherlands Yacht Club by the Medway Yacht Club as a trophy to be competed for between teams of four yachts from each of the two clubs. The British have a tradition of celebrating their defeats, and in 1967 all the main yacht clubs on the river joined together to commemorate the three hundredth anniversary of the Dutch invasion of the Medway by organizing a Dutch Week Regatta. More than sixty Dutch boats, with a naval escort, came over for the week's racing and in company with other yachts we met them in *Meris* at Sheerness to provide an escort up the river to Upnor. Bob Maas, the leading Dutch helmsman, won the race from Holland to England in his sprinter class yacht, *Bem*, and he won the Royal Naval Sailing Association trophy during the week. We were also successful and Miranda attended a reception at Rochester to receive our prize.

When the peace treaty was signed in 1667 the Dutch gave up Sheerness, but the village of Queenborough next to Sheerness was not included. A ceremony was held there when the Dutch sailors paraded in naval uniforms of 1667 and the village was solemnly handed back to the British after 300 years.

The Dutch were entertained every night with dinners and parties. They drank the club bar dry before returning aboard their boats but every morning it was re-stocked as regularly as the milk and papers we delivered to their boats. When we joined our boats in the morning we found that the Dutch had put onboard a case of Heineken beer. At the end of the week they left to sail back to Holland; we escorted them down river and promised to return their visit and race against them in Holland to compete for the Cannonball trophy.

Eight years before the visit of the Dutch fleet two events occurred which led to a change in my life. I failed a medical

196

examination for life insurance because it was discovered that I had a growth in my oesophagus, or gullet, as it is more commonly called. I consulted my doctor, who told me that the X-rays showed the growth was only the size of my thumbnail and he advised me not to do anything about it unless it inconvenienced me. This was probably what the doctor at the village school heard when he examined my chest fifty years before and, in the absence of X-rays, thought I had only one lung. The other event was the news that the Medway Water Board were applying for planning permission to flood the Bewl Valley to create a reservoir where my house and farm were situated.

Although I obtained some relief from my sailing in summer and skiing in winter, the added stress of running my practice single handed caused the growth in my gullet to become active and I was soon fighting on two fronts, for my life and for my home. The growth became so large that it pressed on my lung, I could not breathe properly, and my doctor advised an immediate operation. I had a private room in Nuffield House at Guy's Hospital; I had always paid for private medicine and dental treatment for the family and for the cost of private schooling and university education for the children. After two days on a diet I was given an injection and passed out before being placed on a trolley and wheeled along to the operating theatre to be examined by means of a bronchoscope inserted down my throat into the gullet. I never did see the inside of the operating theatre and when Matron made her rounds the next morning I asked her what they had seen and she replied, 'A lot of pips. You have been eating grapes.' The anaesthetist prepared me for the operation and explained that instead of sawing through the breast bone the surgeon, Professor Brain, would operate from the back, deflating the lung and raising the rib cage to reach the gullet, which could mean forty or fifty stitches but was more likely to be successful in removing such a large growth. After the anaesthetist left there was a knock on the door and a clergyman came in and asked, 'Would you like to take Holy Communion?'

Up to that point I had been quite happy and confident that everything would go well, but seeing the parson raised a doubt in my mind and I do not know whether this influenced my decision when I agreed to his suggestion. He brought in a small table to serve as an altar, laid out the bread and wine, put on his vestments and we celebrated Holy Communion together. After we had prayed I felt at peace, prepared for whatever might happen. The anaesthetist came back, gave me an injection to put me out again and I was taken to the operating theatre. The next thing I knew was sensing a group of people round me, lifting me up, and feeling intense pain, as though a wild animal was tearing me apart with its claws, ripping away the flesh and biting at the inside of my chest. At the same time somebody was shouting and swearing the foulest oaths I had heard sailors use when I went to sea as a boy. I realized it was me; although I had never used those words they must have lain in my subconscious mind. Somebody in the group around me said, 'For God's sake give him another shot'. I felt the prick of a needle in my backside, a warm sea like a tide flooded through my body, I floated off on a white cloud into a wonderful blue sky. Dr Brain telephoned Betty to tell her the operation had been successful and the growth was not malignant. Some days later when he visited me he told me it was as big as a large grapefruit and was now an exhibit in the laboratory at Guys Hospital. I was kept under sedation for four days and when I showed signs of coming to I was given another shot of what I suppose was morphine, especially at night when the nurse who sat at my bedside wanted me to have a good night's sleep. I suspect it was also for the benefit of the nurses on night duty in the ward who came into my room to watch the television I had hired.

When Matron visited me I said to her, 'I hope I was not too much of a nuisance when you were putting me to bed after the operation' and her reply was, 'None of my patients are a nuisance but your threshold of pain was rather low!' I had a great respect for that matron and she certainly lived up to the reputation of the matrons my sisters who had been nurses gave them. She had complete control of her staff and even the doctors stood in awe of her. If she found them in my room she told them, 'Do not touch Mr Brooks. Professor Brain does not like his patients touched.' When she came into the room she ran her finger round the edges of the windows and doors to make sure that the cleaners had done their job, checked the temperature chart and made certain that the prescribed medication had been given.

I was still in great pain when Betty and the children visited me. David had to leave after a short while because the sight of blood and the smell of hospitals always upset him. I arranged with Miranda to collect the post and messages from my office which needed my personal attention and bring them in to me each day, taking back instructions to my staff when she returned to the office. After four days I needed to pass water. I asked the nurse to bring me a bottle but I could not use it lying down. I told her I had to stand upright; she called in two other nurses and they got me to the edge of the bed one each side propped me up and held the flask, which dripped into the veins of my arm high in the air, while the third nurse guided me into the bottle and I was able to relieve myself. They all giggled and laughed when the one holding the flask said, 'I feel like the Statue of Liberty holding her torch up in the air.'

A certain member of the aristocracy whom I had met at the county agricultural shows in the tent of the Country Landowners Association, of which we were both members, was placed in the room next to the one I occupied. Two days later I heard a tremendous row going on in his room. He was shouting, 'What's this rubbish? When am I going to get some real food?' The nurse replied, 'You are here to get your weight and blood pressure down. This is the diet your doctor prescribed.' He shouted back, 'I can't eat this. What's happened to the pheasants my man brought in for me?' The nurse said, 'You are not allowed to have them' and left the room. The next day his Lordship discharged himself.

When my stitches had been taken out, which was a painful process, Betty drove me home to Hook House. After a few weeks I recovered my strength sufficiently to plan a holiday in the sun and Betty and I flew to the Bahamas.

We stayed at the Nassau Beach Hotel with its own private beach close to the town of Nassau, which is also the name of the island and the capital. The most striking aspect of Nassau is the brilliant colours of the blue sky, and buildings, the flowers, the clothes of the people and the various markets, including the dock area where sailing vessels from the neighbouring Out Islands landed their cargoes of vegetables, fish, fruit and conch shells, and the straw market whose stalls are filled with everything imaginable that can be made of straw, straw hats, straw bags, straw toys. The main shopping centre is Bay Street, lined on both sides with quaint shops selling a host of luxury items, watches, jewellery, French perfume and wines, cameras, china, cutlery, cosmetics and women's clothes. At that time the Bahamas was run by the business community who were known as the Bay Street Boys, companies had votes and as each office had hundreds of company registrations on its doors, this enabled them to win the elections. With the coming of independence the business vote has been abolished. Several castles were built on the island as protection against the Spanish and Americans but the most interesting is the ruins of a watchtower used by the notorious pirate Blackbeard; the pirates were not exterminated until the governor hanged eight of the worst of them.

The Bahamas are eighty miles from America and most of the visitors are from the American States, some from the Mid-West who have never seen the sea; when we were on the beach we were even asked if it was safe to paddle in the clear blue water. We sunbathed and swam and I water-skied. I was asked by the young men who ran the water-skiing whether I could manage on one ski. I said I had never tried it and when they suggested I should have a go I said I was not interested. However, they persisted and said that if I could not do it after six runs they would not charge me for them.

Mono-skiing was a new development. There were no special skis then and it involved standing on one ski while being towed by the launch and trying to shake off the second ski to put that foot, when it was freed, behind the foot on the other ski. I made several attempts but I could not complete a successful run back to the beach so it was decided that I had failed and I did not have to pay for them.

The Nassau Beach Hotel was one of the best on the island. The service was excellent and the food was first class but there was too much of it. The steaks over-lapped the plates and the Idaho potatoes were so big they could have supplied enough chips for a whole English family to eat with their fish. The Calypso band which played during dinner and for dancing afterwards was famous for its composition *Yellow Bird*, and was extremely popular.

The American women wore their hair in curlers during the day and took them out in the evening, which I found very strange. I had never run across this habit in a luxury hotel in England. We were the only English people in the hotel and the head waiter always placed us in the middle of the restaurant at dinner so that we could be seen by all the other diners, and when we spoke there was silence while they listened to what we were saying. We were approached by several Americans, who said, 'You speak such beautiful English we have to listen to you'. This was the first time I had been complimented on my speech. My English master would have been pleased to know that all his hard work on a country boy had been worthwhile.

The entertainment in the evening included exhibitions of limbo dancing where the dancer has to bend backwards to get under a rod which is held lower and lower, without touching the ground. It is more an exercise in gymnastics than dancing. The second week we spent in a hotel on Grand Bahama Island from which we made flights to the smaller out islands called 'cays'. On the way back from one of these trips the aeroplane which called to collect us was full up and a small plane carrying six passengers was sent to collect us. The other tourists were American and one small boy said to his father, 'Look Dad, the pilot's a black man. Do you think he can fly this plane?' When we landed the pilot gave me his card and under his name was that of his company, followed by the words, 'Chairman, Chief Pilot, Chief Engineer'. Grand Bahama had a gambling license and a regular air service flew Americans from Miami to the island, where they gambled all night and flew back in the morning.

We had a day deep sea fishing for marlin, tuna and kingfish with another couple who came from Tennesee. The husband spoke in such a strong southern accent that his wife had to translate for us. We sat in the cabin of the motor launch, drinking cold beer, while the helmsman chased after flying fish, hoping to hook one of the larger fish preying on them. One of the crew, who were natives — the owner was a New Zealander — baited our line and when a fish was hooked he called us out of the cabin, strapped us into an armchair at the stern and we took over the rod. It was all like an episode from a film, except that we did not catch any monsters, just two fish of medium size which would have been called large by English standards, but were small by American.

At the end of our holiday we flew back to England to face up to the threat of the loss of our home, Hook House. From the time I first heard of the proposal by the Medway Water

Board to flood the Bewl Valley to create a reservoir, I opposed it, my campaign interrupted only by my stay in hospital. Two surveyors from the water board came onto my land to find sites for boring holes to test whether the sub-soil would hold water. I ordered them off. They said they could get a court order but I told them I would still oppose it. However, other farmers took the £10 a hole they were offered and my land was soon surrounded by bore holes. A committee was formed, of which I was a member. We engaged scientists to advise us on alternative ways of finding water which existed in the underground reservoirs of the chalk and would be safe from pollution, nuclear fall-out and loss from evaporation, and submitted their findings to the water board. We lobbied our MPs and obtained the support of the Ministry of Agriculture, which did not want to see the loss of good farm land.

Arrangements were made for a public enquiry but the water board avoided this by promoting a private bill in the House of Lords, cancelling the public enquiry. The bill had to be fought in the House of Lords, which cost money, and when this was put to the people who were active in opposition they all backed out; after my experience with paying the cost of bringing electricity to the area I might have known how they would react. I decided to go it alone and consulted lawyers who specialized in opposing as well as promoting private bills in Parliament. I paid their costs and they drew up a petition to the Queen, couched in medieval language, in which I told her that I was being oppressed by others of her subjects and begged her to hear my plea and see that justice was done, pointing out that I was her faithful subject who loyally supported the Crown. The Lord Chancellor, acting on behalf of the Queen, therefore appointed five members of the House of Lords to hear my plea against the water board's bill. My lawyers engaged counsel who were experienced in such cases, I was to give evidence and we prepared to do battle. We were defeated before the action started. The Government dropped a bombshell by withdrawing the support of the Ministry of Agriculture from us and saying they proposed to introduce a government bill in the House of Commons on behalf of the water board. I was beaten, there was nothing else I could do. The water board were now determined to get me out and a compulsory purchase order was made on my property.

This was the situation which confronted me when we returned from our holiday in the Bahamas. I appointed a well known firm of estate agents and valuers to act on my behalf in negotiations with the district valuer. I was very disappointed when I learnt that the market value of the farm had not increased since I bought it. Prices did increase later when inflation took off but it was too late for me. The basis of the water board's case had been that water was urgently needed for a rise in the population of the Medway Towns and for the oil refinery being built by BP on the Isle of Grain. Then BP abandoned the oil refinery after a few years when there was excess refining capacity, Chatham Dockyard was closed, together with the naval and marine barracks, reducing the population of the towns, and the town council applied to the Government for a grant as a depressed area. The water board would not agree to us keeping Hook House because they said that the cellar and foundations would be flooded, but it is still there after twenty years, occupied by a tenant. The reservoir has been turned into a leisure centre, the farmworker's cottage is the fishing lodge, hundreds of boats enjoy sailing there in addition to organized boat trips and fishing, bird watching and sponsored walks with toilets and refreshment facilities. I have not been back there but if Queen Mary can say, when the English lost their last stronghold in France after 500 years, that the name of Calais would be found engraved on her heart, then Hook House will be found on mine.

6

THE CLOSING YEARS

I did not have the energy or inclination to look for another house and it all devolved upon Betty to make the effort. Although I had benefited from our holiday in the Bahamas, my operation had left me with a very high blood pressure and difficulty in swallowing my food because my gullet had been narrowed. I had to be very careful what I ate, otherwise I had severe pains in my chest. Remembering how my father looked when he had heart attacks from angina, I used to get up in the night when the pains in my chest were severe and look at myself in the mirror to see whether I had turned blue. After a while I did not bother to look; I went downstairs to get myself a glass of hot water to relieve the pain.

We eventually chose a small house in Cross-in-Hand, a village near Heathfield, halfway between Tunbridge Wells and Eastbourne. It had three bedrooms and I had an extension built to include a studio for Betty and a study for myself, with a shower room and lavatory. It is approached by a drive, with grounds of two and a half acres bounded by a stream, and overlooks the fields of a farm to the south. It is very comfortable, with central heating and double glazing. We do miss the extra rooms and space we had at Hook House, which prevents us from having guests to stay or giving large parties, but I must admit that although we lived at Hook House when Miranda was twenty-one, we gave her a dinner and dance at the Old Barn in Tunbridge Wells instead of at home and David celebrated his twenty-first birthday with a champagne party at Durham University. We did have enough room on the lawn to erect a marquee for Miranda's wedding. The house is called Mariners.

It was built by a naval officer in 1960 and we have not changed the name.

When I returned to the office to supervise my practice I found I could not continue to concentrate for more than two hours and by lunchtime I had such a severe headache that I had to give up and go home. It was no use trying to carry on in that fashion and it was unfair to my clients. I therefore engaged a managing clerk, a chartered accountant with good experience, to run the practice and take the strain off me.

My youngest sister, Barbara, had a stroke which deprived her of her speech, and despite having speech therapy she still could not speak. The effort and frustration of trying to put into words what she was thinking and wished to say brought on another stroke, from which she died. My sister Gladys, who is two or three years younger than I am, was crippled with arthritis when she was forty and had to rely on her husband, Norman, to do everything for her. He became senior night foreman at the engineering company, for which he worked in order that he could look after Gladys and the house during the day. He benefited from his army training and arranged his day to do the housework, cleaning and shopping in the morning when he came home, and after lunch he slept in the afternoon before going back to work in the evening. His company moved their works from Rochester to Strood and he supervised the removal and installation of the plant and machinery from the old factory to the new one. This had to be done with the minimum interruption to production and after it was finished the firm asked him to take two or three weeks' holiday but he refused and continued working. The strain proved too much and he had a heart attack from which he died. Norman had a forceful personality but he was at ease in any company. He was a kind person, always ready to assist anybody who needed help. Gladys moved into a modern flat to be near her daughter, who looks after her, and where she can receive visits from her two granddaughters. We also frequently call to see her and although she cannot go out because of her disability she is always cheerful.

I was approached by John Tyler, whose family owned the Tyler Boat Company at Tonbridge. He told me that one of his customers wished to change his racing cruiser for a smaller boat and asked whether I would be interested. When I found out

Fleetwind racing at Burnham, David (white trousers) checking the spinnaker

that the boat on offer was a new Sprinter Class mark 2 designed by Van de Stadt, a sister ship to *Bem*, the boat owned by Bob Maas the Dutch helmsman, I jumped at the offer and in 1969 exchanged *Meris* for *Fleetwind*, subject to a cash adjustment. *Fleetwind* was thirty-two feet overall with a Royal Ocean Racing Club number 2295. She had accommodation for a crew of five and full equipment for cruising, but as she had not been raced seriously by her previous owners we set about bringing her up to offshore racing standard. I bought a new set of racing sails by Hood, the famous American sailmakers, installed an Electra log distance and speed recorder with twin transducers and auto change, Seafarer echo sounder, Sestral compass, radar reflector and folding propeller. I also added two lifebuoys with McMurdo safety lights, a six man liferaft and an inflatable dinghy.

Fleetwind was not only a fast light displacement racing cruiser but she was a very seaworthy boat, well balanced and easy to handle. She soon showed her paces in our first season, coming in first in all the three races for which she was entered and winning the Medway Regatta Cruiser Championship.

Instead of going to Burnham to end the season we decided to race at Cowes Week. It was a year for the Admiral's Cup races and it was very exciting to sail at the same time as the international teams. Pauline Lashmar, who had crewed for me on the Medway and was staying at the Isle of Wight on holiday joined us, and although we were not familiar with the courses we acquitted ourselves well in the three races which we entered, coming fifth in the Queens Cup, fourth in the Festival of Britain Challenge Cup and fifth in the Coronation Bowl, bearing in mind the number of yachts in each race; for example the Coronation Bowl had forty-seven entries. When we were not racing we sailed along the coast and up to Beaulieu for the day. Some things I did not like about Cowes. It was too congested, we had to have moorings in the Hamble river, because there were none available at Cowes, and sail to and fro for the races. It was only possible to use one of the yacht clubs, the Island Sailing Club, because the other clubs reserved entry for members only and their guests, in contrast to Burnham where all visiting yachtsmen are made honorary members of the clubs, and there was no racing out at sea as there is with East Anglian offshore races because the Cowes racing for our class was confined to the stretch of water between the Isle of Wight and the mainland.

However, it was an experience, although I did not particularly want to repeat it.

I planned a very full programme of racing for 1970, starting with a Royal Navy Sailing Association Race out to the Thames Estuary, in which we came first but were placed fourth on our handicap. We sailed up to Burnham for the start of the race for the Ralph Herring Trophy. Jane, David's girlfriend who later became his wife, joined us and soon became a first class crew, earning her name of 'Muscles Maynard'. The race was from Burnham to West Mersea and after allowing for our handicap we were placed ninth out of twenty-two starters. We returned to Burnham for the Thames Estuary race back to the Medway in which we came second. Our next race was for the Jane's Cup from Upnor to Burnham, coming first in our division and helping the Medway Yacht Club team win the cup. Immediately after the Medway Regatta we sailed to Harwich for the start of the North Sea Race to Ostend. Miranda was a great help in our navigation because she remembered the Morse code she learnt when she was a Girl Guide and was able to pick up the signals from the different radio beacons and identify them. A new member of our crew was a young man named Simon Lyle who took Betty's place. Whilst we were away Betty stayed at a health hydro in Bexhill and when our friends asked why she was not with us we said we had put her in a home.

When we arrived off Ostend at dawn the wind dropped light and we had a frustrating wait outside the harbour for the wind to pick up and the tide to change before we could reach the finishing line. The larger yachts were able to save their tide; several of the yachts in our class gave up but we stayed on and came seventh. The North Sea race was intended as a preliminary to proceeding on to Holland and fulfilling our promise to take part in the Flevo races but the next morning there was a thick fog and I decided to wait until it cleared. The crew nearly staged a mutiny. They argued we would be late for the races and that we would be letting the British team down if we were not in time to join our team competing against the Dutch for the Cannonball trophy. I had to remind them I was captain and I was not going to risk the ship by crossing the entrance to Rotterdam in a thick fog, running the risk of being hit by the cargo vessels and tankers using the port. The crew spent a miserable day waiting for the fog to lift but by the evening they relented and entertained me to a slap up dinner. The wine flowed freely and when we went back on board Simon misjudged the distance and fell from the quay to the deck, fortunately without injuring himself. The next morning the fog had cleared and we set sail with a fair wind. I stood well off the coast until we passed Rotterdam and when Miranda picked up the radio signals from Ijmuiden we altered course and came into the harbour to enter the North Sea Canal.

After fourteen miles passing through locks and several bridges we reached Muiden to tie up at the Royal Netherlands Yacht club and get race instructions and a chart of the Ijsselmeer. The other three yachts of the British team were already there and we were greeted with cries of, 'Where have you been? We thought you were never coming'. But I pointed out we still had a day in hand before the Flevo races started.

Our team consisted of *Xuxu*, owned by D.C. Barham, *Morning Jade*, sailed by R.G. Hollands, which was a sistership to Ted Heath's *Morning Cloud*, myself with *Fleetwind* and the smallest boat, *Puffe*, owned by L.E. Landamore. The Flevo races were run on three days, the yachts racing to a different fishing port on the Ijsselmeer each day. The result of the competition for the De Ruyter Cannon Ball Challenge Trophy was decided on the total number of points scored by each team in the Flevo races.

The day after we arrived my crew visited Amsterdam to spend the day sightseeing, but David and Jane stayed on board to work out the courses to be sailed and make a note of the sailing instructions. When we returned in the evening one of the Dutch officials asked us, 'Did you see the hippies in the square?' These hippies lounged about all day smoking pot, photographed by tourists, and he was very surprised when we replied, 'No. We went to the Rijksmuseum to look at the Rembrandt and Vermeer paintings'.

One hundred and twenty-one yachts took part in the Flevo races, divided into ten classes starting at fifteen minute intervals. There were eighteen yachts in our class and this made the starting line crowded, especially with the next class coming up behind for their start, and once the whole fleet was underway trying to avoid one hundred and twenty yachts while keeping an eye on Bob Maas in *Bem*, which we had to beat if our team was to win the Cannonball Trophy. On arriving at the fishing villages we were entertained at dinner by the inhabitants and the visiting yachtsmen until it was time to go back aboard and get some sleep ready for the next day's race.

The first two days there were light winds and we could only come second to *Bem*, as Bob Maas was able to demonstrate what a superb helmsman he was. The next morning, at the start of the third and final days' racing, the winds were again light but they gradually strengthened and developed into a strong blow. We had to win the last race if we were going to gain the trophy and although the wind was on the quarter and not dead astern we set our spinnaker. *Fleetwind* heeled over and we simply romped away; I am at my best in a strong wind. It was rather dangerous. Jane was apprehensive because she had not raced under these conditions before, but it was exhilarating and exciting and I was sure that the boat would stand up to it if the crew could. They held on to the spinnaker with Simon singing 'Jolly surfing weather' to the tune of the Eton boating song and we crossed the finishing line well ahead of *Bem* and the rest of our class. The final result for the three days racing was British team fifty points, Netherlands team forty-nine points, so we had won the Cannon Ball Trophy. As Wellington said after Waterloo, 'It was a near run thing', and like the soldiers at Waterloo it was won by the crew, under David's direction and encouragement.

After celebrating our success in the traditional yachtsmen's manner we left Muiden to sail back down the North Sea Canal to Ijmuiden and when we had cleared the harbour Miranda set a course for Ostend. We had an easy sail along the coast and arrived off Ostend harbour at eight o'clock the next morning, where we spent the next two days. We left Ostend at four o'clock in the morning of 13 August for Ramsgate with a light wind, and when we sailed through a shoal of mackerel we put a line overboard with a hook on a spinner and soon pulled a dozen on board. Jane gutted them but there was so much blood washing about in the cockpit that some of the crew had lost their appetite when she cooked the fish for lunch. We reached Ramsgate in the evening and tied up alongside the outer harbour wall to await the arrival of the customs officers. When they came on board I told them we had nothing to declare. They went below to search the boat and asked for our ship's papers. When I handed them over, the customs officer examined the passports, looked at us and then said, 'Where is the coloured girl?' We called out, 'Come on Jane' and when she came forward the official did not know how to hide his embarrassment. Jane had been born in Malawi, where her father was in the colonial service and after that episode we dropped the name 'Muscles Maynard' and she became our little 'Picanini', which suited her much better.

The Royal Temple Yacht Club Regatta ran two races for which we had entered, one on Saturday, 15 August, round the Goodwins and the other on Sunday for the Ramsgate Gold Cup. Several of our friends were in Ramsgate for the regatta and the night before the Round the Goodwins race there was a big party at the club. When we reached the starting line and hoisted our sails empty Alka Seltser bottles clattered on to the deck and the crew were feeling rather the worse for wear. However, we had quite a good start and were well placed in our class but it was a long race over fifty-two miles and the wind gradually fell away to nothing. We were sailing against the tide and only two of the larger boats were able to round the outer mark and take advantage of the favourable tide on the way back when the wind ceased. We had to anchor to prevent the tide carrying us backwards. We waited for the wind to pick up but in the end we had to retire, together with seven other boats in our class, only two of the larger boats managing to complete the course out of the ten who entered. The crew pulled my leg, saying they heard the ghostly voices of my two cousins who were drowned when their ship was wrecked on the Goodwin Sands calling out to us, 'Keep away, Reuben. Don't come here. You are in danger'. Perhaps they were right. The following morning a full gale was blowing and the majority of the boats decided it was too rough to go out. The entrance to Ramsgate harbour can be dangerous when there is a strong wind because the tide runs across the entrance and it is difficult to keep a boat lined up in the channel when entering or leaving. The Royal Engineers had to show their mettle by going out and we all went down to stand on the harbour wall and watch them leave. They had their storm sails set and their engine running at full speed to try and get out of the harbour entrance but three times they were thrown back by the force of the waves crashing the boat against the harbour wall. Every time they tried we gave them a cheer and urged them on until eventually they managed to get out, but at what cost to their boat I hate to think. Betty drove

211

over from Bexhill to see us at Ramsgate and we arranged for her to meet us at Burnham where we planned to finish the season.

We had an uneventful sail from Ramsgate to Burnham, carrying the ebb tide to the Whitaker and the flood tide up the River Crouch. Although we had made this journey several times before at low water it was still interesting to watch the seals basking on the sand banks and the wading birds on the flats. We had our usual moorings with Petticrows opposite the Royal Corinthian Club house and this year Ted Heath's yacht *Morning Cloud*, a larger boat, had the mooring next to us. Instead of staying in a hotel we had in recent years, when I owned cruisers, rented a house in the town where all the family could stay. The social events were concentrated at the Royal Corinthian, starting with a champagne reception and continuing with dinner and dancing every night for the rest of the week. The other clubs gave special dinners for the classes of yachts they sponsored. We enjoyed the racing; we didn't win any prizes; perhaps it was a reaction after our efforts in the Flevo races. Ted Heath was very successful.

In a larger boat it was usual to have a tactician who advised the helmsman what course to steer and another man in charge of the crew, deciding what sails to use, trimming and tuning them to the wind, in addition to a navigator. On our boat I was the tactician, David looked after the crew and sails while I shared the navigation with him and Miranda. I was never a pot hunter, although we won our share of prizes, and I preferred racing to cruising, but David was very competitive. When Betty was not quick enough to obey his instructions he caught hold of her by the scruff of the neck and yanked her up on deck, but this did not do much good because they both collapsed with laughter.

We sailed back to Upnor and I laid the boat up for the winter. Although I did not know it this was to be our last Burnham Regatta. David received confirmation that he had a place at the University of Western Ontario and would be emigrating to Canada and Miranda also left for Canada the next year with three girl friends to work in Toronto. I sold *Fleetwind* and following our usual custom we have never been back to Burnham. We had been to the Algarve years before and we decided to take another holiday there with Miranda before she

Villa Luz Bay, Algarve. Betty with Gwen Passmore
on balcony

left for Canada. An airport had been built at Faro since our last visit and we were able to fly there and hire a car to drive westwards and we stayed at a small hotel on the seaside called Donna Anna, near Lagos. We explored the countryside and beaches and found some villas being built at Luz Bay, a village with a beautiful sandy beach enclosed on one side by hills and on the other by rocks, on which stood an old fortress.

The villas were being built by an Englishman whose family had been established in the port wine trade for centuries, and I decided to buy one. We spent time each summer at Donna Anna watching our villa being built and visiting the local workshops and warehouses with an Englishwoman who was an interior designer, choosing fabrics and furniture to match the decor of the typical Portuguese building with its Algarve chimney. There were three double bedrooms downstairs with showers, a bathroom and lavatories and upstairs were the kitchen and utility room and a large living and dining room, opening out onto a veranda overlooking the sea. We had the gardens landscaped and planted with the colourful semi-tropical flowers which grew locally and called the villa Casa Miranda. A Portuguese folk story relates how a king in the old days married a princess from Norway and when she cried because she missed the snow of her native land, he had hundreds of almond trees planted so that their white blossoms would remind her of home, and we included an almond tree in our garden.

Since my operation my doctor had continually pointed out the danger of my very high blood pressure, insisting I should retire, and in 1972 I sold my practice to my managing clerk and resigned all my appointments. I could have amalgamated my practice with another firm, but this would have meant my staying on in the profession and I also thought that by transferring my practice to my managing clerk it would provide continuity and a better service for my clients. After the death of Tom Metcalf in 1970 a new managing director was appointed on a three year contract to run the Metcalf Shipping organization which Tom and I had built up. He had been head-hunted from another company as a professional manager without any experience in shipping and after six months his previous employers wanted him to return to their organization. He obtained the consent of the Metcalf family to dispose of the assets and realize the capital locked up in their business. He sold the wharves at Greenwich and Gravesend, the warehouse and land at Newhaven, the factory at Stevenage and finally the shipbroking business and fleet of modern cargo vessels and tankers, the last one having been built just a few months before the sale. This automatically released the managing director from his contract and he was able to return to his former employer. A year later Betty and I were invited by the Metcalfs to a family luncheon party. We had been friends for forty years and it was a happy occasion to see them all again. We talked about old times and during the course of our conversation they told me how unhappy they were with the result of the sale of the family business. The income they received from the sale of their shares did not match up to the generous salaries they had received as non-executive directors of the company, together with the large dividends they were paid on their shares. They asked me if I would again undertake the management of all their financial affairs but I pointed out that I could not change the agreement they had signed for the sale of the family business, although I had every sympathy with their predicament, and at this stage Betty told them that I was still a sick man with a very high blood pressure, that my doctor had told me not to take on any more work and she could not agree that I should accept responsibilities which would put me under further stress. I therefore declined their offer, but we still see our friends, who live locally at Brighton.

In the spring of 1970, before the sailing season started, Betty and I flew to Paris for two weeks' holiday. We stayed at the Hotel Bradford near the Champs Elysées and bought a book of tickets for the Metro which we used to travel to the various parts of the city instead of using taxis. We visited the art exhibitions, the Louvre of course, the Matisse exhibition which was being staged at the Grand Palais, the Museum of Modern Art and the painters' studios at Montmartre. We did not buy any paintings there but when we were dining at a restaurant one evening a young Japanese came to our table with a folio of pictures which he said he had painted to support himself whilst he was studying in Paris. Betty was always ready to help a fellow artist and bought one of his paintings, which we showed to a friend when we returned to England. She lived in Hong Kong and said that similar paintings could be bought there for next to nothing.

In France it is always best to make use of the services offered by the concierge at the hotel. The concierges were established by Napoleon to spy on people living in the apartments, hotels and inns and report to the police, as part of his policy to control the country. Now they are a mine of information and a great help to visitors. The concierge at our hotel, the daughter of the proprietress, booked lunch and dinner at the restaurants we chose so that there was always a table waiting for us, however crowded they might be, obtained tickets for the show at the Lido night club, despite the number of Americans who were clamouring to get in, reserved our seats for the midnight supper and cruise on the River Seine and arranged our excursions to places outside Paris. We saw the Eiffel Tower, but we did not go up to the top because Betty does not like heights. We also saw the site of the Bastille — there are no ruins — the Petit Palais, the Invalides and tomb of Napoleon, the Arc de Triomphe, the cathedral of Notre Dame, and the market of Les Halles.

On our excursions we visited the palace of Versailles with its wonderful gardens and fountains, where a student conducted us round, condemning the kings who had established it, until I got fed up with her comments and told her that if the monarchs had not built the place she would be out of a job. We went to Fontainebleu, situated in the middle of the forest, and also to Barbizon, the artists' village. We visited Chartres and admired the stained glass windows dating from the Middle Ages, particularly the famous Rose Window, glowing in the rays of the sun when we were there. Our last excursion was to Rheims, where we explored the caves belonging to Moët et Chandon and sampled their champagne.

Owing to its rapid expansion the Medway Yacht Club ran into financial difficulties and the committee could not agree on the measures to be taken to remedy the situation. I had always refused to serve on the committee I am too independent to be a good committee man, but I agreed to become a member of a small sub-committee of three comprising myself, the club treasurer, and John Clay, an investment banker with Hambros, to examine the club's finances and make recommendations to put them on a sound footing. We completed our investigation and advised the committee that subscriptions and other charges, for example the cost of moorings, should be increased by fifteen per cent and that the price of drinks and meals should have a corresponding increase because to attempt economies would mean a lowering of standards. The committee accepted our report and acted on it, our sub-committee was dissolved and I later resigned from the club, as I was without a boat and I did not want to become a barfly.

After selling my boat I bought a motor caravan for touring on land after cruising at sea. It was well fitted out with four berths, cooker, fridge, water tank, lavatory and plenty of cupboard space and lockers. It was powered by a Bedford engine and it was naturally heavier to drive than a car, but Betty could manage it and she earned the admiration of bystanders abroad who watched her parking the vehicle in a congested space. It was also much admired by people who stared into the windows to examine it when we stopped. We used it as a backup on our tours, sleeping in it when we could not find a hotel we liked. David and Jane were married in 1971 and we lent them our caravan for their honeymoon, touring the West Country and visiting Jane's relatives.

In 1972 we flew to Canada to stay with David and Jane for a long holiday in the summer. We flew by BOAC, or British Airways as it is now called, on a VC10 which did not receive the recognition it deserved, some people saying British Airways had to be pressured into buying it by the Government. But we met Americans on the aircraft who had changed their flights from American Boeings to fly on the VC10 because they considered it a better aircraft. One of the pilots on our aircraft was a friend of Miranda's, Tony Colin, and I was invited on to the flight deck for the duration of the flight. The VC10 carried a crew of four, not counting cabin staff, two pilots, a flight engineer and a navigator. I was particularly interested in the navigation across the Atlantic and when the navigator had plotted his position on the chart he called up an American aircraft flying level with us, told them our position and asked them for a check. The American replied, 'Hold on a minute while I press a few buttons', then came back and said, 'You're dead right pal'. We landed at Toronto and entertained Tony Colin to dinner at our hotel. The following morning David picked us up in his car with Jane and their baby, a little boy who had been born in England at Cuckfield, when I paid for Jane to come over so that she could be near her family for the birth of her first child.

We drove up to the Northern Lakes to stay at a cottage owned by one of David's friends. David had hired a camper to tow behind the car but on the way up the mountains the car's gear box gave out and we had to get a lift to the cottage. I paid to have a new gear box fitted, but we decided not to risk towing the camper any more and I said I would pay for all of us to stay in motels during the rest of our trip. David and Jane had gone to a lot of trouble to plan the holiday and after leaving the cottage we drove to Niagara to stay in a hotel owned by an English couple at Niagara on the lake, which had a Bernard Shaw season at their local theatre every year. We crossed over Niagara into New York State — the view of the falls is better from the Canadian side — continued on to Vermont with its splendid scenery and took a cable car ride to the top of the mountains to admire the magnificent view of the forests stretching away into the distance. Some of the most pleasant sights are the white clapboard houses and churches of the villages in the New England states, with their well kept gardens in the green countryside, spaced out between the trees, conveying an impression of quiet prosperity.

When we reached Maine we took the opportunity of having a swim in the sea but although it was midsummer it was very rough and icy cold, so it was a case of quick in and out. From Maine we re-entered Canada and the province of New Brunswick, where we were surprised to see exhibited as antiques in a museum there kitchen objects which were still in use in England. We took the ferry over to Prince Edward Island, but because it was holiday time we found it difficult to obtain accommodation, although we had no trouble staying in motels and guest houses in the United States. The tourist office arranged for us to stay with the family of a sergeant in the Royal Canadian Mounted Police, where we were made very welcome.

It was harvest festival time on the island but instead of being devoted to the produce of the land it was a lobster festival. Each parish provided a lobster supper laid on by the ladies' comprising homemade soup, a main course of lobsters, followed by homemade apple pie and cream. As these meals were provided on different days some visitors went round each parish in turn and had a lobster supper every night. We returned on the ferry to New Brunswick and crossed over the St Lawrence river to

Quebec and met Miranda who had rented an apartment for us there. We explored the old parts of the city, which were very French and included an artists' quarter where we bought a drawing, and we had our meals in typical French restaurants. I visited the ramparts and the Heights of Abraham where Wolfe defeated the French army under Montcalm to bring Canada under British rule.

After spending a day in Ottawa looking round the Government buildings we drove to Stratford on Avon in a car Miranda had borrowed from a friend and went to the theatre there to see *The Tuppenny Opera* with a mainly English cast headed by Anton Rogers. On the way back to Toronto late at night the car Miranda had borrowed broke down but we were rescued by a police car which drove us all the way home. In the morning Miranda telephoned her friend to tell him that the car had to be abandoned on the roadside and he said, 'Just leave it there. I don't want it'. In Toronto we bought an eskimo carving in whale bone of a mother and child, before leaving to catch our flight home. I gave all the dollars I had left to David and Miranda. Tony Colin had arranged to be one of the pilots and I was again invited to travel on the flight deck. What impressed me most was the intense concentration of the pilot on the take off at Toronto and the landing at Heathrow; he was one of the most experienced men in the company.

After skiing in the winter we spent the spring and autumn in our villa in Portugal, leaving the summer free for other activities. Rob and Gwen Passmore were the first of our friends to stay with us in Portugal and we took them to all the interesting places we had discovered and the best beaches. Most of these were to the west of Lagos because since the airport had been built at Faro most of the development on the Algarve was taking place in that area. The only hotel anywhere near us was the Penina where Henry Cotton had built two golf courses and remained as golfing manager, entertaining all the golfing enthusiasts.

We were very fond of swimming and the empty sandy beaches washed by the Atlantic rollers were ideal. I have swum in the Mediterranean off beaches in Spain, France, Italy, Greece, Turkey and North Africa, but they are crowded, very often polluted because it is an inland sea, and without the feeling of space and freshness of the Atlantic. We took our friends to Lagos, with its old houses still bordered by the remains of the ancient city walls, and the church of St Anthony with its gold painted altar. Queen Elizabeth sent her favourite, the Earl of Essex, with an English fleet to Lagos to capture the Spanish ships which were thought to be harbouring their but when Essex arrived they had gone so he sacked the town and stole a library of ancient books, much to the annoyance of Queen Elizabeth and the anger of the Portuguese, who were our old allies.

We went as far as Cape Trafalgar. Nearby at Sagres Prince Henry had established a school of navigation. The lighthouse at Cape St Vincent, scene of a famous British naval victory, is stated to have the strongest light in Europe. The cliffs have a sheer drop to the Atlantic ocean below and the men fishing from the top have a long pull up the face of the cliffs to land the sea bass they catch, losing some which seize the opportunity on the way of jerking themselves free off the hook.

We drove to Monchique in the hills about twenty miles from the coast and visited the quiet of the leafy glade where the Caldas De Monchique is situated. The water from the spring was once distributed by pedlars using carts but this mineral water is now supplied from a bottling plant to outlets all over Europe. Silves is an historical town perched on the mountainside which we took our friends to see. It was the Moorish capital of the Algarve until it was captured by British crusaders, led by Don Sancho 1st, whose massive statue is inside the ruins of the great red sandstone fortress which dominates the town, and close by is the cathedral containing tombs of the crusaders. It is said that the crusaders landed at Portimao before attacking the Moors at Silves. Now it is the main fishing port of the Algarve, where the catches of sardines are landed and canned to be sold. We did not see any bull fights in the Algarve because they are usually held in the summer. The bulls are not killed, they are tormented and irritated until they are tired and then led from the ring.

In the restaurants there is sometimes a performance by a fado singer, usually accompanied by two guitars. Fado is a sad sweet song, moving and melancholy in contrast to the bright tuneful Italian music. The restaurants, boutiques and art galleries were nearly all owned by English people with a smattering of Americans; we bought some pottery and two small figures on horseback.

As Rob Passmore was fond of good food and wine we took

him to a different restaurant each evening which we had used before, and knew that it would come up to his standard. At one small restaurant noted for its cooking he was served with two soles which were fresh from the Atlantic and are smaller than the Dover sole he is used to. He remarked in the hearing of the proprietress that he had never seen such small soles, and when we ordered our brandies the waiter brought Rob a triple over saying, 'A large brandy for a large gentleman with the compliments of the management'. After one slight delay on the way Rob managed the walk back to our villa.

When Betty's mother and her brother, Peter, and sister, Glenys, came out to the Algarve it was the first time Betty's mother had flown in an aeroplane. When one of her friends asked her, 'Aren't you afraid of flying?' she replied, 'At my age what have I got to be afraid of?' She was always willing to try a new experience and she thoroughly enjoyed her holiday with us. There are so many places of interest and monuments that it is difficult to see all of them on a short holiday, but as we spent quite a lot of time at our villa we came to know the Algarve well. There is a little church between Faro and Almasil that not many people see, dedicated to Sao Lourenco, where tiles depict his fate while being burned to death on a grid iron; he is supposed to have said, 'Please turn me, for I am already done on this side'. We always used our caravan for touring on the Continent, taking a different route each time across France and Portugal to reach the Algarve.

I was still unsettled since leaving Hook House and although we were very comfortable at Mariners I was continually looking for another house which might match up to Hook House and provide me with another interest. Now that I was retired I could live anywhere; I looked upon the villa in the Algarve purely as a holiday home, and as I had business interests in Jersey and the Isle of Man we flew there on holiday to look at houses which might suit us but Betty decided against them. She always considered Jersey and the Isle of Man were foreign countries and she had been warned by a fortune teller that she would die in a foreign land if she lived abroad. We toured Scotland and Wales again, going to John O'Groats in the extreme north and visiting a small castle in the Highlands which was for sale. It stood on a hill overlooking the valley and had at one time been the stronghold of 'The wolf of Badenoch', a robber chieftain who raided and terrorized his neighbours. This appealed to my romantic nature. It had been modernized and made into a comfortable home whilst retaining its historical character but Betty decided it was too far away from her family. In Wales we inspected a manor house at one time owned by Owen Glendower, which I liked and would have bought, but Betty said when we were looking round the gardens a ghost kept jostling her from behind and the housekeeper confirmed that years ago a murder had been committed in the house. Betty's family were Welsh, her maiden name was Jones, and I thought a home in Wales might appeal to her, but she turned it down, although her elder sister, Peggy, has since returned to live in Wales.

In 1974 Miranda came back from Canada to take over the business I had bought for her at Shoreham. She joined us for a skiing holiday in St Anton but Betty unfortunately broke her leg and we were not able to visit the Algarve that year.

In 1975 David decided to sail his yacht across the Atlantic to England and I flew to Canada to help him with his preparations, having previously sent him the additional gear he needed. I did not want to sail across the Atlantic with him which I thought would be too monotonous on a small boat for a month with nothing to look at but the sea, and it was therefore decided that David, Jane and I should sail the yacht down Lake Huron, where David would return to finish his term at school, and Jane and I would continue on to New York, a distance of approximately 1,000 miles, and leave the boat there, ready for the crossing to England.

Jane and I sailed the yacht into Lake Erie and met two massive twisting waterspouts on the way which sucked the water from the surface of the lake to a height of hundreds of feet into the air. We took the sails down, closed everything up, switched on the engine and steered away from the path the waterspouts were taking, hoping they would not change course. When we reached the end of Lake Erie we had to negotiate the locks by-passing Niagara Falls. It is necessary to get into the right channel three miles before reaching the locks, otherwise the boat would be carried along by the water rushing towards the falls and swept over the top to be smashed to pieces at the bottom. When we reached the locks we had to wait while a cargo vessel came through; these ships are specially built to fit into the locks with only about two feet to spare either side and fore and aft, and are designed to carry a full cargo of grain from the farms in the Mid-West. We entered the lock and as the water was drained out we sank lower and lower into a dank dark chasm. It was a fall of about sixty feet. We did not have a rope of this length and the men at the top had to lower ropes which we hung on to in order to stop the boat being thrown against the lock gates where the water was being pumped out. We reached the bottom at last, the lock gates were opened and we emerged into the sunlight and fresh air of Lake Ontario.

We sailed during the day and tied up at night, usually finding a small yacht haven or wharf where we could take on fuel and water and buy stores. Everybody was very helpful. On one occasion the man who helped us moor took us into the village and knocked up the owner of the village stores at twelve o'clock at night to serve us. Another time we had a lift in a funeral car, smelling of embalming fluid, to take us to the nearest shop. We called into Rochester on our way through Lake Ontario and entered the marina owned by the Rochester Yacht Club. This was a great contrast to the places we had previously stopped at, an attendant took our lines to moor the boat, came aboard and furled the sails, arranged for the holding tanks to be pumped out and the water and fuel tanks to be topped up. When we came ashore we were greeted by the commodore, who was most interested when we told him we came from Rochester in England. The club was like a country club, with spacious lounges, bars and restaurant, tennis courts and swimming pool in addition to the marina and stores selling everything a yachtsman could require. We had a hot shower, which was a luxury for us, changed into clean clothes and had dinner in the restaurant. Before we left the next day I thanked the commodore for his hospitality. He presented me with one of his club's burgees and I promised to arrange for a Medway Yacht club burgee to be sent to him in return. The USA club's flag now hangs in the lounge of the Medway Yacht Club with dozens of other clubs' various designs and colours which have been collected over the years.

We left Lake Ontario at Oswego and entered the Oswego river which led into the Erie Canal and then the Mohawk river. We fell in with an elderly man who had just retired and was taking his yacht down to Chesapeake Bay with his teenage grandson as crew. He had travelled the same route before and knew the places where we could stop the night and when we had to take down our mast to pass under the bridges. His grandson was a great help constructing a cradle in which to stow it. The Mohawk joined the Hudson River at Albany and we were now on our way to New York, passing Hyde Park, Franklin D. Roosevelt's home and West Point Military Academy, still stopping every night on the way.

When we reached New York we tied up at a wharf on the opposite side of the river at New Jersey to take on fuel and when the pump attendant asked us where we were bound we hold him, 'England'. The man called his foreman over and said, 'Hey boss! Them guys are going to England on that little boat'. The foreman said, 'Yeah, them Englishmen live on an island, they're all good sailors'. I felt it was all worth our long trip to hear somebody say that. The night before we parted company from our friend and his grandson we had a party aboard our yacht. Jane went ashore and bought some beer and snacks, and we had a very jolly evening and invited them to visit us in England if they came over on a holiday.

It reminded me of London to see the empty warehouses and derelict wharves lining the river bank when we passed New York. It was a grey overcast day. The Atlantic Terminal where the ocean liners used to tie up was deserted and altogether it was a depressing picture; even the Statue of Liberty holding up a broken torch was in need of repair and the deserted buildings on Ellis Island completed the atmosphere of decay and neglect as we sailed by.

We tied up at the yacht club on Staten Island at the end of our two week journey and arranged for the boat to be cared for until David could join it with his crew for the voyage to England. I could not have wished for a better crew than Jane and I was confident that she would be an ideal companion for David's trip across the Atlantic and provide the support he would need. Having safely delivered the boat we now had to get back to Canada. We caught a bus from Staten Island to New York and walked across the city to the Greyhound Coach Terminal through very run down streets with sex shops, places showing blue films, overflowing dustbins and suspicious looking characters lounging against the doorways, but we were not afraid of being mugged; we had our old sailing clothes on and carried our gear. We must have looked as if we needed a few coppers ourselves. We booked seats on the coach for Canada, a distance of about 800 miles. We slept part of the way and stopped twice for meals until we arrived home.

David sailed across the Atlantic and telephoned us when he arrived at Falmouth. Betty drove down to Falmouth with me and I joined David to sail with him to the Medway. He stayed a year, teaching at Tenterden School in Kent, but he was under constant pressure to return to Huron High School and he sold his boat and returned to Canada with Jane.

We went to our villa in the Algarve for the autumn. After the death of Dr Salazar, the right wing ruler of Portugal, the socialists took over the government in a revolution which altered the course of Portuguese politics. The British and Americans shut up their shops, abandoned their restaurants and property developments and left the Algarve. We stayed on; the only difference which affected us directly was the rise in wages which meant that we no longer had our personal maid. The cleaning being organized on a group basis, our washing was sent to a laundry instead of being done by our maid, and our garden was maintained by outside contractors. Miranda and Stuart were married in the spring of the following year and Betty and I spent a long holiday at our villa in the autumn, travelling to all the places we knew and noticing the effects of the revolution on the various aspects of life in the Algarve. We did not much like what we saw and in the following spring we gave Portugal a miss and flew to Rhodes for a holiday instead.

We stayed in Rhodes Town at a hotel which was the former summer palace of the King of Greece. It is really two towns, the medieval old town surrounded by the new with hotels and modern shops. The old town is encircled by battlements and palm tree gardens adjoining the harbour where the Collossus of Rhodes once spanned the entrance but which now has the statue of a deer on each side. The main street separating the citadel from the old town's maze of narrow rambling alleys is lined with open fronted shops like one big bazaar, selling gold and silver articles, rugs, clothing, pottery and leather goods which heightens its resemblance to an eastern market. The main sights are inside the medieval citadel — the Hospital of the Knights housing the island's archaeological treasures, the Palace of the Grand Masters, and the Street of the Knights with beautifully restored Gothic inns, one for each of the countries supplying a contingent of nights for the crusades, including England. The governor of the island, appointed by the Italians during the war, was an architect in civilian life and he had the buildings in the citadel repaired and restored.

Further along the coast is Lindos, a town of vivid white houses set against the honey coloured stones of a sheer cliff with the acropolis on top, and at the bottom of the hill a harbour with a sandy beach for bathing. We toured the mountains, including a valley containing a large number of butterflies, and villages where the inhabitants wore Russian boots as a protection against snakes, and bought a plate from a village pottery on which was depicted the tree of life.

We returned to the Algarve in the autumn and were unhappy to see the continued deterioration in standards. The restaurants which had previously been owned by foreigners were now run by Portuguese, the food was uninspiring, the service bad and the lavatories neglected. The villas which had been put up for sale and bought by Portuguese needed painting, and their gardens were overgrown. A café had been built on the beach — the Portuguese are not the tidiest people — and it was surrounded by empty and broken bottles and other rubbish. A small bay which we had discovered could only by approached by a hole in the rocks, leading to a tunnel to the beach. This had been bulldozed out and a bar constructed in the cave, again with its litter of empty bottles. These were some of the things which decided us that it was time to go and we put the villa up for sale in the hands of the club which looked after it for us. They wanted to find a purchaser who would allow them to maintain the villa and the garden to the same standard but they were unsuccessful and in 1979 I sold it to a Portuguese family. The Government in Portugal took months before they gave permission for the money from the sale to be exported to England. In the meantime the Conservatives had taken over the Government, freed the currency exchange of control and abolished the dollar premium, which had the effect of cutting in half the money I received from the sale of the villa. I wrote to the Chancellor of the Exchequer pointing out that I had been refused permission by the Portuguese Government to bring my money to England, sent him the documents to prove it, and asked to be allowed the dollar premium, but he said that he could not make an exception in my case and refused my request. That was the second time — the first being the compulsory purchase of Hook House — that the Government had deprived me of what should have been due to me.

We sold the villa complete with all the furniture, pictures, carpets, linen, cutlery, glasses, crockery and utensils but before handing it over we made one last visit to collect our clothes and personal belongings. Betty and I sailed on the car ferry with our caravan from England to Spain, landing at the port of Bilbao. The weather was fine, the sea was calm as we cruised across the Bay of Biscay along the French coast. From Bilbao we drove to Santander and on to Corunna where Sir John Moore was killed in a battle with the French to hold the port and allow the British troops to be embarked by the Royal Navy for England. Wellington later landed another army in Portugal to drive the French from Spain and history was repeated in the war with Germany when the British army evacuated from Dunkirk by the Royal Navy and invaded France again in Normandy. We continued on the coast road to Oporto where we stopped at a hotel for the night and the following morning visited the lodge owned by Warre, the port wine shippers. After seeing how the wine was matured in huge vats we were seated at an upturned empty cask, a plate of dry biscuits was placed in front of us and we were given a glass of each type of wine in turn, starting with young ruby port and proceeding through all the various ages to old vintage port. We had eaten all the biscuits. Despite this I was feeling rather uncertain about driving, but it was still only ten o'clock in the morning and my head gradually cleared. We arrived at Lisbon late at night, feeling very tired, and decided to stay at a hotel in the middle of the town. I parked the van in the hotel car park where the night porter could keep his eye on it, locked it up, and left our cases inside, taking only overnight bags into the hotel. When we went out to the caravan in the morning we found it had been broken into and our cases had been stolen together with the radio and camera. Apparently during the night a tourist coach had drawn up between our van and the doorway of the hotel, obscuring the porter's view, and the thieves had seized the opportunity to break into our vehicle under cover of the coach. I spent all the morning at the police station reporting the theft and trying to obtain a certificate from them which my insurance company would require before paying out on the claim. It was very difficult because I did not speak Portuguese and the police did not speak English so we had to carry on a three way telephone conversation with an interpreter on another line.

I eventually got my certificate and we spent the rest of the day shopping to replace what had been stolen, which gave us an opportunity to see the town. We drove to our villa and slept the night there. In the morning we loaded our possessions into the van, said goodbye to our friends and started on our way home.

As it would probably be our last visit we decided to take the long way home through Spain, along the coast through Faro, passing Monte Gordo where we spent our first holiday on the Algarve years ago, and crossed over the river at Vila Real de Santo António into Spain. We continued to Seville and afterwards took the green country roads to Granada but before we reached there we ran into violent thunderstorms, which caused a landslide and blocked the route. We were diverted onto a mountain road through a village called La Mancha I thought this was a name invented by Cervantes in his book about Don Quixote, but it was a real place, and after negotiating the mountain roads we came down into Granada where we met several people we had left in Seville who had also to drive a cross country route to reach Granada.

As we went into the hotel restaurant for dinner the pianist saw us and immediately started playing the tune *Granada*. When he finished we clapped him and he gave us a small bow in acknowledgement. The Americans at the next table turned round in surprise; apparently they had never heard of the song. The storm stopped the next morning and we took the opportunity to visit the Alhambra, a former palace of the Moorish Kings with its gardens and avenues, fountains and lily ponds, which we had last visited when we were skiing in the Sierra Nevada mountains at the back of the town. We continued on the green coastal road to Alicante, with its elegant walks along the front, although thousands of people live in caves and holes in the hillsides behind the town. From Alicante we turned inland across the middle of Spain, by-passing Madrid to reach Avila, completely surrounded by massive walls, and drove through the gates to reach the castle, which had been converted by the Government into a parador, a hotel where you can stay for a few days. It had been the former home of the dukes of Avila, one of whom had sailed with the Spanish Armada. It was luxuriously furnished with antiques and paintings of the family and we occupied the former state bedroom with a four poster bed. We were lucky because it is difficult to stay in one of these paradores unless one books ahead; they are usually all taken up by the tourist agencies.

From Avila we turned north to reach the border with France. I wanted to cross the Pyrenees by a small pass not used by heavy traffic and after reaching Pamplona — it was the wrong time of the year to see the bulls run through the town — I chose a small country road to the Pass of Roncesvalles where we stayed at an old inn. This was a beautiful spot with streams cascading down the mountains through the woods to reach the valley; the trees were turning colour and the gold of the leaves provided a wonderful contrast to the green below. When we arrived at the inn a party of three Frenchmen were collecting a picnic provided by the proprietor, including paté, a whole cheese, a ham, a chicken, long rolls of bread, a carton of butter, several bottles of wine and a bottle of brandy. I asked whether they were camping nearby and the maid who was packing their baskets replied, 'No monsieur, they are taking a walk in the forest.' It was a fine day for a walk, sunny and warm, but I could not imagine they got far before starting on their picnic.

Another reason why I chose the Pass of Roncesvalles was the history and romance attached to it I tried to visualize the scene in that quiet and peaceful valley as it resounded to the clash of armour when a Moorich army tried to destroy Charlemagne's forces as they attempted to escape into France hundreds of years before. The rearguard defending the pass was commanded by Oliver who, with his friend and companion, Roland, were acknowledged the most perfect knights in all Christendom, the most chivalrous, the bravest and an example to every knight. Nothing could separate them, they were equal in all things, and if men wished to compare like with like they would say 'a Roland for an Oliver'. The battle for the pass raged all day and when the Moors brought up more and more men to the attack Oliver's forces gradually dwindled as they fought to the death. Oliver was mortally wounded and he turned to his trumpeter and commanded him to sound a call for help to Roland who heard it and turned back to assist Oliver, but when he arrived at the battle scene he was too late, Oliver was dead. But the Moors had suffered so many casualties they were unable to continue the pursuit of Charlemagne's army. As I walked in the evening I fancied I heard the faint distant call of the trumpet, but it was only the rustle of the leaves in the trees as the breeze took over from the heat of the day, or perhaps the cry of a bird.

One's thoughts can play tricks on the senses sometimes. When we left the inn at Roncesvalles we turned right to Carcassonne, an old city founded by the Romans, a perfectly preserved medieval stronghold totally enclosed within defensive walls but with a very comfortable hotel in a garden from which it is possible to still see the Pyrenees. From Carcassonne we turned north to Rodez, where we stayed in a hotel which was formerly the palace of the bishops of Rodez, built on the side of a hill with magnificent views of the countryside. After having dinner in what used to be the chapel or small church in the crypt we went up several flights of stairs to our bedroom and Betty stopped suddenly to ask, 'Can you hear the chanting?' I said no I could not but she insisted, 'I can hear people praying in Latin and I can smell incense'. After a while I admitted that although I could not hear anything I could smell something like incense, but no doubt this was because it was used at the time the bishops lived there and held their services and the scent would become impregnated in the walls of the building. Eventually Betty said the chanting had stopped. We went to bed and I wondered whether her Welsh ancestry made her more sensitive to atmosphere and the spirits of former residents in the old buildings we visited, because she had experienced a similar sensation at the manor house in Wales.

The next morning we made for the Dordogne, driving through Cahors, crossing the river Lot on the old fortified medieval bridge and through the Roman gateway to the old town. We arrived at Bergerac and booked into a hotel there. We spent the next day exploring the pretty villages of the Dordogne and the following morning started our drive home. We were now on a route which we had travelled many times before on our way to and from the Algarve, through Poitiers, across the river Loire at Tours, to Le Mans, Rouen and finally Calais. We stopped on the way but we did not spend any time sightseeing because we were familiar with all the places on the route, and caught the ferry for Dover and home, where I sold the caravan

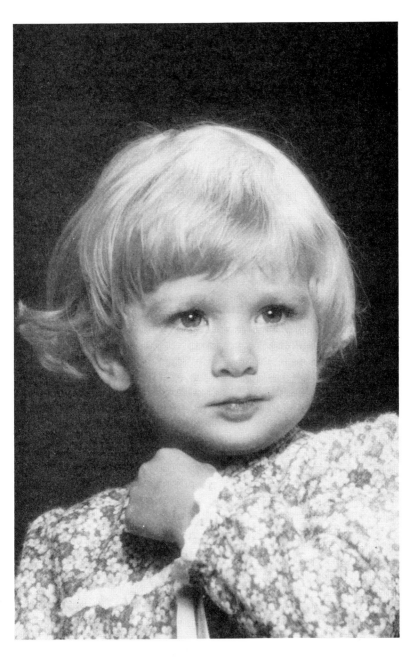

Miranda's daughter, Fiona (Nonie)

and bought another motor car.

After Miranda's first child, a lovely little girl with golden hair and blue eyes, was born in 1978 Miranda could not continue to run the shop at Shoreham and although Betty had been managing it for some time with a staff, it was obvious that Miranda would not be able to return to the business because of her family commitments and we agreed to sell it. Betty organized a closing down sale, cutting the prices until everything was sold, including the plastic fittings which divided up the shelves. These were sold to an elderly man who wanted to make cloches for his garden from them, and when I delivered them to him on my way home, he gave me 50p for a tip. I let the property to a man who wanted a showroom for his engineering products and placed it in the hands of agents to collect the rent. This left us free of responsibilities and we decided in 1980 to spend the money from the sale of our villa on a world cruise.

We joined the P & O liner *SS Canberra* at Southampton on Saturday 12 January 1980. Miranda, Stuart and the baby with our friends, Thelma and Peter Humphreys, were there to see us off. I obtained a bottle of champagne from a steward and everybody drank to our good health and wished us '*Bon Voyage*'. After the visitors went ashore Betty and I stood on the top deck waving goodbye and throwing streamers at the crowd below, while the Royal Marine band played and the tugs slowly drew the ship away from the quayside until the *Canberra* was able to drop the tow ropes and proceed down Southampton water under her own steam. We found our cabin on the promenade deck comfortably furnished with a window, two beds, wardrobes, a writing table, radio, telephone and shower and lavatory. Our steward introduced himself and we dressed for dinner to attend the reception given by the captain, Commodore F.B. Woolley, R.D., R.N.R., and his officers beforehand. Betty kept a scrapbook covering the whole of the voyage with pages setting out the names and photographs of the places we visited, the people and specimens of their postage and coinage, as well as our own snapshots of the passengers and events aboard the ship and an appropriate quotation from the daily newspaper, entitled 'Thought for Today', the first of which was taken from John Masefield's poem *Sea Fever*.

We cruised during the day and put on speed at night. The meals were tremendous and it was necessary to take plenty of exercise to keep fit. I swam in one of the pools in the morning and Betty had a man friend who took her by the arm and walked her round the deck; I forget how many times round equalled one mile. In the afternoon I attended the bridge class and as I am a good card player I was always in demand as a partner by the ladies, who outnumbered the men, and would call me 'Rupert'. Betty went to the art class. We both joined the drama group and after dinner we saw a cabaret show or visited the cinema and ended the day by dancing to one of the bands. Sometimes we played deck cricket or table tennis. All these activities had to be fitted in whilst we were at sea because as soon as we entered port we went ashore on excursions. Our first port of call was Miami and the Everglades, where we saw a marvellous collection of different types of parrots, and when we had a fancy hat competition on board Betty made a wonderful creation with a beautiful parrot perched on top.

The *Canberra* was a tight fit when she was towed through the Panama Canal by small diesel engines running along rails on both sides. We turned north to drop anchor at Acapulco. The town is like many Mediterranean resorts with large hotels and apartment blocks behind the sands. We sailed down a fast flowing river in a small boat to a remote beach surrounded by coconut trees, where I tried to swim out to explore the coral reef, but I was called back before I reached it because sharks were sighted. The river was running too strongly for us to return by boat and a coach was sent to collect us. The next day we saw the young boys dive off the cliffs into the sea hundreds of feet below, a show they put on for the tourists, and after attending a demonstration of folk lore by the native indians we had dinner and saw a cabaret at one of the luxury hotels. This did not end until two o'clock in the morning and when we returned to the beach the captain was waiting there with the boats to take us on board and make sure we were all accounted for.

We continued north to San Francisco but the entrance to the Golden Gate was not very golden. A thick fog covered the bay, which is caused by the cool air off the sea meeting the hot air of the desert and is a frequent occurrence. We explored Chinatown but we could not ride the trains up Nobs Hill because they were broken down and out of action. We took a trip into the mountains to see the giant redwood trees which are the world's oldest living things. We travelled on the Roaring Camp and Big Trees Railroad on one of the old logging trains, crossing the canyons on wooden trestle bridges which look as though they would collapse any minute. You can guess the sort of route we covered by the names of the stations on the way — Roaring Camp, Moskunk Junction, Big Trees, Indian Creek, Grizzly Flats, Deer Valley, Spring Canyon and Bear Mountain. We had a barbecue lunch on top of the mountain and afterwards walked in the woods admiring the trees, some of which were so big that cabins had been built in the hollowed out trunks. The next day we drove south to see the vineyards. California now makes some fine wines, and the old missions established by the Spaniards who first settled in the country, including the Mission San Francisco de Asis, which was named after the founder of the Franciscan Order and gave its name to the city of San Francisco.

The following day we left the harbour and when we had cleared the coast a message was received from the authorities in San Francisco to say that a bomb had been placed on the *Canberra*. We were all informed and asked to search our cabins thoroughly, while the crew examined the rest of the ship. No bomb was found and we steamed on our way, following our usual routine on board after life boat drill. Our next stop was Honolulu. We hired a boat and toured Pearl Harbour, where one of the American warships bombed by the Japanese still lies a sunken wreck, serving as a memorial to the memory of the American sailors who were killed in the attack. We visited the Polynesian Cultural Centre to see the native art and the dancers and Lahaina on Maui Island, where the statue of the Great Buddha stands and the Ukumehame Canyon is situated. We were now near the equator and the sunsets did not fill the sky with clear bright light, they went down in a welter of dark red rays like blood, which spread over the clouds and spilled out to cover the sea.

We crossed the equator on Tuesday, 12 February, receiving a visit from King Neptune, ruler of the seven seas, with his full Aquatic Court, who carried out a most rigorous initiation ceremony of shaving and ducking in the swimming pool those people who wished to cross the equator. Betty received a certificate from King Neptune confirming that 'The Most Noble Cross of the Equator be bestowed on Betty Brooks, who but a mere mortal, hath this 12th day of February 1980, on board S.S. Canberra, accepted with Good Humour and Withstood with Fortitude the most Rigorous Initiation into the Ancient and Moistening Rites of our Aquatic Court — Sealed and witnessed in the presence of F.B. Woolley, Captain'.

We called in to the Fiji Islands and anchored at Suva, where natives demonstrated how they could walk barefooted on red hot coals without being hurt and two men staged a fight with war clubs. I bought a war club in the market which I thought would be useful dealing with burglars in England, where we had already been burgled three times, at my sister's house, at our shop, and in our own house while we were asleep in bed.

Our next stop was Sydney, entering the impressive harbour spanned by the famous iron bridge with the modern buildings of the opera house on one side, looking like a collection of white, broken eggshells. This is half way house for the cruise and the stars who had entertained us, singers, actors, comedians, bands and ventriloquists left to be replaced by other performers flown out from England. Captain Woolley also flew home to be with his wife who had just had a baby, and Captain Gibbs took over command of the ship. We visited the curious group of rock formations called the Three Sisters in the Blue Mountains, which had formed a barrier to explorers who wanted to find a way to the north, and we descended into an abandoned gold mine by a scenic railway, which dropped to the bottom at a speed which stopped our breath, made our hearts beat furiously and left our stomachs behind. The antics of the koala bear amused us but Sydney did not contain any ancient or historic buildings and we did not see any aborigines. Passengers who were staying in Australia left the ship and people who wished to travel to England came on board. Among those who embarked was a frail old lady who was travelling alone to visit relatives and for the first few days she could not find her way about the ship, and we had to help her get to the restaurant for meals. During the voyage home she became progressively worse and one evening while still at sea she rang for the steward and said to him, 'Order me a taxi to take me to hospital'. She was taken to the hospital aboard the ship, which was fully staffed by doctors and nurses, but she died before we reached England. Two or three other people died on the voyage. There were no burials at sea, the bodies were retained in the mortuary to await

235

instructions from the relatives for their disposal.

We became friendly with a lady who was travelling to England for a holiday with her daughter, aged about twenty; the girl met a young man on the ship, and it was obvious that they were attracted to each other. The mother saw danger in the relationship and put as many obstacles in the way of their meeting as she could, but Betty kept the mother interested while the young couple saw each other. The girl keeps in touch with us. She did not return to Australia with her mother, but married her young man and they set up home near Manchester, where she teaches in the local school.

When we left Sydney we sailed for Guam, an American controlled island in the Marianas. The ship was due to refuel there, but as we approached the island we ran into a tropical rainstorm. The rain came down in torrents, blocking out the view from the ship and made worse by spray whipped up by the wind, which enveloped the vessel. The *Canberra* had to stand off the island for six hours until the storm abated, and it was possible to go alongside the oil terminus.

* * *

Our next stop was Yokohama for Tokyo and Mount Fuji in the distance. We visited the Ginza pedestrian shopping street, the Golden Pavilion with each floor surrounded by balconies until the top storey, crowned by a roof shaped like a mushroom curled up at the edges, and the Meiji Jingu shrine which had to be approached through a sacred archway in the South Gate into the Hall of Worship in front of the main shrine.

On a visit to a ceramics design centre we had lunch at a restaurant where each table was built with an electric hob in the centre, on which the waitress cooked the food and handed it to us, sitting round the edge of the table.

From Yokohama we sailed to the Japanese port of Kogoshima. It was the firs time a large cruise ship had visited the city and when we tied up at Taniyama wharf we were given a tremendous welcome. Girls dressed in native costumes paraded on the wharf waving to us, and when we came down the gangway after the official reception on board by the mayor and his council, we were each given a present of a Japanese doll together with a card saying, 'I am a passenger on the cruiser calling at the port of Kogoshima. Please take me back to the ship anchored at Taniyama Wharf' in case we were lost. Once ashore we were greeted by warriors dressed in traditional Japanese armour; the university had given all the students a holiday in order that they could act as our guides, and the young man who accompanied Betty and me asked the inevitable question, 'What do you think of the Japanese?' to which I carefully replied, 'I think they are a very progressive people', and he was very pleased with my answer. We crossed the old bridge in the centre of the town, which had been specially built for the bi-annual procession to pay respect to the shogun, the local ruler, and watched the elaborate ritual of the Japanese tea ceremony, by ladies dressed in traditional costume. At night when we were due to leave, the people of Kogoshima congregated on the wharf, everybody carrying a lantern which they waved slowly to and fro as they sang *Auld Lang Syne* and the ship gradually drew away from the shore. With the lanterns shining in the darkness and the sound of the old Scottish song coming to us across the water, it was a most impressive farewell and in some ways a sad one, as if we parted from friends, although we had only known them for a day.

In 1979, Miranda's baby was christened Fiona to match her Scottish surname and Claire meaning light, in keeping with her golden hair. However, it was discovered that there was something wrong with her heart and whilst we were away on our cruise she was admitted to Great Ormond Street Hospital for open heart surgery. On Wednesday, 5 March we received a radio message from Miranda that Fiona's operation had been successful and she was doing well. We always attended the *Canberra's* religious services on Sundays; I went to the church services at the missions to seamen when I was at sea with my father and, as children, we always included a prayer for those in peril on the sea, so the shipboard services held memories for me, and the one on the Sunday after Fiona's operation was especially significant, as it gave us an opportunity to express our thanks to God for Fiona's recovery.

When we returned from our cruise I went with Miranda to visit the surgeon at Great Ormond Street who had performed Fiona's operation and he told me that he had repaired her heart with Dacron, which was the same material the sails for my yacht were made of.

We left Japan for Hong Kong and berthed at the dock used by cruise liners, which seemed to consist of one huge market place selling the most amazing collection of luxury goods such as watches, cameras, radios, calculators and computers. My lasting impression is of a place teeming with people, in the streets, on the junks and floating restaurants crowded in Aberdeen harbour and the hovels perched precariously one above the other on the hillside over the water, looking as though if the top one fell it would bring down all the others below it, collapsing like dominoes. The only way to get away from the crowds was by taking a ride on the funicular tram up Victoria Peak where it was possible to look down on the island, with its skyscrapers hotels and office buildings and the jumble of boats and junks in the water. *Canberra* had organized two optional excursions from Hong Kong, one to China and the other to Bangkok. We did not fancy China because it had only just opened its borders to foreign visitors, who were taken round in conducted groups to visit schools and factories, and no decent hotels had yet been built.

We therefore flew to Bangkok and stayed in a modern hotel which we made our headquarters. There are so many temples, palaces and Buddhas to see; the Emerald Buddha Temple is one of the most magnificent. It is approached through grounds containing smaller, elaborately carved buildings. The entrance is guarded by two massive gilded statues of figures, which I presumed were intended to be warriors, but it was difficult to tell what they were, because they had faces which were more horrible than the gargoyles carved on the walls of English cathedrals, half man, half devil. Through the entrance is the forecourt of the Chapel Royal of the Emerald Buddha with a row of heraldic beasts carved in ebony, similar to lions in front of the stairs leading to the buddhas. The Emerald Buddha, as its name implies, is a magnificent sight, studded with precious stones in which emeralds predominate, reflected in the electric lights positioned above. The throne room of the palace is decorated with gilded carvings and columns dividing the halls into panels very similar to some of the entrance halls in large country houses in England, which are no doubt copied from buildings in Thailand or India. The throne is elaborately carved and set at the top of a row of steps, behind which is a portrayal of what I assumed was the sun, and in the palace grounds was a statue described as the Image of the Buddha under rainy season attire, looking very miserable. The girls performing their classical dances in costumes and elaborate headdresses encrusted with what looked like pearls were very graceful and pretty and the monks in their saffron robes were a colourful feature of the streets. We had to take off our shoes to enter the temples and one man in our party said that he had seen so many buddhas and taken off his shoes so many times that he preferred to sit on the steps outside. It was possible to buy a buddha in the shops but it was illegal to take them out of the country.

As a relief from sightseeing we toured the canals, or klongs as they are called, which intersected the city. They are floating markets where the country people display their fruit and vegetables on sampans. The motor boats in which we travelled at high speed, pushed the sampans to one side as we ploughed through them and left them in danger of capsizing astern to the shouts and cries of the people on board.

We visited a factory to see the girls making and decorating silk umbrellas and Betty bought a roll of Thai silk to make up into a dress when she returned home. On the last night of our stay we had a Thai dinner of many courses attended by girls in native dress wearing white gloves, who knelt down to serve us as we sat on big cushions. My greatest regret was that I did not have time to go up country and visit the bridge on the River Kwai.

We flew to Singapore to rejoin the *Canberra* and spent a day sightseeing. The two most famous places are Raffles Hotel and the Tiger Balm Gardens. They were both a disappointment. Raffles was run-down, without any of the former attraction it once had and the Tiger Balm Gardens, after entering through an elaborate archway, consisted of a succession of concrete structures interspersed with very ordinary flower gardens.

The trishaws — bicycles carrying three passengers in their side car — were a popular means of transport for a leisurely enjoyable ride through the streets but I was rather irritated by the Chinese we met, who continually referred to the Malays as ignorant people who were not worth educating.

Our next port of call was Madras, where the *Canberra* changed the Indian members of its crew and the new ones came on board with their wives, who were shown round the ship by their husbands. The area of the port is industrial but in the city there are two famous temples, to the gods Shiva and Vishnu, where the devotees come to say their prayers and bathe in the temple tanks, after which they streak their foreheads with scarlet make-up before leaving.

We sailed for Sri Lanka and the port of Colombo where we visited the temple and an enormous statue of Buddha forty feet high, and bought a richly woven tapestry of an elephant, the symbol of Sri Lanka. Looking back it seems that we spent most of our time seeing temples and buddhas but there are so many of them in the Far East that they dominate the towns and countryside and the minds of the people, and it is essential to see them if the visitor wishes to get to know the country in which they are situated.

We crossed the Indian Ocean to Mombasa in Kenya, which had the atmosphere of Arabia rather than Africa. At the ancient port, not used by modern ships, a large Arab dhow was berthed, unloading its cargo from Arabia. Other vessels were being built in the boat yards and the surrounding buildings were of Arab design instead of African. In the old days it was one of the centres of the African slave trade and we visited the medieval castle from which the Arabs controlled the port.

The produce markets were full of exotic fruits. In a workshop we watched men carving models from ebony and bought one of a native woman; the use of ivory was forbidden. Although we were offered an ivory model without the management's knowledge by one of the workmen we refused it. We spent a day in the game park watching the wild animals, mainly various types of deer, and had lunch at a restaurant by the sea where we made a great mistake of eating the local cold fish and salad because it was so hot. The result was that both Betty and I had a very bad stomach upset and could not join the excursion to see the Pyramids when the other passengers set forth in a coach for Suez, accompanied by a medical team to take care of them.

We stayed in bed until we reached Port Said, where the passengers who had been on the trip to the Pyramids rejoined the ship after visiting Cairo. When we went on deck we found the bum-boat men clustered round the *Canberra* like wasps round a honey pot. Their boats were filled with copper and brass articles and ornaments which they were trying to sell to the passengers on deck with a hubbub of shouting and haggling to and fro. One of their number had been sent aboard with a line which he lowered to the boats. A basket was attached and filled with articles in which the passengers showed an interest and hauled up by the man on deck for the passengers inspection and if a sale was made he collected the money. This went on all day until *Canberra* left for Haifa.

We docked at Haifa on the day before Good Friday, and went on a trip to Caesarea to see the Crusaders' Castle and Herod's Tower and to Mount Carmel to visit the monastery perched on the cliffs overlooking the sea. The next day most of the passengers left by coach on the seventy mile drive to Jerusalem but Betty and I still felt unwell and did not like to risk the journey. However, the visit to the Holy Land was the highlight of our cruise and we did not want to miss it. I saw a lonely taxi on the dockside and went down to speak to the two young men sitting inside. I explained to them that we wanted to visit Jerusalem but that we were feeling unwell and it might be necessary to stop on the way, but they said the taxi would be ours for the day and they would do whatever we wished. It was one of the best arrangements I have ever made. One of the young men was a Jew and the other was an Arab, so we were able to visit places where Arabs were barred and mosques Jews could not enter, accompanied by our guides in turn. We drove up to the entrance of the buildings and while one of the young men showed us round the other waited outside in the taxi to take us to the next place we wished to go.

Good Friday is the wrong time to visit Jerusalem and the Holy Land because it is crowded with hordes of people and loses its religious atmosphere in the process. When we came to the Church of the Holy Sepulchre a procession of priests was coming out after a service and the crowds outside tried to push their way in. This degenerated into fighting between the two parties and the police had to intervene to separate them. The trouble is that so many different Christian churches want to have their services at the same place on Good Friday, although there are churches erected over every site which has a possible connection with the life of Christ. The Via Dolorosa with its small shops and crowded with people watching or following the procession must have appeared the same when Jesus carried his cross up the hill for his crucifixion. The Mount of Olives where Christ ascended into heaven has what is supposed to be his footprint

241

preserved there. But it was confusing when our young Arab showed us the footprint to Mohammed, who was also taken up to Allah from the same place. The Wailing Wall was completely occupied by Jews saying their prayers. They arrive in family parties but when they came to the wall they split up, the female members going to the ten per cent of the space reserved for them.

We saw the room of the Last Supper and the tomb where Christ was buried and walked in the Garden of Gethsemane, trying to imagine what it must have been like when Christ walked there. We drove to Bethlehem to see the stable where Christ was born. The Shepherds Field overlooks a large square with churches of different denominations and underneath the Church of the Nativity is a cave, which we entered, conducted by a guide found for us by our young men, and this is the place where Christ is supposed to have been born, not in a stable. Our guide was a horrible old man who kept urging us to, 'Touch the Walls. Touch them. They are lucky'. When we came out, I offered him his fee in sheckels, the Israeli currency, but he refused them and demanded, 'Give me dollars.' I explained, 'I have no dollars. I can give you pounds, but if you don't want to accept them, you'll get nothing'. Our young guides came up and dealt with the man he accepted my pounds and shuffled away grumbling into his beard while we went to a very nice Jewish restaurant for lunch.

We toured the old town and were interested not only in the buildings but also in the fascinating mixture of people there, Orthodox Jews with their fur hats the shape of pancakes on top of their heads, the older Palestinians with white beards, the Arabs in their flowing robes and headdresses, and women in embroidered dresses with long necklaces of beads and what looked like coins, who might have been Jewesses or Palestinian women. We drove back to Haifa in time to reach the *Canberra* before it sailed, after a day which had been full of interest and well worth the effort going, helped by our young guides.

Our last port of call was Palma on Majorca which we had visited before when we were cruising on the *Reina del Mar*, and we spent our time in the old part of the town, walking through the narrow streets and cool leafy courtyards. The cathedral is an impressive building with tall black columns inside reaching to the roof, in contrast to English churches where the pillars are usually white stone, and the medieval coloured glass of the windows is as fine as anything we have seen in other cathedrals. We left Palma for the last leg of our cruise, through the Straits of Gibraltar, passing a British submarine and crossing the Bay of Biscay in calm weather, until we reached our home port of Southampton, where our family and friends were waiting to greet us after a voyage of 34,826 miles.

I was presented with a certificate by the bridge director for my card playing, made out in the name of Rupert Brooks, so the ladies got their way in the end. We said goodbye to the friends we had made on board, the staff and the stars who were leaving the ship. I remembered them all when I sent a telegram to the captain, officers and crew of the *Canberra*, wishing them 'God speed and a safe return' when they sailed for the Falklands War. We were very happy on *Canberra*. It was a luxury hotel afloat with comfortable bedrooms, spacious public rooms, excellent food and service, with the added advantage of free cinema and theatrical entertainment, a casino, sports and pastimes included. As we left the English winter behind in January and steamed south each day was sunny and warm, we were freed from everyday disturbances by unwanted callers, the telephone and the post, it was possible to choose one's companions or to be alone in the library with a good book or just enjoy the sunshine and fresh air on deck. We returned to England at the end of the three months' voyage to the beginning of spring in April, and Betty's last 'Thought for today' in her Scrapbook was from Robert Browning's poem *Home-Thoughts from Abroad*, beginning 'Oh to be in England now that April's there'.

The cruise was the holiday of a lifetime, with well planned excursions to places of interest in the countries where we docked. The changes of scenery, the different architecture symbolic of the history of the inhabitants and their culture, the dress and appearance of the people, all combined to make each call at a new country a wonderful experience. It is not possible to gain more than a superficial impression of a country and its people on a visit lasting only three or four days, but it does serve as an introduction to a longer stay if the visitor's interest is aroused.

7

THE FINAL YEARS

When I returned home I found a mountain of mail waiting for me, including a letter from the widow of the man who had rented our shop, informing me of her husband's death and asking to cancel the lease. There was some rent outstanding but I waived that, took back the lease and put the property up for sale. It was bought by a property developer. We have not been back but I might go to see what has happened some time. It took me the whole of the summer to get my affairs straight because as fast as I dealt with the arrears the daily post kept thudding through the letter box. I had matters under control by the autumn and we decided to take a holiday in Greece.

We flew to Preveza, a small aerodrome occupied by the Greek Air Force and boarded the ferry for the island of Lefkas, one of the greenest and most beautiful of the Ionian Islands. We stayed at the Paradise Taverna in the village of Nidri. The sea lapped only fifteen feet from the terrace where we ate our meals, looking out over the water to the green islands and to the high mountains on the mainland in the distance. The village was quite unspoilt, with a small harbour bustling with boats, old ladies in long black clothes making lace in their doorways while the men sat in the cafes, drinking ouzo and thick black coffee.

We had some very interesting people in our party, a major general and his wife who had a fund of good stories, counterbalanced by a naval captain and a scientist with their wives and a sprinkling of sporting personalities from the cricketing world — Bill Edrich of Middlesex, Richard Hutton from Yorkshire, Brian Johnstone, the cricket commentator and Sandy Gall, the ITV Announcer. Every day, unless we went on an excursion to the mainland, we had a trip by a caique, a small Greek passenger boat, to the other islands and beaches where we landed to sunbathe and swim while the captain's wife cooked us a barbecue lunch. I was surprised when the ladies took off their bathing costumes and swam and sunbathed in the nude or topless. We visited all the islands in turn except Skorpios, which I understand was owned by the Niarchos family and armed guards prevented everybody from landing.

I swam round the other side of one island and as I walked along the beach on the way back to the boat I heard the sound of struggling and scuffling in the bushes, and when I went to investigate I discovered it was a bird caught in some sort of net. I picked it up and found it was a young sparrowhawk tangled in what looked like a fishing line. At first it tried to resist me, but as I cut the line free it gradually relaxed and while I stroked it and smoothed its feathers back into place it perched quite happily on my wrist until I threw it high in the air and it disappeared over the tops of the trees into the woods.

A very plump lady in our party said to Betty, 'I don't think you recognize me' and Betty had to admit that although there was something familiar about her, she could not remember who she was. But when she spoke her name, Betty immediately knew she was the model who had posed for the life class at the art school Betty attended years before. Betty could not say that she had not recognized her because she had put on so much weight; she had married a chef, which no doubt was the reason why she had lost her figure.

We walked through the vineyards at the back of the village up into the hills to visit a waterfall and bathe in the cool waters before returning, eating the bunches of grapes the villagers cut from the vines to give us. One of the sights in the village was to watch the mayor standing in a barrel with his trousers rolled up over his knees, treading grapes to make his wine while an admiring crowd looked on. In the evenings there was always music in the taverna. The best exponents of Greek dancing were the two young English girls who acted as our couriers. When we came in from a caique trip Brian Johnstone was always first in the cake shop while Sandy Gall went to sit up on the roof of the Taverna Villa to continue typing his book.

The last ten years have not been happy ones. Betty's health deteriorated. She has lost weight and constantly complains of

Author at 75

aches and pains, although she has been thoroughly examined by specialists, once at the Royal Berkshire Hospital and again at the Nuffield Hospital in Tunbridge Wells and they could find nothing wrong with her. She has lost her energy and this has depressed her. Instead of spending all her spare time on her painting, she has become engrossed in studying natural medicine, seeking a cure to restore her health, but this only leads her to find little known illnesses in the books and pamphlets she reads and which she then imagines she might have.

She has consulted and been treated by naturepaths,

chiropractors, masseurs, physiotherapists, osteopaths, a hypnotist who could not hypnotize her because she was too strong willed, a woman healer who said she was loose weaved, whatever that meant, tested by a laboratory for allergies which decided she was allergic to Roquefort cheese, although she had never eaten any, and X-rayed, tested and scanned by all the latest medical devices. This expense has cost us hundreds of pounds but I have gone along with it in case there was something wrong and if I had refused to pay for her treatment I would never have been able to forgive myself. Betty cannot reconcile herself to growing older and it depresses her when she finds she has not got the same energy she had when she was younger.

Betty drove into Tunbridge Wells to shop as usual and I was working at home, when two policemen knocked at the door. One asked, 'Are you the owner of a Renault car?' I replied, 'Yes, my wife is driving it into Tunbridge Wells'. The second policeman explained, 'We have found the car wrecked at the side of the road and the driver has been taken to Kent and Sussex Hospital'. My heart seemed to stop still and I was in such a state with the shock that I could not drive my own car and I rang for a taxi to take me to the hospital. Betty had recovered when I got there; she had been examined and was lying in bed. Although she was cut and bruised, nothing appeared to be broken and all she wanted was to be taken home. She discharged herself and came with me to be put to bed at home until she recovered from the battering she had received. The road into Tunbridge Wells was very greasy following a shower of rain after a long dry spell, and the Renault had skidded off the road to hit a pole carrying electricity, which broke in half and crashed down on top of the car, smashing the roof in, but fortunately missing Betty, who had been flung forward against the dashboard by the force of the impact.

Our village policeman called to have a cup of tea and take particulars of the accident. I submitted a claim to my insurance company which decided the car was a write off and paid me out for a total loss, while I paid the electricity board £10 for a new pole. Our doctor at that time practised natural medicine and was president of the Vegetarian Society. He examined Betty and discovered that she had a very slow pulse rate, but said that as Napoleon and athletes had a similar pulse rate there was nothing to worry about. However, we consulted a heart specialist in London who advised that she should have a pacemaker fitted to bring the pulse up to a normal rate. She spent three or four days in Guy's Hospital Nuffield House and had the operation, later visiting the specialist once a year to have a check up. Betty fell down and broke her elbow again and I had her transferred to a private room at the Nuffield Hospital in Tunbridge Wells under the care of the specialist until she was well enough to come home.

In 1981 we spent a holiday on the Isle of Wight with our old friends, Rob and Gwen Passmore, before they emigrated to Australia to join their son and his family outside Perth, where they had bought a bungalow. We still hear from them; they have settled happily in their new home although they find the heat in the summer very trying. Miranda's second baby, another little girl, was born and christened Melissa Jayne. David brought over a cricket team from Upper Canada College to play the southern public schools, and it was a great opportunity to get to know our grandsons and take them to see the Royal Tournament at Earls Court.

When Miranda was a little girl we tried to teach her to say 'Grandpa' when she met Betty's father, but all she would say was 'Pappy', so he was called Pappy by all the rest of the family. When Fiona was beginning to speak we asked her to say her name, but she repeated 'Nonie' and afterwards everybody used that name instead of Fiona. We were not able to see the boys living in Canada, but it was a great joy to us when Miranda's little girls came. Fiona had heard Miranda referring to Betty as 'Mum' and consequently Fiona called Betty 'Mum' but Miranda explained that her mother's name was Betty so Fiona called her 'Betty Mum' and this became her name. When Miranda stopped outside the house I opened the door and saw a little golden haired girl on the doorstep who started dancing up and down, stamping her feet and shouting 'I want Betty Mum. I want Betty Mum', until Betty appeared and carried her indoors.

In 1985 Fiona caught a virus which attacked her heart and stopped it from working properly. The only way to save Fiona's life was a heart transplant, but the difficulty in such cases is to find a new heart compatible with the rest of the organs in the recipient's body. We had to wait until a new heart was found and it was agonizing to watch Fiona gradually fading away. I rented a bungalow near the sea at Greatstone for Fiona, where we had spent many happy holidays in previous years and Miranda also brought Melissa to stay with us. I hoped that the sea air would help Fiona to survive because it was now only a matter of weeks before the situation would be resolved one way or another. Miranda was in radio communication with Great Ormond Street and we just had to wait for news while we made Fiona as happy as possible, hoping every minute that a call would come through to say that a suitable heart had been found, but at the same time feeling guilty that our hopes would only be realized at the expense of some other parents' sorrow on the death of their child.

It was a terrible time, alone with our thoughts, waiting for the call which might never come and seeing Fiona grow weaker. We did not give up hope and at last a police car arrived from New Romney. One of the policemen hurried up the drive and said, 'I have a message for Mrs McKay. A heart has been received at Harefield Hospital and Fiona must be taken there immediately. The police will provide you with an escort'.

Fiona was carried out to Miranda's car and they set off behind the police car, which handed them over to the Kent police at the border, and the Kent police passed Miranda onto the Metropolitan police for the final leg to the hospital.

The operation to transplant the new heart was successfully performed by Professor Yacoub and Fiona made good progress towards recovery. It is amazing how little children can bear pain when they have confidence that those who love them are caring for them. Betty asked Fiona, who was only six years' old, 'Does it hurt?' and she whispered in reply, 'Just a little' and I could not help comparing her quiet whisper with the shouting and commotion I made when I had my operation, and I was a man of fifty! Stuart organized a fund for Harefield Hospital through his Moth Club and one of the members parachuted into the hospital grounds to deliver the cheque. I gave a donation to the appeal set up for the widow and family of P.C. Blakely, who was killed in the Tottenham riots, in appreciation of the assistance the police gave to get Fiona to hospital in time for her operation.

The following year I had not been feeling very well, and when I woke up one morning I could not move my arms and legs. Betty drove me to our doctor who said I had contracted

Author convalescing after first illness of polymyalgia

polymyalgia, which afflicts men who are under stress when they grow older. His cure was to eat only fruit and drink fruit juice and I followed his advice for over a year. My weight dropped from nine and a half stone to seven but I recovered my health.

In 1987 David and Jane brought their three boys with a friend to England for a holiday. I hired two canal barges, seventy feet long and fully equipped to take six people each, from Bridgewater Boats at Berkhamsted on the Grand Union Canal. David and his family had one barge and I had the other with Betty, Miranda and her two little girls. My plan was to continue

Recent Photographs

Grandson Jeremy

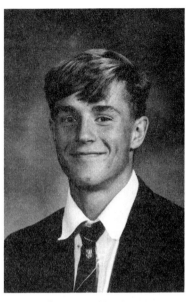

Grandson Matthew

Grandson Benji

Granddaughter Melissa

In the locks

north on the Grand Union Canal to the junction with the Oxford Canal, come back down the Oxford Canal into the River Thames and re-enter the Grand Union Canal below Berkhamsted to return the barges. The owner of the boatyard took us through the first lock a short distance upstream to show us how to run the barges and work the locks and then we carried on through the locks, climbing up the Chilterns until we reached the summit at Cowroast lock. The barges could not exceed four knots an hour and each day we slowly made our way through the countryside, passing an occasional town and stopping soon after lunch alongside a quiet grassy bank for the night, playing cricket in the afternoon, picking strawberries, fishing, visiting interesting churches and villages and walking to the nearest pub for a drink when we finished supper, where the children could play in the garden and have their fizzy drinks with packets of crisps.

Toast for supper ashore from the barges

From the Cowroast Lock we continued through the long wooded cutting that contains the Tring Summit level to Marsworth where there are four reservoirs forming a National Nature reserve which we explored, with many wildfowl and abundant water plants. The first of the Marsworth locks begin to wind down the hill past the reservoirs at the bottom of the flight but these were no trouble to us. All the locks we encountered were sufficiently wide to take two barges and we therefore had two crews to do the work, which made it much easier. David's crew was rather careless with the handles for the lock gates and lost some overboard, but Fiona took good care of ours. Marsworth is the junction with the Aylesbury Arm but we followed the main line which bears round to the North East, falling away from Dunstable Downs and the Chilterns, the hills giving way to open grassland until we reached Leighton

Buzzard, where we stopped to do some shopping and refill our water tanks. From Leighton Buzzard the canal meanders along the Ouzel valley through beautiful scenery past Bletchley as far as Woolstone where it follows the Ouse valley and skirts the suburbs of Milton Keynes, where many of the new houses have inlets from the canal to harbour their yachts. North of Old Wolverton the canal crosses the Ouse high up via an iron trunk aqueduct, a square cast iron trough carried on stone pillars where the water is only inches from the top at the sides and requires careful navigation. A quiet rural stretch followed, passing through open fields following the course of the River Tove for a short distance until we arrived at the seven lock climb to Stoke Bruerne, where the Waterways Museum is situated in an old stone warehouse with a unique collection covering the history of over 200 years of canals. The exhibits include a traditional narrow boat, an example of a butty boat cabin, steam and diesel engines and extensive displays of clothing. Cabinware, paintings, photographs and documents.

Navigating the Aquaduct over the River Ouse

After Stoke Bruerne a deep cutting leads to Blisworth tunnel, at 3,057 yards long the second longest navigable canal tunnel in Britain. There is no towpath, there are no lights and it is pitch black; we had a small lamp which could not penetrate the darkness. I handed over the tiller to Miranda to steer the barge because her eyesight was better than mine and I kept watch up forward as far as I could, shouting instructions to Miranda to prevent the barge from hitting the walls and bumping from side to side. Although we were only proceeding at our slowest speed we appeared to be rushing along at a tremendous pace into a black void, afraid of what might suddenly confront us until daylight appeared at the end of the tunnel and we came out into the sunlight.

We continued on to Gayton Junction where the Northampton Arm joined the main line and discussed our next move. It was obvious that we would not have time to complete our trip down the Oxford Canal into the Thames and re-enter the Grand Union Canal below Berkhamsted to return the barges and the only alternative was to go back the way we came. We therefore re-entered the tunnel and returned to Stoke Bruerne. David had to leave us and fly back to Canada to take up his new post as headmaster in British Columbia and Betty left with him to return home and make way for Stuart, Miranda's husband, who joined us at Leighton Buzzard.

Stuart had no experience of boats, his interest was in aeroplanes, both at work and as a hobby, and I explained to him that while I was in charge of the barge I was responsible for the people on board but when we tied up I could not supervise anybody ashore, which is exactly the same routine followed by an airline pilot. The same applied to Jane, who was now in charge of David's barge and handled it in a very competent manner, with the aid of her three sons and their friend as crew.

Cruising the canals is a wonderful way of seeing the scenery and countryside and providing an activity holiday for children, helping to work the barges through the locks and playing games and visiting places ashore. Fiona took part in everything, helping with the locks, washing the decks and joining in all the games and excursions. While Melissa was fishing from the canal bank with Jane's two youngest sons she fell headfirst into the water and was only saved by the prompt action of the two boys who pulled her out and took her back to her parents. She was very frightened and upset but fortunately not hurt. The weather had been hot and sunny for the whole of our fortnight's holiday and we spent the last day tied up outside Berkhamsted by the open air swimming pool, before returning the barges the next morning on time, after I had paid off the children to reward them for all their hard work as crew.

The following year Betty and I flew to Jersey to spend the Easter holiday in the L'Horizon Hotel at St Brelade's Bay. The weather was fine but there was a bitterly cold north easterly wind, and I was foolish enough to be out in it without a hat, which brought on an excruciating pain in the left side of my head and ear. I always treated doctors as a last resort and hoped that nature would provide its own cure, but the pain on this occasion was so severe that Betty called in a doctor to the hotel after three days to examine me. The doctor was a lady called Dr Sparrow, which reminded me of the character with the same name in the Carry On Films who could not pass his exams, but she was most efficient and informed me that I had cranial arteritis and must take a course of steroids starting at ten tablets a day. When I told her I did not take drugs she said, 'You either take the drugs or you will go blind, and you must report to your doctor when you get home.' My local doctor gave me a blood test and I had to continue to take the drugs and have a blood test every month, which relieved the pain and I was able to organize a holiday for Betty and me to visit British Columbia and stay with David and Jane in Victoria where they had a very nice house.

Before going on holiday we spent a day at Battle and I showed Glenys and Peter, Betty's sister and brother, round Battle Abbey. Glenys is always ready with a joke and when she stood on the spot where Harold was wounded in the eye by a Norman arrow, she suddenly clapped a hand over her eye and shouted, 'Oh! my eye, my eye.' When she drew her hand away the lens of her sunglasses fell out and dropped to the ground, which gave her quite a scare. As we walked back up the road to the village everything I saw from my left eye appeared in a brilliant purple colour, so intense and wonderful it is difficult to describe because I have never seen a colour to match it before or since.

I went to an eye specialist the next day and he informed me that I had a thrombosis of the veins at the back of my eye, brought on by my high blood pressure and the cranial arteritis; he gave me some eye drops to put in my eye to try and disperse it and warned me not to stand up suddenly or turn quickly.

Betty and I flew to Vancouver by Air Canada executive class to lessen the stress of a long distance flight and after landing we changed to the shuttle for Victoria on Vancouver Island, a journey of only twenty minutes, where David, Jane and the boys met us. Victoria is the capital city of British Columbia with a small harbour where ships run a service to Seattle in the USA; there is no industry and the flower gardens lend a bright and colourful appearance to the city. There is a very fine maritime museum and a park displaying Indian totem poles, where we watched the Indian craftsmen carving and painting them and Betty bought an Indian mask and drawing in the market.

Outside Victoria we visited the Butchart Gardens, which have been created in a small valley and have a marvellous display of flowers of all different species, each group contrasting with another, which brings out the colours in both. We went by train up country to see a village which had formerly had a flourishing logging business and when this closed down the inhabitants, to attract tourists, painted murals on the walls of all their buildings, depicting scenes from the old pioneering days which were so life like that the photographs we took looked as if they were actual scenes of places and people.

It was too cold to swim in the Pacific from the beaches at Victoria but we sailed by ferry to the inner islands to spend a day with David and Jane's friends, where the water was wonderfully warm. We enjoyed swimming and the children took a boat out to try their luck at fishing. We watched a baseball game which I found terribly dull; there was not one strike in the whole afternoon.

David was headmaster of two schools. They had previously been separately run and his directive was to bring them together under one management. This involved him in setting up an organization with new buildings and additional finance as well as creating a community spirit amongst the students to form the basis for traditions on which the schools could build for the future.

David still keeps up his main interests in sailing with Jane and playing cricket. He has a yacht. We spent some days sailing and we also watched the cricket matches in which he played. Matthew, the eldest son, is not very interested in sailing but he is a very fine all round cricketer and has now become a member of the Canadian Colts team. Jeremy, the second son, is more academic but he goes in for all the sports as well, while Benjamin, the youngest, has still to make his mark at cricket.

We were entertained at barbecues and parties by David's and Jane's numerous friends, including families from Japan with which David's school has close connections. One lady who had pupils at the school invited us to a tea party and afterwards asked us to take part in a small play. At home we are always dressing up and playing charades, when we decide on a theme, act it out on an impromptu basis and ad lib, but our hostess had followed the American custom, engaging two sisters, professionals, whose name was Snoop, to bring the script of a play and costumes for the guests who were to portray the characters. David had the principal part of an elderly man who was murdered, I was his English secretary and Betty was his alcoholic daughter, Jane was another daughter and other parts were played by some of the guests, while the rest of the party tried to decide who committed the murder. We were supposed to read from the script but we acted our parts in a natural manner, using our own words but keeping to the story of the play, which went down well with the audience and delighted our hostess.

Before we left Victoria I took all the family to the theatre to see an English farce, *No Sex Please We're British*, which they all enjoyed, even the boys, and our last night I entertained David and Jane to dinner at one of their best restaurants. Our partings are always very emotional but while we were waiting for the shuttle to take us to Vancouver an attendant came over and said, 'You can catch the early plane if you like, we have some spare seats.' So our farewells were cut short and we left to catch our aeroplane at Vancouver, where we had sufficient time in hand to have tea.

In 1989 I wanted to give Fiona and Melissa a seaside holiday in a good hotel where they could wear their party dresses and experience what it was like to stay with adults and take part in the events which were organized there. I booked a suite with two interconnected twin bedded rooms at the Pines Hotel, Swanage, which had direct access to the beach, for two weeks in August.

At Easter Miranda came with Fiona and Melissa to stay with us. The girls always enjoyed their visits because we arranged outings for them, to the seaside if it was fine and other places of interest. Betty Mum encouraged them with their paintings and drawings, and we played games and charades. Fiona made up her own play which they acted for us — she had a vivid imagination which she had the ability to put into words. I helped her with her homework to pass the entrance examination for Berkhamsted School for Girls and we played hockey with walking sticks and a tennis ball. Before they left I heard Betty and Fiona whispering at the door of my study where I was working. Fiona was saying, 'He won't like it' and Betty said 'Yes he will. Give it to him'. They came in and Fiona gave me a drawing of myself with a happy laughing face, marked Grandpa. I do not normally laugh very much but I looked at it and said, 'Thank you. It's lovely, I am going to hang it up right away'. I took some adhesive tape and fastened it on the wall behind my chair, where it still looks down on me a year later.

Shortly after she returned home Fiona felt sick and Miranda took her to Harefield Hospital, but despite all the efforts of the staff Fiona died a week later from a kidney failure. When Miranda telephoned us with the news all I could think and say was, 'Why? Why? Why?' A little child had suffered the agony of two major operations, fought for her life for ten years with only three years free from pain and then suddenly to be snatched away was something I could not understand. I have not been a regular churchgoer in recent years — I go to the major festivals and Good Friday with the occasional wedding, christening and funeral — and after Fiona's death I went back to church but I could not find the answer to my question 'Why?' My father, mother, sisters and other relatives and friends have died but they were all old, they had led a full life and I was reconciled to their dying. But I still cannot come to terms with the death of Fiona, an innocent child who had struggled for life and just when it looked as though she had succeeded she was denied it. I also feel sympathy for the parents who donated the heart of their child to save Fiona. If they knew they would suffer the thought of their child dying again.

A thanksgiving service for Fiona's life was held at which the pupils of both schools she attended were present. The headmaster paid tribute to Fiona's courage and determination to take part in all the schools' activities, and read from the essays she had written, describing the thoughts and fantasies which came into her mind. Miranda received a letter a few days later to say that Fiona had passed the entrance examination for Berkhamsted School for Girls.

In May the veins at the back of my left eye gave way under the stress and high blood pressure. I have lost the sight of that eye completely and the eye specialist has told me there is no hope of recovery because the nerves have been destroyed. I have had to give up skiing and I cannot drive on the Continent any more, which has stopped my foreign touring. It needs two eyes to focus on anything properly, especially to judge distances near to, I cannot play cricket or hockey with the grandchildren, and I often find myself putting cups on the edge of the table, thinking they were in the middle and pouring wine outside a glass instead of inside. I also have glaucoma in my right eye, which prevents my seeing in a bad light. I have to put drops in it night and morning and I hope it will hold out. The loss of sight in my left eye may be hereditary because my mother lost the sight in both her eyes in the same way and became completely blind.

Betty and I discussed the question of the holiday we had booked for the children in August and we decided that we should go ahead with it and ask Miranda to come with Melissa, hoping that they would both benefit from the change. The weather was fine and warm, Glenys and Peter came to stay for a week and we had an enjoyable holiday together. We have planted a small corner of our garden for Fiona with rosemary for remembrance and buddleias to attract the butterflies, of which she was very fond. When we were in Eastbourne we always took the children to visit the Butterfly House, where the butterflies used to settle on their hands. On the last occasion the children both bought us little gifts there.

While I was recovering from my operation some twenty years ago I occupied myself by tracing my ancestry back to an ancient family of yeoman through the church registers, which recorded all the births, deaths and marriages, dating from 1557 in the reign of Queen Elizabeth the First. They owned their own land and did not move away from it, but I did not pursue my researches further because before 1557 their wills were written in medieval Latin and deposited in the ecclesiastical courts of Canterbury and Rochester and I did not have the knowledge to translate them. However, I had my pedigree recorded by the registrar of the Most Honourable Company of Armigers and he suggested that in view of my descent from an ancient landowning family I should apply to the College of Arms for a Grant of Arms. I had a meeting with Norroy and Ulster King of Arms who investigated my application on behalf of the Earl Marshal to satisfy himself as to my pedigree and my personal character and standing. This took a year but the Grant of Arms arrived in time for our 1990 golden wedding celebrations. Norroy and Ulster King of Arms also suggested that his staff would be prepared to research my ancestors' wills to take my pedigree back further and I might have this done.

When my Hook House estate was compulsorily purchased to create the Bewl Reservoir, I was left with forty-five acres of grazing land on Pevensey Marsh, used for fattening cattle. The livestock market collapsed and neighbouring farmers ploughed their land to grow corn and take advantage of the high price for cereals. I applied for the usual ploughing grant from the Ministry of Agriculture but the next communication I received was from the Countryside Commission, informing me that my land had been designated a site of special scientific interest I was not permitted to plough or cultivate it and if I wished to sell it I must first offer it to them. I informed the Countryside Commission that as I could not get an income from the land I wanted compensation. After lengthy negotiations which got me nowhere, I told my agents that I was going to strip the turf off the land and sell it. They replied that I would be prosecuted if I did so, but my threat had the effect of bringing them to serious negotiations on my claim for compensation, as a result of which I have signed an agreement they drafted, handing over the whole of the management of the land to the Countryside Commission in return for compensation. This is the third occasion I have had to oppose the Government but at least I have got some satisfaction out of them this time.

1990 was our Golden Wedding Year. Although Betty and I were married on Boxing Day 1940, we decided to hold our celebrations during the summer to take advantage of the fine weather. We commenced our preparations twelve months before because of the difficulty of hiring a marquee and booking a caterer for a date in the summer months, but eventually we were able to fix it for Saturday, 4 August. We left all the arrangements in the hands of Mr Bannerman from Lewes, who organized the whole event perfectly, leaving us free to make our personal arrangements to invite our guests and decide on their seating at the luncheon. We had a large marquee to accommodate ninety guests, which opened out on to the lower lawn with views across the valley to the fields opposite. The weather was sunny and very hot and we placed our garden chairs under the trees to provide some shade from the heat of the sun. The marquee was beautifully decorated with flowers and an internal lining of gold to suit the occasion, and our friends, Mr and Mrs Pearson, who are landscape gardeners and Betty's nieces and nephews brought garden ornaments filled with flowers to line the patio between the house and the marquee. Our guests, including friends we had invited but who could not come, brought or sent us flowers to provide a mass of golden colour in the house. We were given bushes of golden roses from Michael, Stuart's brother and his wife, and a special present of a wine cooler filled with plants and flowers from a group of Betty's oldest friends from her art school days. We were all sorry that Morris Weidman, their art master, and his wife could not come because of ill health, but he sent us one of his own paintings.

We received wonderful presents and it was especially heart warming to be remembered by friends we had not seen for sometime. We had arranged a family dinner party for Thursday night, 2 August, but on Tuesday we received the sad news that Stuart's mother, Margery, had died in hospital. However, Stuart and Miranda came with Melissa to the party and we were able to comfort Stuart and offer him our sympathy on the death of his mother. We had a private dinner party so that we could exchange family presents before our celebrations. David, Jane and the boys joined with Miranda, Stuart and Melissa to give us a fine eskimo print from Canada entitled 'Aerobat', which particularly delighted Betty, and I gave them momentos of my Grant of Arms; a copy of the shield to David as my eldest son and personal copies of my badge to Betty and Miranda, together with illustrated manuscripts of the family's pedigree from 1557.

When Betty and I were married I could not afford both an engagement ring and a wedding ring and I bought her an eternity ring to serve both purposes; I therefore gave her a gold wedding ring suitably inscribed to mark our golden wedding anniversary. I proposed my usual toast on these occasions to the family and this year asked that Fiona and Margery should be particularly remembered.

I had not been feeling well for two or three weeks before the celebrations. I had pains in my right ear and head similar to those I suffered when I lost the sight of my left eye and as the pains increased I visited my local GP on Thursday morning to have a blood test. He telephoned me on Friday afternoon with unpleasant news, 'I have had the result of your blood test and it is very bad. The polymyalgia has flared up again and I must put you back on a crash course of steroids to try and save the sight of your right eye. Please call into the surgery and pick up your prescription'.

I had to take six tablets a day of this dangerous drug for a week, drink no alcohol and have another blood test in six days' time. I acknowledged the toasts in orange juice at our celebration, but the weather was so hot I did not mind. Miranda welcomed our guests and made the men more comfortable in the heat by suggesting they should take off their jackets and ties and Stuart read grace before the meal, which had been specially composed for us by the Reverend Donald Wallace. After lunch David proposed the toast to Betty and me and had a fund of stories about us which I thought were family secrets, ending up with a quotation from Shakespeare, Betty's favourite poet. When I rose to reply I had to point out that I was in the position of a pupil following the headmaster, keeping my speech to a very low key, but after I had thanked our guests for making it such a happy day, I also managed to end up with a quotation from Shakespeare, 'All's well that ends well'.

I had engaged an accordionist to play the type of melodies I had selected for a warm sunny afternoon. He is a very accomplished musician and the guests enjoyed his playing whilst they chatted to new friends they had made at the party and renewed old acquaintanceships. As we moved round the party it was inevitable that we should be reminded of friends we had overlooked and forgotten to invite but we could only offer our apologies for our lapse of memory. It was a happy occasion for everybody, ranging from one year old Jay to my sister Ethel, who is older than I am. After the cake was cut all the photographers among the guests gathered us together to take their photographs and we shall have many pictures to remind us of the climax to a marriage which has lasted fifty years, with the help of our family and friends.

After the golden wedding celebrations I went back to my GP

for another blood test and he asked me to visit an eye specialist for an urgent examination of the condition of my right eye. I was able to get an appointment with the specialist the following day and he confirmed that I had no thrombosis in my eye but that I must continue to take the steroids until the polymyalgia had been eliminated. Unfortunately the specialist has discovered that I have leukaemia as well as polymyalgia and I now have to attend the Eastbourne General Hospital for treatment every month to try and keep it in check. Betty is at her best in a crisis. She visited the doctor who now prescribes her course of vitamins and obtained for me a supply of the vitamins I could take to lessen the side effects of the steroids and leukaemia treatment.

The Reverend Group Captain Donald Wallace, RAF now retired, who composed the grace which Stuart read at our golden wedding celebrations, is chaplain to the de Havilland Moth Club which Stuart founded. He gave great spiritual comfort to Stuart and Miranda when Fiona died and officiated at her funeral and thanksgiving services. The grace expressed our thanks to God for the past and hope for the future in the following words:

> Lord — as our silver years turn to gold — we thank you — for all our yesterdays — for this joyous present — and ask that you — whose years have no end — will keep us company in all our tomorrows. Amen.

I can do no better than end my book with his words.

POSTSCRIPT

In the summer of 1991, Betty and I nearly died as I struggled to save her from drowning in the sea at Bexhill. The red danger flag was flying to warn everybody against swimming in the rough seas but Betty went into the water. She started to swim out to sea when a succession of huge waves caught her and dashed her against a breakwater. I ran down the beach and swam out to her and held her up until several people came to pull her out of the water. I was exhausted but I managed to get back to the shore where I was revived with cups of hot sweet tea. The police called an ambulance and Betty was taken to hospital where X-rays showed that her ribs had been cracked. She was allowed to come home and when I saw her to bed I said 'You owe me one.' But her ribs were too painful to allow her to laugh.